Cixous's Semi-Fictions

The Frontiers of Theory

Series Editor: Martin McQuillan

Available titles:
Reading and Responsibility:
Deconstruction's Traces
Derek Attridge

Of Jews and Animals
Andrew Benjamin

Working with Walter Benjamin: Recovering
a Political Philosophy
Andrew Benjamin

Not Half No End: Militantly Melancholic
Essays in Memory of Jacques Derrida
Geoffrey Bennington

Dream I Tell You
Hélène Cixous

Insister of Jacques Derrida
Hélène Cixous

Volleys of Humanity: Essays 1972–2009
Hélène Cixous

Poetry in Painting: Writings on
Contemporary Arts and Aesthetics
Hélène Cixous, ed. Marta Segarra and
Joana Masó

The Poetics of Singularity: The Counter-
Culturalist Turn in Heidegger, Derrida,
Blanchot and the later Gadamer
Timothy Clark

About Time: Narrative, Fiction and the
Philosophy of Time
Mark Currie

The Unexpected: Narrative Temporality and
the Philosophy of Surprise
Mark Currie

The Post-Romantic Predicament
Paul de Man, ed. Martin McQuillan

The Paul de Man Notebooks
Paul de Man, ed. Martin McQuillan

Geneses, Genealogies, Genres and Genius
Jacques Derrida

Cixous's Semi-Fictions: Thinking at the
Borders of Fiction
Mairéad Hanrahan

Scandalous Knowledge: Science, Truth, and
the Human
Barbara Herrnstein Smith

To Follow: The Wake of Jacques Derrida
Peggy Kamuf

Death-Drive: Freudian Hauntings in
Literature and Art
Robert Rowland Smith

Veering: A Theory of Literature
Nicholas Royle

Material Inscriptions: Rhetorical Reading in
Practice and Theory
Andrzej Warminski

Ideology, Rhetoric, Aesthetics: For de Man
Andrzej Warminski

Against Mastery: Reading and Other Forces
Sarah Wood

Forthcoming titles:
Readings of Derrida
Sarah Kofman, trans. Patience Moll

Visit the Frontiers of Theory website at www.euppublishing.com/series/tfot

Cixous's Semi-Fictions

Thinking at the Borders of Fiction

Mairéad Hanrahan

EDINBURGH
University Press

To Peter

© Mairéad Hanrahan, 2014

Edinburgh University Press Ltd
The Tun – Holyrood Road
12(2f) Jackson's Entry
Edinburgh EH8 8PJ
www.euppublishing.com

Typeset in 10.5/13 pt Sabon by
Servis Filmsetting Ltd, Stockport, Cheshire
and printed and bound in Great Britain by
CPI Group (UK) Ltd, Croydon CR0 4YY

A CIP record for this book is available from the British Library

ISBN 978 0 7486 4228 1 (hardback)
ISBN 978 0 7486 9664 2 (webready PDF)

Contents

Acknowledgments   vi
Series Editor's Preface   vii

1. Introduction   1
2. Fictional Analysis: *Dedans*   19
3. An Elementary Deconstruction: *Les Commencements*   56
4. The Illegitimate Mother: *Souffles*   94
5. Vital Tragedy? *Déluge*   127
6. The Time of Hospitality: *Les Rêveries de la femme sauvage*   157

Works Cited   185
Index   195

Acknowledgments

I am grateful to University College Dublin for a President's Fellowship in Spring 2002 during which the idea of this book was born, and to the Irish Research Council for the Humanities and Social Sciences for a Senior Fellowship in 2003–4 during which much of the archival work was carried out. A section of Chapter 6 was originally published in French under the title '*Les Rêveries de la femme sauvage* ou le temps de l'hospitalité', in *Expressions maghrébines*, 2:2 (2003), 55–69, and I am grateful to the publisher for permission to reuse this material.

This book has accompanied me for such a long time that it is impossible to do justice to all those whose contributions helped to make it what it is. I owe so much to so many over that period that I cannot name them all; the support and stimulation of numerous colleagues – some bare acquaintances, some close friends – have enriched my work in widely varying ways over the years. Nevertheless, some particular debts must be acknowledged. Sincere thanks go to Martin McQuillan for supporting this project. Mireille Calle-Gruber, Ginette Michaud and Judith Still deserve special gratitude for the generosity of spirit that ensures dialogue with them is always a happy as well as a fruitful experience. Though my dialogue has inevitably been more with Hélène Cixous's texts than with her person while writing this book, as always I deeply appreciate her exceptional intelligence and kindness, not least in allowing me to translate, or fail to translate, passages from texts not yet published in translation. Finally, thanks are most due where most they fail. I can never thank enough Aisling Hanrahan, Deirdre Hanrahan, Róisín Hanrahan, Peter Neary, Máire Ní Annracháin, Tadhg Ó hAnnracháin and Violette Santellani, to whom I owe the life in which I could write this book.

Series Editor's Preface

Since its inception Theory has been concerned with its own limits, ends and afterlife. It would be an illusion to imagine that the academy is no longer resistant to Theory but a significant consensus has been established and it can be said that Theory has now entered the mainstream of the humanities. Reaction against Theory is now a minority view and new generations of scholars have grown up with Theory. This leaves so-called Theory in an interesting position which its own procedures of auto-critique need to consider: what is the nature of this mainstream Theory and what is the relation of Theory to philosophy and the other disciplines which inform it? What is the history of its construction and what processes of amnesia and the repression of difference have taken place to establish this thing called Theory? Is Theory still the site of a more-than-critical affirmation of a negotiation with thought, which thinks thought's own limits?

'Theory' is a name that traps by an aberrant nominal effect the transformative critique which seeks to reinscribe the conditions of thought in an inaugural founding gesture that is without ground or precedent: as a 'name', a word and a concept, Theory arrests or misprisions such thinking. To imagine the frontiers of Theory is not to dismiss or to abandon Theory (on the contrary one must always insist on the it-is-necessary of Theory even if one has given up belief in theories of all kinds). Rather, this series is concerned with the presentation of work which challenges complacency and continues the transformative work of critical thinking. It seeks to offer the very best of contemporary theoretical practice in the humanities, work which continues to push ever further the frontiers of what is accepted, including the name of Theory. In particular, it is interested in that work which involves the necessary endeavour of crossing disciplinary frontiers without dissolving the specificity of disciplines. Published by Edinburgh University Press, in the city of Enlightenment, this series promotes a certain closeness to that spirit: the continued exercise of critical thought as an attitude of inquiry which counters modes of closed or conservative opinion. In this respect the series aims to make thinking think at the frontiers of theory.

Martin McQuillan

Chapter 1

Introduction

Where do we situate Hélène Cixous? Where is her place? I deliberately begin this book at a tangent, since place will not be its core preoccupation, nor even a dominant line of inquiry. These questions of place could furthermore be deemed out of place in other ways. Their ontological form, which presupposes that a categorical answer exists, may seem an inappropriate way to approach a writing that passionately and powerfully resists any attempt to pin it down, as anyone who has ever opened one of Cixous's texts must immediately be aware. If she has a place, it is one that is always more than one, a place of connection between different places. For example, what Cixous terms the 'sol originaire, le pays natal de [s]on écriture' ['the originary ground, the native country of [her] writing'][1] is above all a space of intersections: not only does she owe her existence to a chance encounter in Paris between her Sephardic North African father and Ashkenazi European mother,[2] but the Oran in which she grew up was a space 'au bord de l'Afrique du Nord' ['at the edge of North Africa'],[3] where the North meets the South, where Catholics, Arabs and Jews were in constant contact with each other and her ear was daily nourished by a diversity of languages. The world which formed her was an irreducibly plural space, as exemplified in the name of her grandfather's shop:

> *Aux Deux Mondes*, The Two Worlds. So the boutique was dedicated, and I with it, to a universe with two worlds. But I never knew in a clear, explicit or decisive way which the two were. The world was two. All the worlds were two and there were always two to begin with. There were so many two-worlds.[4]

In addition, this differential, relational space was double in another crucial sense. The 'paradis' ['paradise'][5] of her childhood was also always already exile; as we shall explore in Chapter 6, her place of origin was never *hers*.

The place of origin at stake in the quotation above is specifically the native country, not of Cixous herself, but of her writing. A disconcerting aspect to this metaphor is that writing originates (metaphorically) in Cixous's own 'real' birthplace: its metaphorical place of origin is a place which is not a metaphor (or at least not only a metaphor). The unexpected substitution calls attention above all to the uncertain boundary that separates the person 'Hélène Cixous' from the work signed by that name. When I ask what her place is, I am interested in the place occupied by the latter. Foregrounding the question of place is paradoxically a way of highlighting both how necessary and how insufficient an approach it is to her writing, how impossible it is to account for Cixous's 'work' in purely spatial terms. Of course, traces of the formative intersections of Cixous's childhood can be recognised in the most insistent spatial figures in her work, which are precisely figures of passage: the 'entre' or in-between, the door, the angle, etc. They can also be recognised in the interstitial position occupied by her texts, one of whose most striking characteristics is the relentless way they defy categorisation. As Verena Andermatt Conley already remarked in the very first monograph devoted to the author's work, 'Cixous writes at the interstices of fiction, criticism, psychoanalysis, and philosophy without enclosing herself in any of them.'[6] What matters most, however, is how Cixous's writing always *transforms* its originary 'ground'.

One of the most revealing aspects of the early reception of Cixous's work was the extent to which a writing which never encloses itself within any disciplinary or generic limits was forcefully enclosed within them from the outside. A further reason for my beginning with the question of place is to pay homage to a landmark discussion of Cixous's work which investigates the implications of the very categorical way Cixous was labelled, especially in the Anglophone world, as a theorist rather than a writer. In 'To Give Place: Semi-Approaches to Hélène Cixous', Peggy Kamuf explores the limitations of constructions of Cixous as a 'French feminist theorist'. She shows definitively how attempts to account for her work in this way in effect posit an opposition between 'a politics and a poetics of "women"'[7] and how the privileging of the former over the latter not only fails to engage with what is most original in Cixous's writing, but is furthermore blind to the *ethical* implications of the way her writing exceeds the theoretical. Picking up on Toril Moi's characterisation of Cixous's work as 'theoretical (or semi-theoretical)',[8] Kamuf turns around the disparagement suggested by Moi's parenthesis to argue that '"theory" is always semi-theory'[9] insofar as it is never fully independent from the political, contingent, differences it seeks to theorise. Moreover, this implication of theory in the processes it describes is by no means a weakness; rather, it represents the greatest ethical opportunity. In contrast with a fully general theory that would, by definition, exclude the inscription of the differences that make up the other's singularity,

> 'The semi-' would be here an impossible name, a semi-name for that which each time must be addressed differently. With its hyphen, or *trait d'union*, it signals the space within the name of a heterogeneity, that for which there is no common measure other than the minimal mark of coappearance – minimal, almost weightless as it waits for the other's approach. A spacing . . . that which gives place to writing.[10]

The 'semi-' is less a space than a *spacing*; it is as a space of encounter, of 'giving place' to the other, that it 'gives place' to writing. Kamuf stresses that 'to give place' is not an idiomatic use of English.[11] Only in a writing – that is, in a practice of language that dares to venture outside pre-existent categories, that doesn't feel the need to enclose what it names in the confines of the already-known, to translate what it names into terms it already recognises – can the 'semi-' find its place, find *a* place.

For Kamuf, Cixous's writing is admirably attentive to the question of how to write '*on*' the other without her own discourse proving 'ruthlessly crushing'.[12] She considers Cixous 'one of our age's greatest semi-theoreticians'[13] precisely because the theorising in which her texts are engaged seeks to 'give place' to the differences constitutive of the other. Her texts have exemplarily assumed 'the necessity of thinking, in terms that are as rigorous as possible, the semi- (semi-theoretical, semi-translatable, semi-referential, semi-fictional), there where a difference crosses with the generality of the concept'.[14]

We are now approaching the central concern of this book, which explores the 'semi-fictional' quality of Cixous's texts. Before I develop what we might understand by a 'semi-fiction', however, I would like to summarise some of the ambiguities inseparable from the term 'fiction'. Firstly, fiction functions as a marker of literarity. Indeed, for Gérard Genette fiction and poetry are the only categories with a 'constitutive' literarity; it is enough for a text to be marked 'du sceau générique, ou plutôt archigénérique, de la fictionalité et/ou de la poéticité' ['with the generic, or rather the suprageneric, seal of fictionality and/or poeticity'][15] for it to be recognised as a work of literature. This obtains regardless of any evaluation of its merit; a 'bad' fiction or poem nonetheless remains a work of literature. In contrast, a text from another domain – for example, philosophy or history – can be recognised as having a 'conditional' literarity because it has some formal (or 'rhematic') characteristic that elicits an aesthetic response in the reader. But, as indicated in the shift from 'generic' to 'suprageneric', the classing together of fiction and poetry as genres *within* literature is complicated by the fact that both genres have also served on their own, for very different reasons, to represent the genre *of* literature. As evidence of the view that poetry offers a figure of literature itself, Genette quotes Jakobson: 'La poésie, c'est le langage dans sa fonction esthétique' ['Poetry is language in its aesthetic function'].[16] The other, even more widespread, view holds that 'la fiction, et plus précisément la fiction narrative, et donc aujourd'hui par excellence le roman, représente la littérature même' ['fiction, and more precisely narrative fiction, and thus today, par excellence, the novel, represents literature itself'].[17] Interestingly, these views are orthogonal to each other; neither can be amended or expanded to encompass the other. As synecdochal representations of the space of literature, they at most intersect.

Secondly, not only is fiction's status as genre or archigenre uncertain, but the grounds on which its claim to a constitutive literarity is based are irreducibly heterogeneous. On the one hand, by fiction we understand a work of the imagination. Fiction in this sense is defined *thematically*, by the invented nature of its content. It is a space where usual considerations of truthfulness are suspended:

> L'énoncé de fiction n'est ni vrai ni faux (mais seulement, aurait dit Aristote, 'possible'), ou est à la fois vrai et faux: il est au-delà ou en deçà du vrai et du faux, et le contrat paradoxal d'irresponsabilité réciproque qu'il noue avec son récepteur est un parfait emblème du fameux désintéressement esthétique.

> [Fictional utterances are neither true nor false (but only 'possible', as Aristotle would have said), or else they are both true and false: they exceed or fall short of truth and falsity, and the paradoxical contract of reciprocal irresponsibility that such an utterance maintains with its receiver is a perfect emblem of the well-known posture of aesthetic disinterestedness.][18]

The imaginary nature of the referent suspends and makes irrelevant the distinction between 'truth' and 'falsity'. It is often pointed out that fiction shares the etymology of the verb 'to feign': both derive from the latin *fingere*. It is in this sense that fiction picks up most closely on the Aristotelian notion of *mimesis*, to which the notion of imitation is central. For Aristotle, and counter-intuitively in terms of our use of these words today, the poet is a poet insofar as he invents a good *story*: 'the poet must be a maker of plots rather than of verses, since he is a poet by virtue of his representation [*mimesis*], and what he represents is actions'.[19] When he quotes this passage, Genette translates *mimesis* with 'fiction' and 'feint' (feigns),[20] accentuating the fact that for Aristotle *poiesis* was *mimesis*. Poetry *was* fiction.

On the one hand, then, fiction shades into the work of the imagination per se. On the other hand, fiction also shades into narrative. Once more, Genette provides us with key reference points. In 'Frontières du récit', he sets out to map the borders of narrative, an enterprise again complicated by the unavoidable need to engage with terms that are not only temporally but linguistically specific. (In addition to the various ways that he shows *mimesis* can be (has been) translated, the 'récit' of his own title exceeds its English translation as narrative insofar as the French term is on occasion better rendered as 'story'.) The same terms in fact meant different things even to Plato and Aristotle. Plato distinguishes narrative (*diegesis*) from imitation (*mimesis*), which he restricts to characters' direct speech. For Aristotle, as we saw, there is only imitation; *diegesis* is subsumed as a subcategory of *mimesis*. Aristotle reformulates Plato's distinction as the difference between indirect imitation (which, like Plato, he terms *diegesis*) and direct imitation. Genette then goes on to demonstrate that, as inherited in the Western tradition, 'La représentation littéraire, la *mimésis* des anciens, ce n'est donc pas le récit plus les "discours": c'est le récit, et seulement le récit [. . .] *Mimésis, c'est diégésis*' ['Literary representation, the *mimesis* of the ancients, is not, therefore, narrative plus 'speeches': it is narrative and only narrative [. . .] *Mimesis is diegesis*'].[21]

How can the equivalence between *mimesis* and *poiesis*, on the one hand, be reconciled with that between *mimesis* and *diegesis,* on the other? Genette's answer, in effect, is that they cannot. In *Introduction à l'architexte*, Genette shows how no one system of classification has ever succeeded in fully accounting for the diversity of literary forms. Thus, for example, far from being the origin of the triad of genres (lyrical-epical-dramatic) often mistakenly believed to encompass the space of literature, Aristotle's *poiesis* entirely excluded the form we would today expect it most immediately to translate, the lyric poem. Especially, Genette establishes how the discussion of *genre* has always been traversed and complicated by questions of enunciatory *mode*:

> Il y a des modes, exemple: le récit; il y a des genres, exemple: le roman; la relation des genres aux modes est complexe, et sans doute n'est-elle pas, comme le suggère Aristote, de simple inclusion. Les genres peuvent traverser les modes (Œdipe raconté reste tragique), peut-être comme les œuvres traversent les genres – peut-être différemment: mais nous savons bien qu'un roman n'est pas seulement un récit, et donc qu'il n'est pas une espèce du récit, ni même une espèce de récit.

> [There are modes (for example, the narrative); there are genres (for example, the novel); the relationship between genres and modes is complex and

doubtless not, as Aristotle suggests, one of simple inclusion. Genres can cut across modes (Œdipus recounted is still tragic), perhaps the way individual works cut across genres – perhaps differently; but we do know that a novel is not solely a narrative and, therefore, that it is not a species of narrative or even a kind of narrative.][22]

Literary space is defined not by an overarching categorization but by a series of transversals or intersecting lines. In consequence, there is no single point at which they all meet, no single unifying principle according to which literary forms can be classified.

As this brief discussion shows, the term 'fiction' is in itself the epitome of uncertainty. In different contexts, it can be interpreted as congruent with 'narrative', 'novel', 'work of literature', 'work of the imagination'.[23] Fiction, in other words, is always more than fiction.[24] What, then, of 'semi-fiction'? In what ways and at what levels might Cixous's fiction be said to 'give place' to its others?

The first level at which Cixous's texts open onto a 'beyond fiction' is that of genre. To the extent that they declare a genre, that genre is: 'fiction'. Prior to 1975, Cixous's books were specifically marked as 'romans' (novels) when initially published, although that label was dropped from the cover of the later Éditions des femmes re-editions (though not from the Seuil re-edition of *Tombe*). The texts published for the first time with the Éditions des femmes bore no generic mention; however, they were retrospectively labelled 'fictions' in 'By the Same Author' lists of subsequent texts, including those published by the Éditions Galilée, who became Cixous's principal editor in 2000, as well as those published by the Éditions des femmes. The other labels used were 'essai' (essay) or 'théâtre' (theatre), indicating that the use of the term 'fiction' is characterised by the uncertainty of status outlined above.[25] 'Fiction' serves in these lists both as a marker of genre (a literary work that is not theatre) *and* as a marker of literarity (a literary work as distinct from an essay). The texts published for the first time by Galilée have no such labels; nevertheless, some of their subtitles invite reading as generic classifications of varying degrees of unconventionality. As recognisable literary or artistic forms, the 'Lettres de la préhistoire' [Letters of Prehistory] of *Manhattan* or the 'Prédelles' [Predelles] of *Philippines* appear to offer a metaphorical description of the (kind of) book they entitle as much as of its content. Even more strikingly, the force of the title *L'Amour du loup, et autres remords* [*Love of the Wolf, and Other Remorses*], and still more so that of *Le Rire de la Méduse, et autres ironies* [*The Laugh of the Medusa, and Other Ironies*], each of which contains a text with the same title as the volume as a whole along with other texts, derives in large part from the fact that the subtitle seems to invent a new genre. The 'remorse' in one case, 'irony' in the other, suggests a new way of classifying the 'other texts' included in the volume as much as it refers, metaphorically or otherwise, to the book's content.

While the vast majority of Cixous's texts may resemble 'fictions' more than they resemble anything else, however, they are above all distinguished by the comprehensive way they exceed the constraints of generic codification. They restlessly straddle several genres: for example, we shall see in Chapter 4 that *Souffles* presents itself also as a (very non-Cartesian) 'meditation'. In text after text, her writing borders on other forms such as the diary, the elegy, the fable, etc.[26] Autobiography merits particular mention. Designating her books as 'fictions' can in fact be argued to function in the opposite way to an autobiographical pact, by stressing their imaginary nature. Cixous's narrators frequently warn against the danger of believing that *any* text can unequivocally tell the truth of the author's life. For example, the narrator of *Le Livre de Promethea* exclaims:

> Je ne redoute rien autant que l'autobiographie. L'autobiographie n'existe pas. Mais tant de gens croient que cela existe. Alors je déclare solennellement: l'autobiographie n'est qu'un genre littéraire. Ce n'est pas un genre vivant. C'est un genre jaloux, décepteur, – je le déteste.

> [I fear nothing as much as autobiography. Autobiography does not exist. But so many people believe it exists. So I solemnly declare: autobiography is only a literary genre. It is not a living genre. It's a jealous, deceitful genre, – I hate it.][27]

Cixous takes the precaution of prefacing 'Albums et légendes' ['Albums and Legends'], the short memoir at the end of *Hélène Cixous, Photos de racines* and her most overtly autobiographical work to date, with a similar warning: 'Toutes les biographies comme toutes les autobiographies comme tous les récits racontent une histoire à la place d'une autre histoire' ['All biographies like all autobiographies like all narratives tell one story in place of another story'].[28] Yet in the same text she stresses the link between the autobiographical and writing in general: 'Ce que je raconte ici (oublis et omissions compris), c'est ce qui pour moi n'est pas dissociable de l'écriture. Il y a une continuité entre mes enfances, mes enfants, et le monde de l'écriture – ou du récit' ['What I am recounting here (including what is forgotten and omitted) is what for me is indissociable from writing. There is a continuity between my childhoods, my children, and the world of writing – or of the narrative'].[29] Her writing, then, is not just autobiographical in the way and to the extent that, for example, Paul de Man theorised.[30] Cixous's work draws singularly intensely on biographical events (such as the death of her father and son) and elements, for example setting the names of the most significant figures of her childhood to work repeatedly in her writing. In doing so, however, she transforms them, freely changing even such 'factual' elements as dates of birth, with the result that the limit between the autobiographical and the fictional remains totally undecidable.

It is noteworthy that one genre Cixous has not practised is poetry: she has never published a collection of poems. Yet, just as her texts can broadly be deemed 'fictions', their virtuosity and extraordinary lyrical density equally justify classifying them as poetry in the large sense of the earlier quotation from Jakobson, as language used in its aesthetic function. Her texts may not be poems, but they are manifestly exceptionally *poetic*. It is no surprise not only that she should more often select the term 'poet' to describe herself than 'writer', but that others too should do so, as notably Jacques Derrida did when introducing the second of her 1990 Wellek Library lectures: 'Hélène Cixous is today, in my view, the greatest writer in what I will call my language, the French language if you like. And I am weighing my words as I say that. For a great writer must be a poet-thinker, very much a poet and a very thinking poet.'[31] Derrida's link between poet and thinker helps to shift the discussion of semi-fictionality away from the level of genre to that of the interstice observed by Conley, between fiction in the sense of 'literary writing' and its others: criticism, psychoanalysis, philosophy. We can note that these are all discourses traditionally (that is, before the paradigm shift of deconstruction) considered 'theoretical' to the extent that they aspire to abstract a truth, a knowledge, from the material words in which they are grounded. In this book, I take 'theory' to mean a practice of language that reaches some form of intellectual conclusion, a result or outcome that lends itself to translation out of the context in which it is presented for a more general application.

Most Cixous scholarship has attempted to reckon in one way or another with how Cixous negotiates the border between poetry and theory (including her own (semi-)theory).[32] Recent work has moved far beyond the early considerations of her as primarily a theorist who practises theory lyrically/poetically/metaphorically, to offer readings which take as their point of departure the need to be attentive to the richness of her extraordinary practice of writing.[33] I aspire to continue in this direction, starting from the premise that the borders Cixous's writing most repeatedly and insistently crosses are not The Frontiers of Theory but the frontiers of fiction. In doing so, I am elaborating on a remark made in another of the landmark readings of Cixous to date, Derrida's 'H. C. pour la vie, c'est à dire . . .':

Bien que tous ces textes soient transis de fictions, et de fiction à la puissance *n*, le fictionnel ne domine pas, en dernière instance, pas plus que rien n'y domine, qu'on l'appelle le narratif, le romanesque, le théâtral, l'autobiographique. Sa poétique traverse tout cela à la fois et autre chose. Son hyperréalisme fictionnel pose à la classification des modes et des genres le plus redoutable, le plus inouï et le plus intéressant des problèmes.

[Although all these texts are transfixed with fiction, and with fiction to the nth power, the fictional element does not dominate, in the last instance, more than anything else does, whether it be called narrative, novelistic, dramatic, autobiographical. Her poetics runs through all that at the same time and something else. Her fictional hyperrealism poses to the classification of modes and genres the most formidable, the most unheard-of, and the most interesting problems.][34]

To paraphrase Derrida, Cixous's work is *absolutely semi-fictional*. But Derrida considers that semi-fictionality only at the level of genre. What difference does it make if we stress fiction as much as poetry as the marker of the literarity it endlessly exceeds?

The main difference concerns the fact as outlined above that fiction is inextricably linked with the notion of narrative. My starting point in this book is that the narrative impulse is an insistent motor of Cixous's writing. The desire to tell stories is as intrinsic a part of her writing practice as her poetic discourse. The title of one of the most discursive texts Cixous has written is revealing: the first piece she wrote about Derrida, exploring the differences between them, is an essay entitled 'Contes de la différence sexuelle' ['Tales of Sexual Difference']. Of course, the title is highly relevant to the discussion of sexual difference the text contains, where Cixous reflects on the truth of sexual difference as the kind of truth derived from shared stories, a 'récit oral' ['oral narrative'] or 'conte' ['folk tale']. But she also explicitly explains, in a characteristically untranslatable play on words, that the way she feels most comfortable in approaching the question is as a fairytale, the narrative form par excellence: 'si c'est un conte de fées, alors c'est la fée qui fait la différence, *la fée différence*. Oui, je m'aperçois qu'en en parlant comme d'une fée j'ai un petit peu moins peur' ['if it is a fairy tale, then it is the fairy that makes the difference, the *difference fairy*. Yes, I realize that in talking of a fairy I am a bit less afraid'].[35] We can note, moreover, that this predilection for narrative is a site of greater difference between Cixous's work and Derrida's than her linguistic virtuosity: while Derrida's discourse is just as much as Cixous's a writing that gives place to the semi- (the semi-theoretical, the semi-philosophical, etc.) and plays as much as hers does on the words it uses, it rarely ventures into the narrative. He has little desire to tell stories.

Narrative is, above all, inseparable from the question of time. As Paul Ricœur has argued, it is the primary way we make sense of time: 'le temps devient temps humain dans la mesure où il est articulé de manière narrative; en retour le récit est significatif dans la mesure où il dessine les traits de l'expérience temporelle' ['time becomes human time to the extent that it is organized after the manner of a narrative; narrative, in turn, is meaningful to the extent that it portrays the features of temporal existence'].[36] We *make* sense of time: narrative is a fundamentally dynamic process. That is, it is a *process*, which is why a purely spatial approach to Cixous's work is necessarily insufficient. Narrative takes time, as Peter Brooks establishes so cogently in *Reading for the Plot*; the plot cannot be understood without the plotting that produces it, the story told without consideration of the telling. This temporal dimension is in my view central to the fact that Cixous has never written 'poems'. As Brooks points out, lyric poetry 'strives toward an ideal simultaneity of meaning, encouraging us to read backward as well as forward (through rhyme and repetition, for instance), to grasp the whole in one visual and auditory image', whereas not only does the reading of narrative typically take time but narrative stories depend on 'meanings delayed, partially filled in, stretched out'.[37] Narrative, in other words, is the sphere of interstitial time: the time after something has begun before the end comes to decide the outcome. As Barthes had suggested with his description of the text as an 'espace dilatoire' ['dilatory area'],[38] narrative is the deferral of the ending, which retrospectively determines the meaning of the deferral. Frank Kermode had earlier proposed to read fictional endings as a grappling with the final ending, death:

> Men, like poets, rush 'into the middest,' *in medias res*, when they are born; they also die *in mediis rebus*, and to make sense of their span they need fictive concords with origins and ends, such as give meaning to lives and to poems. The End they imagine will reflect their irreducibly intermediary preoccupations.[39]

Building on this, Brooks deploys the insights of psychoanalysis to argue that the condition of mortality structures not only the story, but the telling of the story. Narrative is the plotting of desire: 'If the motor of narrative is desire, [. . .] the ultimate determinants of meaning *lie at the end*, and narrative desire is ultimately, inexorably, desire *for* the end.' Just as the satisfaction of desire is also its death, so the meaning narrative longs for, propels itself towards, signals its end. Hence, for Brooks: 'If we ask where and how we find this insistence of past desire most powerfully alive within the signifying chain of narrative, we may want to answer that first and last it lies in the very project of telling.'[40]

I shall return to the question of the final determination of meaning in Chapter 2. Here I want especially to stress the *reprioritisation of the middle* effected by both Kermode's and Brooks's analyses. This is particularly evident in Kermode's discussion of the importance of peripeteia in narrative,[41] and in Brooks's mapping of Freud's view as expounded in *Beyond the Pleasure Principle* that life is a detour on the road to death, a return to a previous quiescent state that seeks to prolong itself as long as possible, onto narrative as a desire for the end it defers.[42] This renewed focus on the middle and the relation to time it necessarily implies is in my opinion very suggestive for reading Cixous. It is true, on the one hand, that Cixous's narratives are singularly lacking in 'narrativity', that is the sense 'of someone "telling a story", of a performance, of narrative "for its own sake"'.[43] If poetry has been used to describe Cixous's work so much more often than fiction, it is doubtless because the reader rarely has the impression that the story 'predominates'.[44] The linguistic virtuosity of her writing, as manifest in its ubiquitous wordplay and creative subversion of grammar and syntax, concentrates the reader's attention at the level of texture rather than narrative structure. Indeed, at the macrotextual level, the main organising principle is rhythm: 'Ainsi chaque texte un autre corps. Mais dans chacun la même vibration: car ce qui de moi marque tous mes livres rappelle que c'est ma chair qui les signe, c'est un *rythme*. Médium mon corps rythmé mon écriture' ['So for each text, another body. But in each the same vibration: the something in me that marks all my books is a reminder that my flesh signs the book, it is *rhythm*. Medium my body rhythmic my writing'].[45] Cixous's texts are highly organised, but as organic sequences rather than totalisable system. Not only is it often difficult to ascertain 'what' the text is about but the reference points that classically guide us in structuring our reading – 'who', 'when', 'where', etc. – also remain uncertain, with the result that the plot typically defies any attempt to abstract it.

On the other hand, nevertheless, a constant in her 'fictions' is that they invariably create a diegetic universe, however uncertain and fluid it may be. Frédéric-Yves Jeannet sees the desire for narrative emerging relatively late in Cixous's writing career; he posits a shift between Cixous's early work and her books from *Manne* onwards in terms of a movement from a poetic to a more novelistic writing: 'Dans les [livres] précédents, comme dans (comme s'ils étaient) des recueils de poèmes, il n'y avait pas toujours ce sentiment d'un fil, sauf celui de l'écriture, des affres et joies de la rédaction. Seriez-vous en train de devenir romancière, à la longue (romancière de votre vie, je veux dire)?' ['In the preceding books, as in (as if they were) collections of poems, there wasn't always this feeling of a thread unspooling, save that of the writing, the throes and joys of composing. Would you be becoming a novelist, at long last (a novelist of your life, I mean)?']⁴⁶ We will consider the question of the periodisation of Cixous's writing in greater detail in Chapter 6; here I want to propose, contrary to Jeannet, that a narrative impulse has always been inseparable from Cixous's writing endeavour. As we shall have occasion to see in the different texts studied in this book, from the outset her texts have typically begun *in medias res*, plunging the reader into a story, conjuring up an immediate relation with a character or characters, inventing an imaginary world. That is, *imagining* a new world. Telling stories, in the sense both of making things up and of relating them to time, has always been irreducibly part of what she does.

The premise from which this book starts is that Cixous is called to tell stories that do more than tell stories. Let me recall that the word 'narrative' derives from *gnarus*, from the Proto-Indo-European root **gno*; it thus shares the etymology of both the French *connaître* and the English *knowing*. Telling stories has always been a mode of knowing, of seeking the truth, as well as an inventive artifice. What I want to suggest is that, far from being incidental, the narrative dimension to Cixous's writing needs to be reckoned with as a key component of the way she troubles the border between fiction and its others. Narrative is not securely on one side of a divide between imagining and understanding, between story and knowledge, between 'fiction' and 'theory'. Narrative also unsettles that divide. Cixous's fictions do not *minimise* their narrative dimension; on the contrary, the particularly exuberant way they exploit and exceed conventional fictional limits can be read as *maximising* a potential always already existent in narrative.

The next five chapters which compose this book each focus on how a different fictional text can be read as a 'semi-fiction', that is a fiction that 'gives place' to something other than itself. My project is neither to read Cixous's fictions in the light of her own theory nor, especially, to suggest that they contain a clear, or even a clearly discernible, theoretical discourse. That would be tantamount to reducing the plurality and hybridity of Cixous's work to a continuum between two poles which would ultimately would have no place for any frontier, any border. It would further run the risk of reducing the performative power of her writing by subordinating it to a set of predetermined conceptual parameters. Rather, picking up on the sense in which for Derrida a great writer must be a 'poet-thinker', my purpose is to show how in each case *fiction thinks*. Each text is therefore approached in relation to a particular theoretical question or discourse. Needless to say, the same text could often be used to stage an encounter with a different theory, or a different text deployed to address a particular question. The analyses which follow seek not to offer an exhaustive account of any aspect of Cixous's writing, but rather to show how her fictions elaborate a thinking with theoretical implications, often complicating the assumptions and categories of the theory or discourse in question. In particular, as the verb *elaborate* suggests, the work of this thinking is a dynamic one, hence the decision to take specific texts, rather than theories, as my point of departure. I have argued elsewhere for the need to take account of the distinctness of Cixous's different texts as well as of the continuity of her writing, to do justice to the unique singularity of each individual work.[47] The reason for exploring a few books in depth is not only to enable a greater engagement with the *poetic* stakes that, as Derrida suggested, make each book a 'vivant singulier et irremplaçable' (HC, 74) ['singular and irreplaceable living entity' (HCE, 77)] or, as Cixous says, 'the textuality, the textility, the fabric, the style, [. . .] which, in fiction, is the beginning and the whole'.[48] It is to facilitate an engagement also with the specifically *fictional* dimension of the text: with how the textual fabric unfolds.

Chapter 2 questions the relationship to the authority of knowledge as an important site of difference between literature and psychoanalysis, via an in-depth study of Cixous's first book, *Dedans* [*Inside*]. Chapter 3 offers a reading of *Les Commencements* [*Beginnings*] to argue that a difference in relation to the desire for knowledge, the desire to go *beyond* fiction, similarly constitutes a difference between Cixous's work and the deconstruction of Jacques Derrida. An analysis of *Souffles* [*Breaths*], the fiction written at the same time as the polemical 'Le Rire de la Méduse' ['The Laugh of the Medusa'] with which Cixous was identified for so long in the Anglophone world, and engaging with many of the same issues, provides an angle in Chapter 4 from which to approach, or re-approach, the question of Cixous's 'semi-theory' of sexual difference. I then tack to the question of genre in Chapter 5 with *Déluge* [*Deluge*], discussing the extent to which 'tragedy' can be generically circumscribed and the implications if it is the case that a tragedy is always 'more' than a tragedy. Finally, the question of narrative time explicitly guides the analysis of *Les Rêveries de la femme sauvage* [*Reveries of the Wild Woman*] in Chapter 6. Each chapter thus seeks to show how the text in question both *is* a fiction and is *more* than a fiction. Cixous's fiction, in other words, is always a semi-fiction: fiction in an encounter with something beyond itself.

Including, of course, the reader. This book necessarily represents *my* encounter with Cixous's fiction's encounter with its others. To conclude this Introduction, let me draw a contrast between two representations of reading which both figure it as a walk, yet evoke a radically different experience. In a letter to Fliess, Freud describes the path along which he has led his reader in *The Interpretation of Dreams*:

> The whole thing is planned on the model of an imaginary walk. At the beginning, the dark forest of authors (who do not see the trees), hopelessly lost on wrong tracks. Then a concealed pass through which I lead the reader – my specimen dream with its peculiarities, details, indiscretions, bad jokes – and then suddenly the high ground and the view and the question: which way do you wish to go now?[49]

Freud gleefully – wishfully?[50] – graphs the process of reading his book as a linear emergence from the darkness to the light, from confusion to clarity, from error and erring to a clear sense of direction. Cixous's notion of reading, on the other hand, undermines the possibility of any totalising perspective:

> À aucun moment je n'ai prétendu qu'il faille lire mes textes compte tenu de la culture, du savoir. C'est comme tous les textes. De toute manière, ils traversent le temps et ils sont lus comme ils peuvent être lus. Là où il y a des gens qui connaissent le Moïse de Michel-Ange, ils en aperçoivent quelque chose; là où il y en a qui connaissent Freud, ils en aperçoivent quelque chose, mais, à vrai dire, un texte c'est comme une ville, comme un musée: on s'y promène et on perçoit ce qui nous revient. Je perçois ce avec quoi je suis dans un rapport quelconque, ce qui m'a affectée.

> [At no moment did I ever pretend that my texts need to be read in terms of their culture, their knowledge. It is like all texts. Anyway, they go through time and are read as they can be read. Where people know Michelangelo's *Moses*, they will notice something of it; those who know Freud will notice something of him, but, to tell the truth, a text is like a city, a museum: you walk around and you perceive what reaches you. I perceive whatever I have some relation to, what has affected me.][51]

Where for Freud the reader follows a path determined by the author, for Cixous no preordained path exists: what one sees depends on what one has oneself already seen and known – and *felt*. 'Ce qui m'a affectée' ['what has affected me']: it is in Cixous's model rather than in Freud's that reading is affected by affect, by the forces that exceed knowing, as well as by 'savoir', knowledge. Reading, in other words, must needs be *partial*, in both senses of the word: incomplete, and inflected by the reader's likes and desires.

What follows, then, are readings that aspire to tell *a* truth about the thinking to which Cixous's texts 'give place'. A humble aspiration, but one I hope may do at least partial justice to the extraordinary event represented by the creation of Cixous's semi-fictions.

Notes

1. Mireille Calle-Gruber and Hélène Cixous, *Hélène Cixous, Photos de racines* (Paris: Éditions des femmes, 1994), 183; *Rootprints: Memory and Life Writing*, trans. Eric Prenowitz (London and New York: Routledge, 1997), 181.
2. As noted in a famous footnote in Cixous's most famous text: 'Mon père, sépharade, – Espagne-Maroc-Algérie – ma mère askhenaze – Autriche-Hongrie-Tchécoslovaquie (son père) + Allemagne (sa mère) – traversant par hasard un Paris éphémère . . .', Catherine Clément and Hélène Cixous, *La Jeune née* (Paris: 10/18, 1975), 244 ['My father, Sephardic – Spain-Morocco-Algeria – my mother, Ashkenazi – Austria-Hungary-Czechoslovakia (her father) and Germany (her mother) – passing by chance through a Paris that was short-lived', *The Newly Born Woman*, trans. Betsy Wing and intro. Sandra M. Gilbert (Minneapolis and London: University of Minnesota Press, 1986), 131].
3. *Photos de racines*, 183; *Rootprints*, 182.
4. 'My Algeriance, in other words: to depart not to arrive from Algeria', trans. Eric Prenowitz, *Stigmata: Escaping Texts* (London and New York: Routledge, 1998), 153–72, at 164.
5. *Photos de racines*, 196; *Rootprints*, 196.
6. Verena Andermatt Conley, *Hélène Cixous: Writing the Feminine* (Lincoln, NB and London: University of Nebraska Press, 1991), 12.
7. Peggy Kamuf, 'To Give Place: Semi-Approaches to Hélène Cixous', *Yale French Studies*, 87 (1995), 68–89, at 75.
8. Toril Moi, *Sexual/Textual Politics: Feminist Literary Theory* (New York: Methuen, 1986), 102.
9. 'To Give Place', 74.
10. Ibid., 81.
11. Ibid., 89.
12. Ibid., 69.
13. Ibid., 74.
14. Ibid., 79.
15. Gérard Genette, *Fiction et diction* (Paris: Éditions du Seuil, 1991), 26; *Fiction and Diction*, trans. Catherine Porter (Ithaca, NY and London: Cornell University Press, 1993), 16.
16. Roman Jakobson, 'La nouvelle poésie russe', in *Questions de poétique* (Paris: Éditions du Seuil, 1973), 15, quoted in *Fiction et diction*, 24; 'Modern Russian Poetry: Velimir Khlebnikov [Excerpts]', in *Major Soviet Writers: Essays in Criticism*, ed. Edward J. Brown (Oxford: Oxford University Press, 1973), 62, quoted in *Fiction and Diction*, 14.
17. *Fiction et diction*, 19; *Fiction and Diction*, 9.
18. *Fiction et diction*, 20; *Fiction and Diction*, 10.
19. Aristotle, 'On the Art of Poetry', 1251b, in *Aristotle, Horace, Longinus: Classical Literary Criticism*, trans. T. S. Dorsch (Harmondsworth: Penguin, 1965), 44.
20. *Fiction et diction*, 17; *Fiction and Diction*, 7. Genette cites Käte Hamburger (*Logique des genres littéraires* (Paris: Éditions du Seuil, 1986) [*Die Logik der Dichtung*, 1957]) as having proposed a similar translation.

21. Gérard Genette, 'Frontières du récit', *Figures II* (Paris: Éditions du Seuil, 1969), 49–69, at 55–6; 'Frontiers of narrative', *Figures of Literary Discourse,* trans. Alan Sheridan with intro. Marie-Rose Logan (New York: Columbia University Press, 1982), 127–44, at 132–3.

22. Gérard Genette, *Introduction à l'architexte* (Paris: Éditions du Seuil, 1979), 75–6; *The Architext: An Introduction,* trans. Jane E. Lewin with intro. Robert Scholes (Berkeley: University of California Press, 1992), 71.

23. An additional association specific to our contemporary period is that fiction now connotes writing in prose. Here again, its relation to its outside is not simple. It is probably the case that 'prose fiction' is used more often to differentiate a text from 'prose non-fiction' than from 'poetic fiction', a category which has nearly entirely disappeared. Nevertheless, at the risk of sounding alarmingly like Monsieur Jourdain's philosophy teacher, it remains significant that in the very era when the poetic function is generalised across literary space (as distilled in the quotation from Jakobson above), fiction continues to be considered exclusive of poetry.

24. I recall here Jacques Derrida's analysis, in a similar vein, that genre is always more than genre. He argues that a generic trace, while possible in any kind of text whatsoever, is 'absolument nécessaire et constitutive dans ce qu'on appelle l'art, la poésie ou la littérature' ['absolutely necessary for and constitutive of what we call art, poetry, or literature']. But although there is no such thing as a genre-less literary text, one that would not bear the mark of one or more genres, a text also always exceeds the genre(s) to which it belongs: 'Un texte ne saurait *appartenir* à aucun genre. Tout texte *participe* d'un ou de plusieurs genres, il n'y a pas de texte sans genre, il y a toujours du genre et des genres mais cette participation n'est jamais une appartenance' ['a text cannot belong to no genre, it cannot be without or less a genre. Every text participates in one or several genres, there is no genreless text; there is always a genre and genres, yet such participation never amounts to belonging'], Jacques Derrida, 'La loi du genre', in *Parages* (Paris: Éditions Galilée, 1986), 249–87, at 263–4; 'The Law of Genre', in *Critical Inquiry,* 7:1 (Autumn, 1980), 55–81, at 64–5.

25. It is interesting that no such analogous uncertainty attaches to Cixous's theatre, which is considerably more respectful of generic conventions than her fictional writing. The exception to this exception is arguably *Portrait de Dora,* a play culled from *Portrait du soleil* at the behest of Simone Benmussa. Cixous's theatre has to date attracted less attention than her fiction; the only book-length study of it currently remains Julia Dobson's *Hélène Cixous and the Theatre: The Scene of Writing* (Bern: Peter Lang, 2002).

26. I have explored this question with respect to the diary in 'Cixous's *Le Livre De Promethea*: A Diary in an Other Form', *French Studies,* 55:2 (2001), 195–206.

27. *Le Livre de Promethea* (Paris: Gallimard, 1983), 28. See also Cixous's interview with Mireille Calle-Gruber, *Photos de racines,* 95–6; *Rootprints,* 86–7.

28. *Photos de racines,* 179; *Rootprints,* 178.

29. *Photos de racines,* 206; *Rootprints,* 203–4. Most of the recent publications dealing with autobiography in Cixous have focused on her relationship with Algeria. For discussions adopting other perspectives, see Mary E.

Schipa, 'Hélène Cixous: Sur la piste d'une autobiographie féminine', *Romance Review*, 5:1 (1995), 29–37; my 'Of Altobiography', *Paragraph*, 23:3 (2000), 282–95; Claudine G. Fisher, 'Cixous's Auto-Fictional Mother and Father', *Pacific Coast Philology*, 38 (2003), 60–76; Claire Boyle, *Consuming Autobiographies: Reading and Writing the Self in Post-War France* (Oxford: Legenda, 2007); Sissel Lie and Priscilla Ringrose, 'Personal and/or Universal? Hélène Cixous's Challenge to Generic Borders', *European Legacy*, 14:1 (2009), 53–64. Susan Sellers's *Hélène Cixous: Authorship, Autobiography and Love* (Cambridge: Polity Press, 1996) does not address this issue, notwithstanding the mention of 'autobiography' in the title.

30. 'Autobiography, then, is not a genre or a mode, but a figure of reading or of understanding that occurs, to some degree, in all texts. [. . .] [A]ny book with a readable title-page is, to some extent, autobiographical. But just as we seem to assert that all texts are autobiographical, we should say that, by the same token, none of them is or can be.' Paul de Man, 'Autobiography as Defacement', in *Modern Language Notes*, 94:5 (1979), 919–30, at 921–2.

31. See the front cover of Hélène Cixous, *Three Steps on the Ladder of Writing*, trans. Sarah Cornell and Susan Sellers (New York: Columbia University Press, 1993).

32. For example, the monograph whose title promises the closest relation to my own approach aims explicitly to 'souligner les contradictions et les paradoxes de la fiction et de sa théorie chez Cixous' ['underline the contradictions and paradoxes between fiction and her theory in Cixous's work'] (Martine Motard-Noar, *Les Fictions d'Hélène Cixous: Une autre langue de femme* (Lexington: French Forum, 1991), 12).

33. In particular, I would like to single out Mireille Calle-Gruber's *Du café à l'éternité: Hélène Cixous à l'œuvre* (Paris: Galilée, 2002) and Ginette Michaud's *Battements du secret littéraire: Lire Jacques Derrida et Hélène Cixous 1* and *Lire Jacques Derrida et Hélène Cixous 2* (Paris: Hermann, 2010). Although not often cited in this book since they concentrate on different texts from those I deal with, their analyses have enriched and nourished my thinking.

34. Jacques Derrida, 'H. C. pour la vie, c'est à dire . . .', *Hélène Cixous: Croisées d'une œuvre, Actes du Colloque de Cerisy-la-Salle*, ed. Mireille Calle-Gruber (Paris: Galilée, 2000), 13–140, at 34; *H. C. for Life, That Is to Say . . .*, trans. with Additional Notes Laurent Milesi and Stefan Herbrechter (Stanford: Stanford University Press, 2006), 28–9. Future references are to these editions, and will be placed in the text preceded by HC for the French version and HCE for the English translation. The French text was subsequently reprinted separately as *H. C. pour la vie, c'est à dire . . .* (Paris: Galilée, 2002).

35. Hélène Cixous, 'Contes de la différence sexuelle', in *Lectures de la Différence Sexuelle*, textes réunis et présentés par Mara Negrón (Paris: Éditions des femmes, 1994), 31–68, at 42, 52 and 35; 'Tales of Sexual Difference', trans. Eric Prenowitz, *The Portable Cixous*, ed. Marta Segarra (New York: Columbia University Press, 2010), 48–60, at 53, 54 and 48.

36. Paul Ricœur, *Temps et récit 1* (Paris: Éditions du Seuil, 1983), 17; *Time and*

Narrative 1, trans. Kathleen McLaughlin and David Pellauer (Chicago: University of Chicago Press, 1984), 3.

37. Peter Brooks, *Reading for the Plot: Design and Intention in Narrative* (Cambridge, MA: Harvard University Press, 1984), 20–1.

38. Roland Barthes, *S/Z* (Paris: Éditions du Seuil, 1970), 82; *S/Z*, trans. Richard Miller (New York: Hill & Wang, 1974), 75.

39. Frank Kermode, *The Sense of an Ending: Studies in the Theory of Fiction* (Oxford: Oxford University Press, 1967), 7.

40. *Reading for the Plot*, 52 and 58.

41. *The Sense of an Ending*, 18.

42. See chapter 4 of *Reading for the Plot*, 'Freud's Masterplot': 'If in the beginning stands desire, and this shows itself ultimately to be desire for the end, between beginning and end stands a middle that we feel to be necessary (plots, Aristotle tells us, must be of "a certain length") but whose processes, of transformation and working-through, remain obscure' (*Reading for the Plot*, 96).

43. H. Porter Abbott, *The Cambridge Introduction to Narrative* (Cambridge: Cambridge University Press, 2002), 22.

44. Ibid., 31.

45. Hélène Cixous, *La Venue à l'écriture*, in *Entre l'écriture* (Éditions des femmes, 1986 [1976]), 64; 'Coming to Writing', in *'Coming to Writing' and Other Essays*, with intro. Susan Rubin Suleiman, ed. Deborah Jenson and trans. Sarah Cornell, Deborah Jenson, Ann Liddle and Susan Sellers (Cambridge, MA: Harvard University Press, 1991), 53.

46. Hélène Cixous and Frédéric-Yves Jeannet, *Rencontre terrestre* (Paris: Galilée, 2005), 123; *Encounters: Conversations on Life and Writing*, trans. Beverley Bie Brahic (Cambridge: Polity, 2013), 130.

47. See my 'Long Cuts', *parallax* 44, 13:3 (2007), 37–48.

48. Hélène Cixous, 'Enter the Theatre', *Selected Plays of Hélène Cixous*, ed. Eric Prenowitz (London: Routledge, 2004), 25–34, at 31.

49. Sigmund Freud, *The Complete Letters to Wilhelm Fliess (1887–1904)*, ed. Joseph M. Masson (Cambridge, MA: Belknap Press, 1985), 365.

50. The idea that the journey was planned from the beginning is contradicted in another letter from the previous year in which Freud claims: 'I did not start a single sentence knowing where I would end up' (ibid., 319).

51. Hélène Cixous, 'Entretien avec Françoise van Rossum-Guyon', *Revue des Sciences humaines*, 44:169 (Octobre-Décembre 1977), 479–93, at 489.

Chapter 2

Fictional Analysis: *Dedans*

'What is the interest of psychoanalysis for the non-analyst?', Cixous asks in her contribution to a recent volume arising from a conference discussing the place of psychoanalysis in her work and that of Jacques Derrida.[1] She presents herself explicitly as a non-analyst: 'I imagine – but maybe I am mistaken – that none of us here is an analyst'.[2] This non-analyst, who is also on record as a non-analysand, nonetheless opens her piece with the assumption that she and her audience 'are all, all of us, fellow para-practitioners', and later asserts: 'I'm telling you about *lay-analysis*, which we – all of us – somehow practise. We are all lay-analysts, beginning with the first analyst who was a lay-analyst, since Freud was an analyst before analysis, the pre-analysed, pre-analytical analyst.'[3] She thus in effect situates herself at the borders of psychoanalysis: both outside and inside it.

Cixous's (atypical) totalisations in this quotation ('none of us', 'all of us') are of especial interest. It is no surprise that she should situate her own work at this border, notwithstanding the fact that she personally has no clinical experience of psychoanalysis (as was also the case with Derrida). Although her first response to Freud's text was negative,[4] her discovery of *The Interpretation of Dreams* a few years later launched a dialogue with psychoanalysis which has lasted throughout her writing career. A whole series of texts engage explicitly and extensively with its precepts and principles, often deploying insights gleaned from psychoanalysis to critique its own blind spots.[5] Others leave little doubt as to the admiration Cixous felt for Freud's intellectual adventurousness and candour; as she herself reminds us, he is often a character in her texts, 'usually as an uncle. He is a nuncle.'[6] This sense of a familial relationship is motivated by their shared Jewish identity; Cixous specifies that the formative 'primal scene' that she, Freud and Derrida had in common had less to do with the origins of sexuality than with Judeity.[7] But Freud figures for Cixous above all as the thinker of the unconscious.

Shakespeare was her 'first Freud'[8] in that his work supremely explores the passions that drive the human animal. In retrospect, it can be seen already to express Freud's major intuitions. Freud's immense achievement was to theorise for the first time what writers through the ages have thought through their work. The unconscious is now *known*: the difference in writing today from when Shakespeare, Stendhal, Balzac wrote is that it is no longer possible to write as if unaware of the unconscious. Cixous's work is remarkably of its time, I would argue, less because it gives a free rein to the unconscious – poets have done so for time immemorial – than because of how it knowingly acknowledges its existence.

The extent to which Cixous's writing obliges its reader to recognise an excess over what can be known rationally is one of its most distinctive aspects. The welter of puns, profusion of contradictions and dense narrative thicket that make her texts such a fascinating reading experience function in a way strongly reminiscent of the processes Freud identified as constitutive of the dreamwork (condensation, displacement, etc.). This endows her writing with a markedly oneiric texture, which is reflected thematically in the proliferation of references to dreaming throughout her work.[9] Many of her narrators discuss their dreams; passages are often presented as reworked dreams; the publication of a selection of her dreams in 2003 revealed that numerous passages not presented as dreams in her fictions also developed initially from a dream.[10] Her work is so bound up with dreaming at every level that it profoundly troubles any notion of a clear distinction between writing and dreaming: the one cannot be thought without the other. Yet, as Derrida signalled in his reflections on *Rêve je te dis*, the very fact of writing a dream down alters its status.[11] Writing (or reading) a dream is not the same as dreaming. Just as the dream is not an immediate expression of the unconscious but rather its translation into a form able to attain consciousness, so writing 'as if' dreaming involves a further level of translation.[12] However directly her texts may seem to inscribe the unconscious relative to those of other writers, it is important to bear in mind that any such inscription is necessarily mediated through language. The unconscious is only ever accessed in translation.

Why emphasise this? Why stress at the outset that Cixous's texts do not deliver us her 'raw' unconscious, but rather involve a process not only of secondary revision but of tertiary, quaternary, even quinary revision, to judge from the archives deposited at the Bibliothèque Nationale de France, which suggest that her texts are no less worked over in the light of day than those, for example, of Beckett, another writer whose rhetorical force was definitively recognised only after many decades?[13] The point is certainly not to propose that in her texts a conscious agency dominates the unconscious, but rather to highlight that Cixous's texts are as much the site of an active *thinking* about the unconscious forces which complicate and contradict her (forces also variously designated as the unknown, the secret, the ineffable, even the divine . . .) as they are the site in which those forces find expression.

Cixous's thinking manifestly takes a very different form from psycho-analytical theory, the standard discourse used to think about the unconscious over the last century. For this reason, her output offers a particularly rich terrain of investigation for consideration of the relationship between 'literature' and 'psychoanalysis', especially given that she can be argued to occupy as uncertain a place with respect to the former as she does to the latter. Let us return here to Cixous's designation of all the members of her audience at the conference along with herself both as non-analysts and as 'fellow para-practitioners' of analysis, 'lay-analysts'. Reading this as a metonym for all those who are interested in analysing texts rather than people, it suggests that the position we have seen her adopt at the margins of psychoanalysis is not unique to her, but generalisable to all those interested in 'literature' in its broadest acceptation, in writing. However, Cixous's relation to her audience is scarcely one of identity; textual analysts clearly do not all 'para-practise' in the same way. As the only participant whose work was also the object of the conference, she is unavoidably both inside the 'us' she makes reference to and outside it. She is both *part* of what for the sake of brevity and at the risk of over-schematisation I shall call a critical community that analyses texts, and *apart* from it in that her work foregrounds an irreducibly literary dimension. The reason why her work merits the holding of a symposium to discuss its relations with psychoanalysis is grounded in this exceptional juncture. Far from being supernumerary, the work of the writer is inextricably linked with the work of analysis.

This question of the writer *as* analyst forms the focus of this chapter. By this, I of course do not mean that either Cixous or the narrators of her texts engage in a fictional psychoanalysis, in the sense that *À la recherche du temps perdu* can be considered a fictional autobiography. I am interested rather in exploring the extent to which literature and psychoanalysis are congruent – or incongruent. Over the decades of Cixous's writing career, theoretical explorations of the relationship between the two have moved far beyond the psycho-biography (whether in the form of psychoanalysing characters or of studying the psychogenesis of the work) of earlier psychoanalytical criticism. Critiquing the privileging of content over form, work from the 1970s onwards stressed that it is in the workings of textuality itself – in the texts of psychoanalysis as much as in literary ones – that unconscious forces can most

productively be analysed.[14] Cixous's work anticipates these develop-
ments to an astonishing degree. Her texts, as self-reflexive as her narrators are self-reflective, foreground for the reader both explicitly and
implicitly associations of the sort criticism often contents itself with
discovering in other authors. Since her narrators themselves incessantly
excavate the side of themselves which escapes their conscious control,
critical investigations that sought in turn to determine their unconscious
motivations would run the risk of redundancy or paraphrase. When a
writing already maximally exploits many of psychoanalysis's fundamental insights, the notion of a psychoanalytical reading (however sophisti-
cated/subtle/attentive it may be) that would come from the outside,
speak from a place not already included within the text, necessarily
becomes even more problematic than it would otherwise be. Cixous's
work is thus ideally placed to provide a springboard from which to
explore the 'inter-implication' that, for Shoshana Felman, characterises
the relationship between literature and psychoanalysis:

> The relation of *interiority* conveyed by the inter-implication of literature and
> psychoanalysis is by no means a simple one. Since literature and psychoanaly-
> sis are *different* from each other, but, at the same time, they are also 'enfolded
> within' each other, since they are, as it were, at the same time outside and
> inside each other, we might say that they compromise, each in its turn, the
> interiority of the other.[15]

For Felman, one way this inter-implication troubles the tendency of
previous psychoanalytic criticism to consider literature as a body of
language to be interpreted and psychoanalysis as a body of knowledge
that can be used to interpret it is by displacing the opposition, viewing
the literary text as 'the very place where meaning, and *knowledge* of
meaning, reside'.[16] Another is that

> literature, by virtue of its ironic force, fundamentally deconstructs the fantasy
> of authority in the same way, and for the same reasons, that psychoanalysis
> deconstructs the authority of the fantasy [. . .] Psychoanalysis tells us that
> the fantasy is a fiction, and that consciousness is itself, in a sense, a fantasy-
> effect. In the same way, literature tells us that authority is a *language effect*,
> the product or the creation of its own *rhetorical* power: that authority is the
> *power of fiction*; that authority, therefore, is likewise a fiction.[17]

At issue, in other words, in the difference between literature and psychoanalysis is a different relationship to the authority of knowledge.
Elsewhere, in *Jacques Lacan and the Adventure of Insight*, Felman
develops Lacan's recognition that psychoanalysis is constantly *forgetting* the mythical, that is fictional, dimension of its own access to truth.

Thus, for example, Lacan deemed it no accident that Freud went beyond himself in *Beyond the Pleasure Principle* 'at a point where the psycho-analysts, engaged in the path that Freud has taught them, believe they know. Freud has told them that desire is sexual desire, and they believe him.'[18] Lacan came to a 'dramatic, tragic understanding that psychoa-nalysis is radically *about expropriation*'; his own expulsion from the International Psychoanalytic Association was symptomatic of a compul-sive repression of the insight that psychoanalysis can never come to 'any final rest in a knowledge guaranteed by the self-possessed kingdom of a theory.'[19] The repressed of psychoanalysis is that its truth is of mythical status: *its truth is a fiction*. If psychoanalysis keeps needing to rediscover this, it is because, despite itself, it persists in believing the unconscious can be known.

And literature, which manifestly shares the 'structure de fiction si véridique' ['very truthful fictitious structure'][20] of the psychoanalytical experience? Felman does not explore the attitude literature adopts to the irreducibly fictional nature of the truth to which it aspires. It is precisely in this respect, however, that Cixous's work seems to me to point up forcefully the difference between literature and psychoanalysis. This chapter will broach discussion of this question via a reading of Cixous's first full-length fiction, *Dedans* [*Inside*],[21] the book which won her initial literary acclaim when it was awarded the Prix Médicis in 1969. The author was already thoroughly familiar with the work of both Freud and Lacan when she wrote it, having even attended the latter's seminar for two years. While the book makes no direct mention of either think-er's texts, it deals through and through with 'psychoanalystuff',[22] the material with which psychoanalysis (like dreams) is concerned. Cixous's own references to *Dedans* in later texts indicate her opinion that it reveals her 'inaugural scene, from which writing sprouted',[23] the death of her father when she was still a child. Her discussion of such 'inaugural scenes' in *Three Steps on the Ladder of Writing* states unequivocally: 'The first book I wrote rose from my father's tomb. [. . .] I said to myself that I wouldn't have written . . . I wouldn't have had death, if my father had lived. I have written this several times: he gave me death. To start with.'[24] Death was there from the beginning; but also, as the punctua-tion stresses, death was to prove *a* beginning. As early as *La Venue à l'écriture* [*Coming to Writing*], the author declared that she had 'd'abord écrit en vérité pour barrer la mort' ['in truth first written to block death'].[25] While such statements clearly articulate Cixous's belief in a connection between her father's premature death and her own urge to write, the actual form this connection takes is by no means clear; the link between 'having' death (of which more later), on the one hand, and 'blocking' it, on the other, remains to be explored. The uncertainty of the distinction between ending and beginning, death and life, is reflected spatially in yet another formulation, which casts the writing of *Dedans* in terms of the border between inside and outside: 'c'était d'une certaine manière dans la tombe et hors la tombe de mon père' ['it was in a way both inside and outside my father's tomb'].[26] Writing is both 'inside' and 'outside' the experience in which it originates.

Dedans covers the same ground as a psychoanalysis in many respects. As we shall see, it revisits a traumatic experience through language. Its structure emphasises the degree to which the narrator seems bound to repeat the past in the present, and directs the reader's attention to the determining role of her Œdipal configurations. Yet in other respects Cixous's exploration of family dynamics fundamentally disrupts the Freudian model. The Œdipal triangle is represented not as a crucible in which stable identities are forged but rather as a kaleidoscope of multiple identifications. Especially, *Dedans* enables us to think about the different ways 'literature' and 'psychoanalysis' relate narrative to truth. In exploring how the kaleidoscope of identifications and the identities they make possible are functions of language, it builds on the (Lacanian) insight that we are above all spoken by language. But Cixous's writing bears no trace of the resistance to the unknowable that Felman showed to be contradictorily at work in psychoanalysis. However much Freud and others struggled to rediscover otherwise, a fundamental precept of traditional psychoanalytical practice is that psychoanalysis seeks to defuse the unconscious. 'Wo Es war, soll Ich warden', 'Where Id was, there Ego shall be':[27] according to Freud's famous maxim, the point of an analysis is that once identified and verbalised, the unconscious motivations which produce the patient's symptoms lose their force. For Freud, the purpose of going over the past in language is to recognise unconscious formations 'as belonging to the past' so that they can 'lose their importance and be deprived of their cathexis of energy';[28] it aims to leave the prison of the past behind. For Cixous's narrator, too, the past is a prison. However, in contrast with Freud, *Dedans* displays no desire to situate language 'outside' the unconscious scenes it opens up. It has no difficulty acknowledging the fictional nature of the stories it needs to tell, or in accepting that beyond the story is . . . another story. At issue in this chapter is the difference between a desire to escape from the prison of the past, and a desire to transform the prison itself from an enclosure into a source of possibility.

The Stuff of Psychoanalysis

Dedans tells a story which in numerous respects corresponds to the psychoanalytical notion of trauma, a distressing experience so overwhelming as to resist any attempt at the time to symbolise or narrativise it, and which only achieves a symptomatic representation retroactively, when something happens to repeat it.[29] The narrator declares herself driven by a legacy of pain: 'Car je vis sur mon héritage de douleur, et je dors sous les toits depuis longtemps quittés, et c'est la perte qui fait battre mon cœur' (152) ['For I live on my legacy of pain, and I sleep under roofs long since abandoned, and it's loss that makes my heart beat' (98)]. The sense of an ongoing, unresolved grief is reflected in the text's narrative structure. The book is divided into two parts, the first focusing on the narrator's childhood relationships (with her father, especially the imaginary father she invents after his death, grandmother and, to a lesser extent, her mother and brother); the second on her adult relationships with various 'amis' or lovers. The question of the repetition of childhood experiences in adult life is thus central to the book's concerns, although the relationship between the two parts is never directly articulated. One of the text's most disconcerting aspects is the constant shifting between present, *passé composé* and *passé simple* which makes it impossible to establish a diegetic chronology either of the childhood events related in Part I or of the adult experiences treated in Part II.[30] An exception which draws attention to this general rule is the shift from Part I to Part II, whose beginning unequivocally marks a jump in diegetic time: 'Je suis de nouveau dans ma première ville. [. . .] Je suis assise dans un fauteuil; après vingt févriers' (139) ['I am once again in my first city. [. . .] I am sitting in an armchair, twenty Februaries later' (91)]. The temporal indeterminacy of Part II therefore repeats that of Part I, just as the various 'amis' – 'mon dernier ami' (144) , 'le plus jeune' (162), 'un amant distrait' (176) ['my last lover' (94), 'the youngest' (104), 'an absentminded lover' (115)] – appear to be substitutes for the narrator's father: 'J'ai mal partout où j'ai pensé à lui, j'ai mal à toute ma vie, j'ai mal à tout ce que j'avais fait bien ou mal pour lui, j'ai mal à chacun des amants qui n'ont pas été lui' (191) ['I hurt wherever I thought about him, my whole life hurts, everything good or bad I did for him hurts, every lover who wasn't him hurts' (125)]. All her life and with all her lovers she has been repeating the suffering the father's loss caused her.

However, the focus on the narrator's lovers means that the masculine third-person pronoun in Part II cannot automatically be taken to refer to the father, as seems evidently the case in Part I. For example, the 'lui' that her lovers were not could also be interpreted as the proximate cause of her pain, the lover for whom she has just cut off her finger. This unde-cidability of the masculine pronominal reference is most manifest in relation to the narrator's 'dernier ami' ['last lover'] in a chapter itself beginning 'QUI? LUI:' ['WHO? HIM:']:

> Nous sommes là-bas où il nous a laissés il y a dix ans en Amérique, et nous sommes où il nous avait laissés dix ans avant en Afrique. Car mon amour et mon père sont un, et ils m'ont tenue dans leurs bras, il y a vingt ans, il y a dix ans, et j'ai eu d'autres hommes depuis, mais nul n'a eu mon âme, ni ma bouche, car j'attends qu'il revienne et me donne les baisers de sa bouche.
> En mon dernier ami meurent tous les hommes qui n'ont pas été lui. (161–2)

> [We're there where he left us ten years ago in America, and we're in Africa where he'd left us ten years before that. For my love and my father are one, and they held me in their arms, twenty years ago, ten years ago, and I've had other men since, but none has had my soul, or my mouth, for I'm waiting for him to return and give me the kisses of his mouth.
> All the men who have not been him die in my last lover. (104)]

The disconcerting use of the same pronoun, 'il', to refer to both father and lover is no sooner explained by the declaration that they are 'one' than their (singular) identity is troubled by the plural '*ils* m'ont tenue' ['*they* held me']. Moreover, the later loss (of the lover ten years earlier in America) textually precedes the earlier one (of the father twenty years earlier in Africa); the later comes first and the first comes later. 'En mon dernier ami meurent tous les hommes qui n'ont pas été lui': this 'last' lover may refer either to the most recent lover, that is, the last of the series of men, or alternatively to the first, the 'amour' who held her in his arms ten years previously and whose repetition of the father apparently inaugurated the series. Similarly, the 'lui' that all the other men were not can be read as either the last lover or as the father to whom no other man has lived up.

Through the series of lovers (in which it is impossible to determine who came first in time, order or importance), then, the narrator has been repeating a prior repetition. This last lover, 'un homme jeune qui pouvait avoir vingt-cinq ans ou soixante' (145) ['a young man who could have been twenty-five or sixty' (95)], is himself first introduced in the context of a 'répétition', that of the cabin crew of an aeroplane requesting the passengers 'de ne rien laisser à bord [. . .] qui vous soit personnel' (142) ['not to leave on board [. . .] any personal belongings' (93)]. In effect, the question for the narrator is to find a space in which her personal 'baggage', to borrow an opportune English expression, can be left behind. 'Non, non, nous ne laisserons rien à bord qui nous soit . . .' (142) ['No, no, we will leave nothing of ours . . .' (93)]: the ellipsis endows the French with an ambiguity not easily conveyed in translation, since the final clause also echoes with the meaning 'nothing that is us'. The narrator goes on to image her interior life as an airport, a prime example, because of its mobility and transience, of the anonymous 'non-places' that Marc Augé distinguishes from traditional places in which social and historical attachments anchor a subject's identity:[31] 'Tous mes aéroports décollent dans ma tête, du premier au dernier au premier. Tous gracieux. Un homme dans chaque aéroport, non un homme toujours le même' (144) ['All my airports take off in my head, from the first to the last to the first. All of them graceful. A man in every airport, no a man always the same' (93–4)]. Note the extent of the mobility: not only is there circulation between first and last but the airports themselves circulate, 'take off'! 'Un homme dans chaque aéroport': the metonymy linking airport and man suggests that the narrator's relational history is one of repeated detachments and separations (another meaning of 'décoller'). But her situation is the opposite of that of the proverbial sailor who loves and leaves a woman in every port. With each airport she repeats a primary experience of loss, each man being the latest incarnation of the 'man always the same' who left her: 'je le perdis comme j'avais perdu mon père et mon seul et seul et seul et même amant' (146) ['I lost him the way I had lost my father and my only and only and only and same lover' (95)].[32]

The traumatic nature of the father's death can thus be read in the pattern of loss the narrator keeps reproducing. The book suggests that the father's overwhelming loss deploys its effects retroactively, with the later loss of the lover whose effect in turn derives from the previous loss: 'il me semblait parfois que je ne le connaissais pas mais le reconnaissais et que je ne le connaîtrais jamais dans le présent' (145) ['it sometimes seemed to me that I didn't know him but recognized him and that I would never know him in the present' (94)]. It stops her from living in the present, as a bitter exclamation towards the end of the book elaborates: 'Être? Il y avait longtemps que je n'avais pas été (avais été) (suis) (être). A été: "un accompli", mais avec quelles conséquences, quelles! dans l'actuel! C'est le genre d'accompli qui rend l'actuel éternel' (192) ['To be? I had not been (had been) (am) (to be) for a long time. Has been: "an accomplishment", but with what consequences, what consequences! for the present! It's the kind of accomplishment that makes the present go on forever' (125)]. This is an instance where any translation must find itself insufficient. In French, 'un accompli' designates a verb in the perfect aspect, signalling that the event being referred to was completed at the time of reference. The recourse to impersonal linguistic terminology thus conveys a powerful sense of disappropriation on the part of the narrator from her present self. She is not railing here at the spectral relation to time as analysed, for example, by Derrida,[33] at the fact per se that the past haunts the present; rather she is lamenting that the past has *immobilised* the present, left her with a timeless eternity instead of a present. As she says in relation to another lover: 'Il est déjà passé. Nous parlons, mais tout s'écrit déjà, je lis, et tout est à l'imparfait: c'était' (176) ['He's already in the past. We talk, but everything we say is already written down, I read, and it's all in the past tense: it was' (115)]. The problem is that the past appears to have *prescribed* what can happen in the present.

'Comment un vivant peut-il vivre avec un mort?' (197) ['How can someone alive live with someone dead?' (128)]: this question, formulated in the penultimate chapter of *Dedans*, distils the narrator's predominant concern. How to live when time has stopped? How to wrest something living from a deathly stasis? The father's death appears at one level to have given the narrator an experience of time having stopped, of all being already 'accompli' or accomplished, of no further change being possible. Hence her anguish, for example, each time she realises again that an event makes no difference: 'Le soleil s'est levé ce matin. Mais rien n'avait changé. Trois et trois six et trois neuf' (181) ['The sun rose this morning. But nothing had changed. Three and three six and three nine' (118)]. Hence also the equivalence between immortality and death:

> Je retrouvais mon père du côté de notre silence, à l'intérieur de notre immor-talité sans mots. Corps à corps, tout danger, toute perte étaient abolis; dans l'instant où il m'encerclait et je l'embrassais, je ne désirais plus rien sauf la mort. Si nous étions morts ainsi, nous ne serions plus séparés. Et tant que nous étions enfermés dans l'anneau, nous étions immortels, ou bien morts, ce qui ne faisait pas de différence, puisque ainsi nous étions hors d'atteinte. (82–3)

> [I would go back to my father in our private silent space, within our word-less immortality. Body to body, all losses, all dangers were abolished; in the moment he held me in his arms and I kissed him, I no longer wanted anything but death. If we were to die this way, we would never be separated again. And as long as we were inside the closed circle, we were immortal, or else dead, it made no difference, since this way we were out of danger. (54)]

There is no difference between death and immortality insofar as neither is a *time of difference*. In contrast, where there is difference, there is life: 'Ce qui vit c'est ce qui n'est pas mort. Dans mon corps je pouvais installer toutes les différences et tant qu'il y aurait une différence, une seule, j'aurais la vie' (53–4) ['What is living is what is not dead. In my body I could establish all the differences and as long as there was one difference, just one, I would hold on to life' (33)]. The only difference that makes a difference, in effect, is the difference between life and death: 'La seule différence incontestable n'est pas celle des sexes ou des âges ou des forces, mais celles des vifs et des morts' (121) ['The only incontestable difference is not that of sex or age or strength, but that of the living and the dead' (79)].

The challenge of 'living with someone dead', then, is to find a way to relate to them that does not further immobilise the past. The narrator's horror of visiting her father's grave with her wailing grandmother is intensified by the flowers the family placed there, not because their transience contrasts with the unchanging granite of the tombstone but on the contrary because they have been carefully selected not to wither too quickly, unlike the scented violets he loved while he was alive. Similarly, the photograph mounted on the grave serves only to reify him. The 'yeux immobiles' ['fixed look'] with which he unchangeably surveys the visitors highlights the discrepancy between the living man she had known and his image: 'C'était lui. Ce n'est pas lui' (92) ['It was him. It's not him' (60)]. But the rotting body contained within the grave does not contain him any better: 'Mon père qui pourrit n'est pas dans l'appartement de granit, il est là où il est. J'ai de la peine pour la vieille bête qui gronde le cadavre par habitude. Je lui dis: – Il n'est pas mort *ton fils*, pourquoi gronder un tas pourri, ton fils est dans toi' (87–8) ['My father who's rotting is not in that granite apartment, he is where he is. I feel sorry for the old cow scolding the corpse out of habit. I tell her: – *Your son* is not dead, why are you scolding a rotting pile, your son is in you' (57)].

The assertion that the dead son survives 'in' his mother – or his daughter – invites an analogy between the 'inside' at stake in *Dedans* and the process of encryption theorised by Maria Torok and Nicolas Abraham (in the years immediately following the publication of Cixous's text), whereby a loss too traumatic to be assimilated is incorporated in a 'crypt' inaccessible to the rest of the psyche, and not subject to temporal disinvestment.[34] The work of Torok and Abraham is particularly pertinent to this chapter in a further respect. 'L'Écorce et le noyau', the article which gave its name to the collection of writings now known under that name, took issue with the very project of Laplanche and Pontalis's 1967 *Vocabulaire de la psychanalyse* [*The Language of Psychoanalysis*] for seeking to fix the meaning of psychoanalytical terms.[35] By failing to recognise that these terms 'designify' more than they signify because the formations they refer to belong to the realm of the unconscious, the *Vocabulaire* in effect downplays one of psychoanalysis's key insights, which is that unconscious formations are irreducibly unknowable. (Or, to reformulate in words that stress the relevance to the argument of this chapter: the way language is all too often used within psychoanalysis – as a means of naming the unconscious, closing down meaning rather than opening it up – can in its own way represent a prison, a word which derives from the Latin *prēnsiō*, 'the action or power of making an arrest', from *prehendere*, 'to lay hold of'.) In contrast, what Torok and Abraham term an 'anasemic' practice of language directs attention away from its meaning and insists on the fundamental unknowability of its object.[36]

Cixous's language is manifestly anasemic. Her narrator seeks release from the past: 'Le passé ne cache plus qu'il a été ma prison' (76) ['The past no longer hides that it has been my prison' (49)]. But her priority is not to attain an unchanging immortality, either 'without words' (as in the cocoon enclosing her with her father) or with them. 'Ici rien n'arrive, il faut passer là où les mots n'enferment plus' (87) ['Here nothing happens. You have to go where words no longer imprison' (57)]. An attempt to circumscribe the past will just repeat the prison; what is needed is for the repetition to transform the prison it explores into a site of passage. The paragraph quoted above in which the narrator declares that she lives on her legacy of pain continues: 'Car il y a eu un commencement, et il y a eu la fin, et je me nourris de l'un et de l'autre' (152) ['For there was a beginning, and there was an end, and I feed on both' (98)]. The question is not to set death at a distance, but rather how to make it sustain life.

The Language of Prison, the Prison of Language

Part I of *Dedans* opens with an image of enclosure which both is and is not a prison:

MA MAISON EST ENCERCLÉE. ELLE EST ENTOURÉE PAR LE GRILLAGE. DEDANS, nous vivons. Dehors ils sont cinquante mille, ils nous encerclent. Dedans je suis quand même chez nous: je suis sûre qu'ils n'oseront pas rentrer. Mais il faut bien que je sorte tous les jours. (11)

[MY HOUSE IS SURROUNDED. IT IS ENCIRCLED BY THE IRON GRATING. INSIDE, we live. Outside, they are fifty thousand, they surround us. Inside, all the same, I'm home: I'm sure they will not dare come in. Yet I must go out every day. (7)]

The hostile encirclement makes the house both a space of security and one of captivity. The ability to cross the border between inside and outside is what stops it from being only a prison.

This 'inside' has generated a number of readings from a psychoanalytical perspective, with critics typically interpreting the narrator's somewhat reluctant leaving of her house as not only a symbolic birth, but a birth into the symbolic. This perspective is supported by the association the narrator explicitly makes further on between her father and language: 'J'ai peu de mots. Mon père qui les avait tous, est parti si précipitamment, qu'il n'a pas eu le temps de me les donner' (52) ['I don't have many words. My father, who had them all, left in such a hurry that he didn't have time to give them to me' (32)]. Thus for Morag Shiach, 'inside' represents the Imaginary in both its positive and negative aspects insofar as it offers a space of both imprisonment and security. The narrator is caught in the conflict of wanting 'neither to be trapped in the Imaginary, nor silenced by the Symbolic', a conflict which ultimately remains unresolved in that her attempt to 'move beyond the categories and limitations of language' can succeed 'only linguistically'.[37] For Susan Sellers also, the 'inside' is a 'metaphor for the state prior to separation', although unlike Shiach she reads the movement of the text linearly, as a progressive differentiation of the narrator's self. The role she attributes to language in bringing about the narrator's 'emergence from this "inside"' suggests an equivalence with a movement from the Imaginary to the Symbolic, although she uses neither term directly.[38] Anne-Marie Picard, on the other hand, reads *Dedans* explicitly as the replacement of the 'imaginary father' by a 'symbolic father'.[39]

These readings share a common assumption of the priority (at least in the sense of the antecedence) of the 'inside' over the 'outside' or of the Imaginary over the Symbolic. Yet *Dedans* profoundly challenges the assumption that the 'inside' is more originary than the outside. The house was not initially besieged; the narrator and her family were not yet 'tout à fait encerclés' (11) ['completely encircled' (7)] during the period when the old family friend in relation to whom the father's death is first mentioned visited them. In a later account of a trip to the zoo with her father, the narrator specifies that 'la maison n'était pas encore encerclée, et dehors les cinquante mille autres ne s'opposaient pas à notre marche' (45) ['the house was not yet surrounded, and outside the fifty thousand others did not keep us from taking our walks' (28)]. The house was therefore only gradually surrounded, the final encirclement – and consequently the opposition between inside and outside – appearing to take place after rather than before the father's death.

The opposition between inside and outside is key to the violence Cixous recalls as the main characteristic of her 'Algerian scene' in a short text published nearly thirty years after *Dedans*:

'My house is encircled', is the first sentence of my first fictional text, *Inside*. It swooped down on me when I started writing. [. . .] The encirclement, the Circle, the siege, are primitive figures of my Algerian scene. Our familial and social movements were attempts to enter, to be admitted, to go through the doors, to pass the thresholds of intolerance. [. . .] The circles intersected. To be inside was also to be outside. Entering gave on to exclusion.[40]

Rather than an initially undifferentiated space from which it was imperative that the narrator emerge, 'inside' represents an already differentiated space, the product of a particular mode of differentiation or symbolisation which, by opposing inside and outside, makes them mirror images of each other. A pure 'inside' is inconceivable; 'inside' is only what it is because of the 'outside'.

Significantly, the sentence Cixous quotes above is not, in fact, the first sentence of the book.[41] In the published text, Part I is preceded by a paragraph-long prologue which is presumably a late addition, as no trace of it is evident in the material relating to *Dedans* held at the Bibliothèque Nationale. Examination of these archival documents reveals that – unlike for Cixous's other texts – a similar process of retrospective framing extends throughout the book. In ways, *Dedans* is more similar to the short stories that preceded it than to the longer fictions that followed; it is Cixous's most broken text, its two parts each being divided into smaller sections, the first into twenty-two short, unnumbered and untitled chapters, the second into nine. Many of these sections were originally written and arranged in a different order from that of the published text, suggesting that what is at stake in the writing process is less a progressive exteriorisation than a crossing backwards and forwards between inside and outside. In particular, it is noticeable that a disproportionately large number of the handwritten additions to the typescripts relate to the first and last sentences of a chapter (seven and nine changes respectively). For example, in the typescript of the second chapter (21–5/13–15), the last sentence – 'Ainsi je sus qu'il y avait moi et qu'il y avait toi, et que je pouvais être l'un ou l'autre' (25) ['Thus I learned that there was me and there was you, and that I could be one or the other' (15)] – is a manuscript addition. The genetic material thus shows that the writing of *Dedans* is a process privileging the *production of borders*, the generation of exchanges between outside and inside. Moreover, another typescript shows that the second chapter was first conceived as a separate story, under the title 'Dehors' ['Outside'], now the first word within the chapter. The border between the 'inside' and the 'outside' is unremittingly mobile.

This mobility is strikingly obvious in the lyrical prologue mentioned earlier which constitutes the text's first border after the title, occupying a position both inside and outside the text it introduces.[42] Just as the 'inside' of the title is unlimited by any reference to an outside or context, the prologue posits an 'inside' conspicuously not limited by traditional oppositions:

> Le soleil se couchait à notre commencement et se lève à notre fin. Je suis née en orient je suis morte à l'occident. Le monde est petit et le temps est court. Je suis dedans. On dit que l'amour est aussi fort que la mort. Mais la mort est aussi forte que l'amour et je suis dedans. Et la vie est plus forte que la mort, et je suis dedans. Mais Dieu est plus fort que la vie et la mort. On dit que la vie et la mort sont au pouvoir de la langue. Dans mon jardin d'enfer les mots sont mes fous. Je suis assise sur un trône de feu et j'écoute ma langue. [. . .] Je ris à cause des mots. (7–8)

> [The sun was setting in our beginnings and is rising as we end. I was born in the east I died in the west. The world is small and time is short. I am inside. It is said that love is as strong as death. But death is as strong as love and I am inside. And life is stronger than death, and I am inside. But God is stronger than life and death. It is said that words have power over life and death. In my garden of hell words are my fools. I sit upon a throne of fire and listen to my language. [. . .] It is because of words that I laugh. (3)]

To considerable rhetorical effect, the 'I' three times declares itself 'inside' – but inside what? The word has no clear spatial referent, with the result that instead of specifying one place as distinct from another, it appears to signify a link between the terms of the various binaries evoked: sunrise/sunset, beginning/end, East/West and, especially, life/death. But these terms are themselves already in movement. The reference to the sun establishes a parallel between *Dedans*'s prologue and the introduction to the book of Ecclesiastes: 'The sun rises and the sun sets, and hurries back to where it rises' (1: 5). The message in Ecclesiastes, however, is that no mobility is possible. The past is fixed, and the dead therefore are doomed to oblivion:

> What has been will be again,
> what has been done will be done again;
> there is nothing new under the sun.
> Is there anything of which one can say,
> 'Look! This is something new'?
> It was here already, long ago;
> it was here before our time.
> No one remembers the former generations,
> and even those yet to come
> will not be remembered
> by those who follow them.
>
> (1: 9–11)

In contrast, the way Cixous invokes the sun is itself already evidence that there *can* be something new under the sun. In a reversal of the usual association sunrise/beginning, sunset/end, the sun sets at the beginning, *before* it rises in the end. The ending can be a beginning. Furthermore, the spatial uncertainty echoes in a temporal confusion, exemplified in the use of the verb *mourir* (to die) in the perfect tense, which situates the subject in relation to both past and present. *When* the narrator speaks is as difficult to situate as *where*. She has already died at the beginning of the book, yet her death is inscribed as part of an ongoing process. Death is not the end, but rather an inseparable part of the cycle of life. 'Le monde est petit et le temps est court' ['The world is small and time is short']: 'inside' appears to be the sphere of space and time, that is of life, but life of which death is an integral part.

Especially, the opacity of the prologue's opening highlights that the novelty in question is irreducibly a matter of language. Though the series of assertions establishes a complicated hierarchy between love, life, death and God, above all it flaunts an exuberant excess over the logical relations it asserts. Is the narrator's position 'inside' the same in all three instances of the word? Is the proposed hierarchy, with God at the top as the strongest, to be accepted as a logically defensible construction or is it to be taken as an article of faith? The text's beginning forcefully reminds the reader that the narrator is primarily *within language*, even before language emerges at the level of theme with the assertion that life and death are subject to its power. This makes its position analogous to that of God, since God is stronger than life and death: 'On dit que la vie et la mort sont au pouvoir de la langue' ['It is said that words have power over life and death'].

The power of language is presented explicitly as beyond the narrator's control. Words are her 'fous', admirably rendered in the English translations as 'fools' in a way that preserves the resemblance hinted at from the beginning between the narrator, sitting on a throne, and King Lear.[43] Words are a madness belonging to her yet separate from her, speaking through/to her rather than spoken by her: on her throne, she listens to 'her' language. She is both *with* and *in* language. But language is what makes it possible in the first place to conceive of being simultaneously outside and inside. The prologue's foregrounding of its own textuality, together with the narrator's emphasis on her linguistic condition, thus highlights from the very beginning that, rather than a state or body before language, 'inside' is above all a linguistic space, an irreducibly *textual* space.

The prologue's final sentence presents words as the source of the narrator's pleasure: 'Je ris à cause des mots' ['It is because of words that I laugh']. From the outset, words figure as a counterweight to suffering, as a force with power over life and death – and especially over death. The father's loss transforms the narrator into someone for whom death happens *to others*: 'Quant à la mort je savais bien qu'elle n'était qu'un mot. Autrefois je me demandais pourquoi certains avaient peur de mourir alors que personne ne peut mourir sauf les autres' (19) ['As for death I knew very well it was just a word. In the past I used to ask myself why some people were afraid of dying when no one could die except the others' (12)]. As 'just a word', her own death holds no fear for her. Feeling herself to be immortal, the only limits on life are those she imagines: 'Dans ma vie il n'y avait pas de place pour la mort: ma vie avait l'immensité de l'imaginable. La mort mourait dans son propre nom, comme "rien," comme "Dieu," comme "certain," et tout ce qui était inimaginable' (20) ['In my life there was no room for death: my life was as vast as the imaginable. Death died in its own name, like "nothing," like "God," like "certain," and everything that was unimaginable' (12)].

This, we may presume, is the sense in which the father's early loss 'gave' Cixous death: she knew from experience that death can be *survived*, can give way to life. Faced with the destruction of the world as she knew it, the narrator's response is to live on, to extend the boundaries of life by inventing an alternative world: 'Enfin je repoussai la limite de la vie de part et d'autre du présent: le passé n'étant qu'une histoire, je me raconterais un passé à la place de celui que ma mère n'avait pas conservé' (19) ['Finally I pushed aside the limit of life on both sides of the present: the past was just a story, I would tell myself another past instead of the one my mother had not preserved' (12)]. Or, as she states towards the end of the book: 'Il m'a planté dans l'âme les graines de l'immortalité. Désormais nous vivons contre la mort. [. . .] La seule arme de l'homme, c'est la force de l'imagination. Qui ne veut pas s'en servir pour harceler le présent, celui-là est mort' (200) ['He has planted in my soul the seeds of immortality. From now on we will live against death. [. . .] Man's only weapon is the strength of the imagination. If you don't want to use it to badger the present, you're dead' (130)]. Death is to be resisted imaginatively, by 'harassing' or skirmishing with the present, challenging the inevitability with which it follows from the past. The metaphor of 'seeds' of immortality is aptly paradoxical: at issue is an *organic* immortality, an eternity subject to change.

The photograph of the father was inadequate to represent him because it unchangingly repeated the past. In contrast, words are the cause of Cixous's narrator's laughter because language allows her to repeat the past *with a difference*, to create a living past. For her, the issue is to invent something other than the oppositional relation between her 'inside' and the fifty thousand surrounding the house: 'S'il existait une autre forme de relation, je ne la connaissais pas; c'était eux ou moi' (54) ['If there were another form of relationship, I wasn't aware of it; it was them or me' (34)]. The contrast is stark between this exteriority and the uncertain boundary that characterises her relation with her imaginary father:

> L'inattendu et l'attendu s'épousent comme lui et moi, il fait jour dedans la nuit, [. . .] peu à peu j'annexe le futur à notre intensité, il était déjà là puisque nous avions déjà tout et que j'étais lui et qu'il était moi. Le passé ne cache plus qu'il a été ma prison. (76)

> [The expected and the unexpected are wedded as he and I are, inside night it's daytime, [. . .] little by little I connect the future to our intensity, it was already there since we already had it all and since I was he and he was me. The past no longer hides that it has been my prison. (49)]

Note the use of the perfect aspect: if the past no longer hides that it (or 'he': both possible translations are valid) 'has been' her prison, it means that is no longer the case. In addition, if the past is no longer a prison, it is because other relations have opened up: day is inside night, outside is inside inside, she is inside him and he is inside her . . . *Puisque j'étais lui et qu'il était moi* clearly recalls the famous line from Montaigne: 'Par ce que c'estoit luy; par ce que c'estoit moy' ['Because it was he; because it was I'].[44] But whereas for Montaigne the sentence reflects a friendship where two souls 'se meslent et confondent l'une en l'autre, d'un melange si universel, qu'elles effacent et ne retrouvent plus la couture qui les a jointes' ['mix and work themselves into one piece, with so universal a mixture, that there is no more sign of the seam by which they were first conjoined'],[45] for Cixous the mingling does not abolish the difference between them: 'Mais si nous étions un, il n'y aurait plus d'espace entre nous deux, où Dieu pourrait se glisser. Si j'étais lui, s'il était moi, s'il était moi, si j'étais lui, qui aurait pu nous interrompre?' (81) ['But if we were one, there would be no more space between the two of us, for God to creep in. If I were he, if he were me, if he were me, if I were he, who could have come between us?' (53)].

Far from yearning for the fusional unity Lacan associated with relationships in the Imaginary, then, Cixous's narrator's most intimate desire is for *proximity*. Her pleasure lies not in abolishing boundaries, but in setting them in motion. The fluidity of the border between herself and her father is developed explicitly when her musing over the fixity of his tombstone photograph ends in her apostrophising him directly, at one of the previously mentioned chapter endings added retrospectively (itself therefore representing a shifting border):

> J'aurais voulu être née de toi, avoir vécu longtemps sinueuse dans tes veines au creux du genou, bercée dans ton sang, lovée dans une membrane transparente, moïse au nil rouge. La fille du pharaon le regarde glisser entre les roseaux, et c'est Moïse qui décide d'approcher la rive où l'attend la femme vêtue de blanc. C'est moi moïse en ton sang mais je ne veux pas aborder. (94–5)

> [If I'd had my way I would have been born out of you, I would have lived for a long time creeping through your veins in the hollow of your knees, rocked by your blood, coiled in a transparent membrane, moses in the red nile. The Pharaoh's daughter watches him slip between the reeds, and it is Moses who decides to approach the shore where the woman wearing white awaits him. I am the moses in your blood but I do not wish to reach the shore. (62)]

The narrator's fantasy of being cradled within her father, coiled up within a membrane in fluid, has unmistakable amniotic connotations; she clearly yearns to have known her father from the inside, as intimately as a child experiences the mother who carries it. At the same time, the extract defies any schematic interpretation in terms of a nostalgic desire to return to an earlier enclosure, insisting rather on the displacements involved. Veins take the place of the womb, the father that of the mother, while Moses' (substitute) mother features as Pharaoh's *daughter*. In particular, the abrupt comparison of the narrator in her father's veins to Moses in the basket in the Nile suggests that the inside in question is also an outside. At every level, meaning *floats*. As both container and contained, the transparent 'membrane' in the river is reminiscent of Proust's carafes in the Vivonne, a famous example of a troubled border between the solid and the fluid, the inside and the outside. But the most obviously mobile border in the quotation concerns the difference between common noun and proper name. In French, 'moïse' designates what in English is called a Moses basket after the prophet who gave it his name. The absence of a capital letter for the name of the river Nile in 'moïse au nil rouge' calls attention to the fine line distinguishing 'moïse' from the 'Moïse' it appears to call up, with the result that when the narrator declares 'C'est moi moïse', it is impossible to determine whether she is in the place of the inanimate basket or the living baby it contains. Moreover, the Moses with whom the narrator identifies is not the baby in the basket, who 'decides' to approach the shore, but rather the *dying* Moses, the one who does not enter the Promised Land.[46] Just as Cixous's writing keeps returning in practice to the border, the desire not to 'aborder' or reach the shore reads here as a desire to remain in transit, in transition.

Unlike the photograph on the father's tomb whose stillness exacerbates her grief at his loss, in the narrator's fantasy there is place for her relationship with her father to evolve. In *Dedans*, the border between life and death is not an irrevocable passage. But this is not the only border the creative freedom which was the legacy of the father's loss leads the narrator to rethink. It also leads her to engage imaginatively with broader questions of identity, especially with the implications of the (psychoanalytical) idea that identity is fundamentally a function of language.

In Language, in Motion: Œdipus Unbound

Given the emphasis in Part I on the narrator's early familial relationships, it is no surprise that her reflections on language should focus on the part it plays in the construction of identity. The narrator remains anonymous throughout; indeed, *Dedans* is exceptional in Cixous's writing, which typically displays a pronounced onomastic inventiveness, in that it has practically no proper names. None of the places are specified, and the only time a character's name is mentioned is when the narrator explains that the father's name did *not* definitively differentiate him: 'Mon père était le quatrième ou le cinquième Georges' (70) ['My father was the fourth or fifth George' (45)]. The fact that the characters are referred to not by name but by their relationship to the narrator ('my father', 'my grandmother', 'my last lover', etc.) makes the 'I' the linchpin of the narrative. But this 'I' is far from a haven of stability. At times, it suddenly shifts reference, forcing the reader to realise that the apparent sameness of the pronoun masks a discontinuity. In the first obvious shift, in the short chapter introduced by the word 'EXERCICE' ['EXERCISE'], the narrator suddenly begins to run and speak as a dog:

Chien, je cours [. . .] Je cours, je cours, je cours, je cours vite, si bien, mes quatre pattes brûlantes, dures parcourues d'un liquide en effervescence, la droite devant à peine un peu raidie par l'appréhension, mais les autres si fines, si nerveuses que le petit défaut est une élégance qui me distingue du commun, sans diminuer ma vitesse, je cours, je cours, je cours si vite que je n'entends plus les bruits des poules et des gens, flp, fllp, fllpp, henham, henham, henham. (40)

[I, the dog, I run [. . .] I run, run, run, I run fast, so well, my four hard, burning paws coated with a bubbly liquid, the right one in front just a little

bit stiff from anxiousness, but the others so splendid, so spirited that this
small defect is a refinement which sets me apart from the ordinary, without
slowing down, I run, I run, I run so fast I can't hear the noises of the hens or
the people anymore, flp, fllp, fllpp, dedum, dedum, dedum. (24–5)]

The reason for the running is to build up speed in order to 'prendre mon
premier vol' ['take off for the first time'], so that the narrator can prove
to her brother that she has no master and that her freedom is limited
only by physical considerations: 'seul le corps nous retient' (42) ['only
the body keeps us back' (26)]. This context, especially in the light of the
dog's concern to convey the noise of the running onomatopoeically, that
is to translate it into language, invites us to read the dog's attempt to
test the limits to its freedom as a figure of the narrator's first attempt to
reach beyond herself in language. The 'exercise' the narrator is exploring in this chapter can be read as a figure of writing itself. As a practice
whose only constraints are physical, writing is limited only by what is
conceivable in language.

Most pertinently for my discussion, the enunciative shifts shake up the
distribution of family roles. This is particularly the case with a long
sequence where the narrator becomes the echo-chamber of her dead
ancestors (the 'cent voix de la mémoire' (103) ['hundred voices of
memory' (67)], and the narrative voice becomes that of the grandfather.
The typescript shows that much of this sequence – 'Un jour je m'éveillai
[. . .] je me tus' (103–7) ['One day I woke up [. . .] I stopped' (67–9)] –
was a later insertion into the narrative, as the supports for the text
immediately preceding and following were originally one page cut in
two at the point of the insertion. The shift in voice is introduced by the
words 'Il dit:' ['He said:'], followed by a gap of some lines. Because of
this framing, it is initially unclear if the sequence after the gap consists
of his words or if the gap figures what he said. The first indication the
speaking subject has changed is when the 'I' refers to its wife (104/68).
Since the characters are identified by their relationship to the narrator,
this means that the textual identity of *all* the characters changes each
time the enunciation shifts: 'my grandmother' becomes 'my wife', etc. As
a function of a deictic (the possessive adjective), the identity therefore
even of characters designated by the third person is a matter of endless
repositioning within a network of relationships.[47] And, as the following
quotation makes clear, this repositioning is not constrained by logic; its
only bounds are those of language:

> Mon père m'appelle 'ma fille', et son père et sa mère m'appellent aussi 'ma
> fille' et ils appellent mon père 'mon fils' ou 'ton père'. (74–5)

[My father calls me 'my daughter,' and his father and his mother call me 'my daughter' too and they call my father 'my son' or 'your father'. (48)]

As this suggests, the principal effect of these narrative shifts in *Dedans* is to call family roles profoundly into question. One particular passage, where death is imaged as the Sphinx, highlights the specifically Œdipal implications of the structure in question:

> Je vais d'abord à la fenêtre tirer la langue à la Mort. Je l'ai eue. Et chaque jour je la vole. Elle s'étale dehors, sans yeux, sans bouche, sans forme, géante pitoyable vautrée sur la ville et le pays, sur les animaux et les peuples, gavée, gâtée, mais encore tourmentée de désirs. (76)

> [First I go to the window to stick my tongue out at Death. I've tricked her. And every day I steal from her. She sprawls outside, eyeless, mouthless, shapeless, pitiful giant dragging herself over the city and the country, over animals and peoples, gorged, spoiled, but still tormented by desire. (49)]

The scene is manifestly an Œdipal scene, but one in which the usual Œdipal triangle is oneirically displaced: here death is the third term threatening the narrator's union with her father. On the one hand, it builds on Lacan's reformulation of Freud's Œdipal triangle as a set of relations between instances (the subject, the object of its desire and the figure of the Law or paternal metaphor) rather than people (the child, mother and father). Here, instead of the father figuring as the third term separating the child from the mother, death is the figure threatening to interrupt the child's relation with her father. But Cixous's writing complicates this schema even as it takes shape. First of all, death can be interpreted as the object of desire as well as what forbids it, especially in the light of Cixous's comment many years later that she wouldn't have 'had' death if her father had not died. 'Je l'ai eue. Et chaque jour je la vole' could be translated by 'I had her. And each day I steal her' as well as by 'I tricked her. And each day I steal from her'. Secondly, the comparison of death to an old woman 'still tormented by desires' places it in the position of the subject of desire. And indeed this passage introduces a chain of signification that links death with the father's mother. Death is designated in the following paragraph as a 'vieille Bête' ['old Beast'] and an 'immense vache aux mamelles desséchées' (77) ['enormous cow with withered tits' (49)], and later as 'la Grand Mort' [Great Death]: 'L'autre [rumeur] était le souffle de la Grand Mort qui habite au cœur de la ville, non loin du port' (81) ['The other was the nasal wheezing of the Great Death who lives in the heart of the city, not far from the port' (53)]. The genetic material shows that this sentence earlier read 'la Grande Vache qui habite au cœur de la ville, non loin du port' ['the Great Cow who lives in the heart of the city, not far from the port'], then 'la Grande Ville qui rumine, non loin du port' ['the Great City that ruminates, not far from the port'], before being fixed in its final form. The link between the paronyms 'mort' and 'mère' thus links death with the 'grand-mère' whose cries on the death of her son lead the narrator to call her a 'Bête' ['beast'] who 'rugit' (67) ['roars' (43)], a word sharing the same etymology as 'rumeur'.

These displacements foreground the complexity of the relations involving the narrator, her father, mother and grandmother, a complexity which reminds us that at issue in these scenes is an Œdipal *complex*, a network of familial relations which does not necessarily become fixed once the subject has emerged as an individual. One of the principal challenges facing *Dedans*'s reader is that while Cixous's known familiarity with Freudian and Lacanian theory invites a psychoanalytical reading, her text already displaces the analytical schema provided by the theory. In the last quotation, the 'paternal' instance was the father's mother who is also a beast. In the narrator's fantasy of being cradled in her father's blood, the father is represented as the object of desire within a dual relationship more usually associated with the pre-Œdipal relationship with the mother.[48] Other scenes, as when the narrator is in bed with her mother, place the mother more conventionally in the position of object of desire: 'Dedans il fait brun, et chaud, nous sommes seuls, le corps et moi' (63) ['Inside it's dark, and warm, we're alone, her body and me' (40)]. Yet the hostility the narrator displays towards her mother ('Parce que je la hais, ma mère n'est plus' (65) ['Because I hate her, my mother is no more' (42)], especially her fury at discovering that 'ce n'était pas mon père qui occupait l'esprit de ma mère' ['it was not my father who occupied my mother's thoughts'] and that she had 'égaré notre passé' (15) ['mislaid our past' (9)]), places the mother rather in the position of the third term, the figure of the Law prohibiting access to the object of desire.

Dedans is thus full of Œdipal triangles, *constantly shifting* Œdipal triangles, where the points rotate between figures such as death and the city as well as the different members of the narrator's family. Whereas in the orthodox Lacanian psychoanalytical model Œdipal triangulation leads to the stabilisation of an initally uncertain identity, in Cixous's text the triangles bear witness to an identity that never stabilises.[49] It is as though the father's death presented the narrator with a searing experience that positions in an Œdipal scenario are precisely *positions*, always subject to change. Indeed, the narrator states explicitly that the troubling of her identity followed (rather than preceded) her father's death:

'jusqu'à la mort de mon père, je pensais que chacun était chacun pour soi comme pour les autres, que j'étais une petite fille, et que toutes les petites filles sont identiques' (66) ['up to my father's death, I believed that everybody existed for themselves the same way they existed for the others, that I was a little girl, and that all little girls are alike' (42)]. His loss opened the way for her not to become a little girl – she already considered herself a little girl – but to multiply her identifications.

The narrator's lability reads thus as a response to loss, rather than a fluidity preceding the Œdipal structuring of identity of psychoanalytical theory. It is an act of memory, reaching a climax when she stops 'resisting' the hundred voices of memory (the first of which was the sequence when the 'I' became the grandfather), and becomes caught up in a veritable whirlwind of voices. Significantly, she listens to these while sitting between her grandmother's legs, 'assise en tailleur à l'entrée de la maison ouverte de mes pères' (102) ['sitting cross-legged in the entrance of the house of my fathers' (67)],[50] 'posée à l'entrée de la Bête' (103) ['poised in the entrance to the Beast' (67)]. Her threshold position allows her to channel the voices from the past she hears inside:

> Ecoute fils-fille de notre fils écoute (j'écoute), écoute enfant de notre enfant, j'écoute tandis que les vagues sucent et frappent chacun de mes petits os, l'espace en rotation rapide efface le monde extérieur qui tourne au blanc, le temps en déroulement rapide efface les âges extérieurs, tout est mêlé je vacille, je suis le fils, la fille, mon père, son père et mon propre fils, sans cesser de me souvenir de moi-même, je me succède sans m'oublier, ils me disent: 'Sache', et 'Souviens-toi' et je sais, ils me disent: 'Deviens' et 'Reviens'. Alors la voix m'invite à venir: 'Viens voir, viens voir.'
>
> Je vérifie dehors: la bête n'a pas bougé; je sais ou me souviens que je suis dans l'espace sans temps, oreille de la mémoire. Je vais faire un voyage dans un monde autrement mesuré; entre le temps où la bête ouvre la bouche pour soupirer et le temps où elle referme ses lèvres sur un grand morceau d'air, j'ai le temps de passer trois âges et d'assister à trois naissances et trois morts, au-delà du labyrinthe. Je vois naître mon père et son père et moi-même. (120–1)

> [Listen son-daughter of our son listen (I'm listening), listen child of our child, I listen as the waves suck and beat against each of my little bones, fast spinning space is blotting out the outer world which is turning to white, fast unfolding time is blotting out the outer ages, all of it mingling, I stagger, I am the son, the daughter, my father, his father and my own son, never ceasing to remember myself, I am heir to myself, never forgetting that I am me, they tell me: 'Know' and 'Remember' and I know, they tell me: 'Become' and 'Come back.' Then the voice invites me to come: 'Come look, come look.'
>
> I look outside: the beast hasn't budged; I know or remember that I am in timeless space, ear of memory. I will travel through a world that is measured differently; between the time the beast opens its mouth to sigh and the time

it closes its lips upon a great hunk of air, I have time to live through three generations and time to attend three births and three deaths, beyond the laby-rinth. I see my father being born and his father and myself. (78–9)]

Unlike the grandfather's earlier voice, framed visibly as a shift in enunciation, here the lack of inverted commas distinguishing between the various voices forcefully reproduces for the reader the impression of being caught up in the swirling waves the narrator describes. The vacillation of her identity accelerates. All is indeed 'mêlé' or mingled at every level: sexual, temporal, genealogical. The declaration 'je suis le fils, la fille, mon père, son père et mon propre fils' ['I am the son, the daughter, my father, his father and my own son'] recalls Artaud's line, 'Moi, Antonin Artaud, je suis mon fils, / mon père, ma mère, / et moi' ['I, Antonin Artaud, am my son, / my father, my mother, / and me']:[51] the narrative voice is entwined with others intertextually as well as with those echoing from her past. She specifies twice that she remembers herself along with them: she is herself as well as the other generations and genders that speak through her.

'Je me succède' ['I succeed myself']: 'I' is a *succession of voices* which become audible as the 'outer world' and 'outer ages' whirl away. Reading *Dedans* as the journey announced here into this interiority, 'espace sans temps' ['space without time'] or 'monde autrement mesuré' ['differently measured world'], writing becomes literally a venture into the mouth of the beast, into a space where time knows no limits. This timeless space evokes the Freudian unconscious, characterised by the absence of any temporal organisation. But here the lack of temporal progression is not represented as a problem to be resolved; on the con-trary, it appears to offer a resource. In the interval between the beast's opening and closing her mouth, *any* time is possible. 'J'ai le temps de passer trois âges' ['I have time to live through three generations']: these ages evoke the three ages of man in the Sphinx's riddle as well as the three generations mentioned (the narrator, father and grandfather). In this momentary space, time is elastic, contracting[52] and dilating like a sphincter (a word which shares the etymology of 'Sphinx', deriving from the Greek *sphingein*, to bind tight). The succession of voices functions as an entry to a space where succession need not take place, where ages coexist rather than replace each other. *The present is the place of time.* In the present, she can order (narrativise) time as she desires.

The narrator gleans from the other voices she allows to speak through her that both age and sex exceed logical determination. The final section of the chapter describes a dialogue she overheard between unspecified voices which appear to belong to a mother and son. The reader assumes these to be the voices of the narrator's grandmother and father, reminiscing about the latter's childhood passion for the former. The narrator is thus herself in the position of third term in a conversation which logically would have taken place many years before. The dialogue recalls a classical Œdipal scenario: the intensity of the child's love is outlined when we learn that the feminine voice's 'petit garçon' ['little boy'] always wanted to come into her bed when his father had gone out; that he loved her and wanted to marry her; that he wanted to lick her everywhere (122–3/79–80). However, within the overheard scene, the (grand) father's negative response to his son's question casts him as interrupter of the dyad:

> C'est mal, dis-je? Mon père dit non.
>   Le père de mon fils l'air posé comme le premier matin, quand il m'avait donné l'arum volé au jardin voisin, dit: non. (128)

> [– Is it bad I say? My father says no.
>   The father of my son looking as solemn as on the first morning, when he gave me the lily stolen from the neighbour's garden, says: no. (83)]

The colon before the final 'non' has the effect of generalising the negative; as the one who says no in the absolute, the (grand)father in the classic position of prohibiter.

The grandfather thus takes up the position of third term first adopted by the narrator: 'voici ce que j'entendis' (122) ['this is what I heard' (79)]. In turn, the 'I' shifts antecedent between all the different points of the Œdipal triangle over the seven-page sequence as a whole. Initially in the position of third term in the framing narrative, within the dialogue it alternately refers to the boy (in the place of subject of desire) and his mother (object). More significantly, even in the few narrative interventions interspersed throughout the dialogue, the first person changes reference. Above, it's the grandmother who says 'The father of my son . . .'. Elsewhere, the 'I' crosses sexual as well as generational boundaries, being clearly marked as the boy's voice: 'Une fois trouvé, je danse, je suis fou de joie, trouvé quoi je ne sais pas, trouvé toi maman' (127) ['Now I've found it I dance, I'm wild with joy, found what I don't know, found you mama' (82)]. The last narrative instance of an 'I' within the sequence even thematises its own shift in identity: 'Je n'ai plus de limite, c'est elle, j'avais toujours voulu l'épouser, mais elle ne m'avait pas pris au sérieux' (125) ['I have no more limits, she's the one, I always wanted to marry her, but she never took me seriously' (81)]. Only the use of the verb *épouser* in relation to a feminine object invites the reader to posit this *je* as masculine. The message of the sequence as a whole, in effect, is that 'I' has no limits: the speakers have no identity – gender, age, familial position – other than can be inferred from what they say.

Some moments suggest the overheard conversation is already triangulated. The simplest way to make sense of the sequence 'je t'aimais. / – Et toi? / – Je t'aime' (122) ['I loved you. / – And what about you? – I love you' (80)] is to posit three rather than two participants in the conversation. Similarly, there are two intervening speakers, not just one, between lines that would logically seem to be uttered by the same person: 'Mais moi, moi, je suis ton petit garçon. Tu sais? ça sentait mauvais dans ton lit, l'âcreté de ton mari' ['But *I, I* am your little boy. You know? There was a bad smell in your bed, your husband's acrid smell'], and: 'Arouar, je suis ton petit garçon-lion' (123) ['Aahrr, I am your little boy-lion' (80)]. The attempt to figure out who is speaking sets the reader searching for a trio which could conceivably be the source of these words (for example the narrator, her brother and her mother). In other words, the text foregrounds the process of construing the identity of the speakers from what they say. There are no limits to the roles they can assume. A 'girl' can 'be' in succession a grandmother, a boy . . . or a lion, as in the line quoted above, a line which links its speaker both with the grandmother's roars on the death of her son – 'RRRaRRRaRRa [. . .] AarrrA aarrAarr' (67/43) – and with the Sphinx, especially given that the lion in two of the other three inscriptions of the word in *Dedans* is winged: 'lions aux ailes rigides' (144) ['lions with wings standing out stiffly' (94)], 'lion de marbre, aux ailes enguirlandées de glycines' (195) ['marble lion, with wisteria hanging over its wings' (128)]. Significantly, the final mention of a lion instances yet another configuration in the narrator's Œdipal fantasies: 'A nouveau je l'attends, mon lion blanc, ma rose, mon père-époux' (175) ['Now I wait for him again, my white lion, my rose, my father-spouse' (114)].

Listening to the voices within her, then, gives the narrator access to a complex of relations in which no bounds are placed on the identities one may assume other than what is conceivable in language. The extensibility of the narrator's identity is a corollary of its linguistic nature; it can shift so spectacularly because it emerges from relations mediated by language. Instead of putting an end to the narrator's uncertain identity, language is what makes it possible. Language represents an *ongoing* process of triangulation, one in which relations are endlessly unsettled by a third term whose intervention serves not to terminate a dialectic, but rather to set the triangle in circulation, in 'rotation'. As we have seen, the third term is often figured as the Sphinx: it is interesting that the sole explicit inscription of the word in *Dedans* relates not to a statue graven in stone but to the hawkmoth, 'papillon appelé sphinx tête de mort' (132) ['the night butterfly they call death's-head moth' (86)], a figure of death in flight.

Unapologetically Narrative

The narrator's infinitely extensible identity is reflected in *Dedans*'s extreme lack of narrative closure. The book remains hauntingly, oneirically, opaque all the way through, ending on a new return, a repetition whose meaning yet again defies any attempt at elucidation. The return which takes place in the final two chapters reiterates the message that the narrative gives access to no knowledge outside itself, that the only 'beyond' of the story is another story still untold:

> IL EST REVENU.
> – Viens, dit sa voix, allons en prison, tout seuls nous deux ensemble, viens, dit-elle.
> Comme je l'entendais mal et sans le voir, je le cherchais partout.
> – Répète, dis-je. Où es-tu? dis-je. Allume, allume, dis-je. (193)

> [HE HAS RETURNED.
> – Come, says his voice, let's away to prison, we two alone, come it says.
> Since I could barely hear him and couldn't see him, I looked for him everywhere.
> – Say it again, I say, Where are you? I ask. Turn on the light, turn it on, I say. (126)]

This return cranks up uncertainty at the exit to the book rather than resolving it. For example, critics have been able to make varying assumptions as to whether this 'he' refers to the narrator's lover or her father.[53] The further detail that he had come back 'pour la dernière fois' (204) ['for the last time' (133)] could mean either that she and he will never again be parted, or that they will be together no more. Given that 'IL EST REVENU' immediately follows the passage in which the narrator bemoans the limitations of the 'accompli' or perfect aspect, the use of the perfect calls attention to itself, yet the completedness of the return it describes is cast into question. While the statement initially suggests that he and she are now together, the narrator herself returns later in the chapter ('Je suis revenue' (200) ['I have returned' (130)]) to join 'him' (is it the same 'him', then, or a different one?). More precisely, it is not clear whether she *will* join him or whether she *has already done so*. The following quotation offers a perfect example of the bewildering sequence of tenses that characterises the narrative:

Je peux venir, mais je ne peux pas rester, même si tu es gentil, puisque toi tu
ne restes pas.
   Tant que tu seras forme je resterai. Quand tu seras poussière je reviendrai.
   Quand il fut poussière je revins, par la même route. (197)

[I can come but I cannot stay, even if you're nice, since *you* are not staying.
   As long as you are form I shall remain. When you are dust I shall return.
   When he became dust I returned, by the same route. (128)]

In the French, all the verbs in the second line (*seras, resterai, reviendrai*)
are in the future. The sudden shift to the past in the following line con-
nects the two tenses; future and past belong to the same time, a time
explicitly related some lines later to the time of writing when, musing
over the coexistence of temporal incompatibilities, the narrator inter-
rupts herself: 'je n'aurais pas dû écrire ça' (198) ['I should not have
written that' (129)]. As in the alternative past she proposed to 'tell' for
herself, the borders of the present extend on either side.[54] It seems that
writing is the space where the future can precede the past, where the past
can *have* a future, one that is not already programmatically determined
by what has happened. Unlike in Ecclesiastes, something 'new under the
sun' is possible; the past is 'eternal', immortal, not because it was fixed
'long ago [. . .] before our time', graven in stone, but because it can be
infinitely rewritten.

   The narrator returns again to Ecclesiastes in these final chapters: 'Un
temps pour jeter les pierres, un temps pour les assembler. Un temps,
un temps, un temps pour étreindre, un temps pour refréner l'étreinte. Un
temps, un temps, un temps, un temps' ['A time for throwing stones, a
time for gathering them. A time, a time, a time for hugging, a time for
holding back. A time, a time, a time, a time']. In the Bible, the idea is that
there are separate times for these activities:

There is a time for everything,
and a season for every activity under the heavens, [. . .]
a time to scatter stones and a time to gather them,
a time to embrace and a time to refrain from embracing.
                                        (Ecclesiastes 3: 1–5)

In contrast, in *Dedans* they take place at the same time: '– Viens, dit-il,
tous les deux ensemble. Un temps pour étreindre le même temps pour
refréner l'étreinte' (200) ['– Come, says he, the two of us together. A time
for hugging the same time for holding back' (130)]. The book's ending
is enigmatic in part because different versions of the story, and different
stages of its action, share the same time-space. We learn that the narrator disintegrates into dust without leaving any trace (203/132), only to

read on the next page that she feels she should disappear. She joins the man awaiting her (199/129), then again sets off, a few pages later, 'vers les eaux tendres de mon père-époux' (207) ['towards the sweet waters of my father-spouse' (134)]. Contradictions abound at every level.

The singular lack of narrative resolution means that no sense of finality is produced at the end of the diegesis. Cixous's text is of course not alone in this respect; for example, Beckett is another obvious instance of a writer whose texts comprehensively subvert the expectation that the ending will bring narrative closure. What is distinctive about *Dedans*, however, is that the ending suddenly and unexpectedly strikes a different tone. *Dedans* thus surprises its reader with a happy ending, albeit an unconventional one. A sense of unlimited potential is created by the insistent repetition in the last chapter of the words 'je pouvais' ['I was able'] (eight times in one long paragraph alone (204–5/133–4)), reaching a climax at the end of the penultimate paragraph: 'Or j'en ai marre des bords de mort et j'en ai marre des remplaçants [. . .] je me réjouis de pouvoir parler, que j'aie dix ans, trente ans ou soixante, et de pouvoir dire merde merde merde à la mort' (208) ['Now I'm sick and tired of standing at the shores of death and I'm sick of substitutes [. . .] and I rejoice in my power to speak, in the fact that I am ten years old, thirty years old or sixty, and that I can say kiss off kiss off to death' (135)]. The narrator's sudden joyful, upbeat attitude is not attributed to any diegetic development; it appears to be her 'power to speak' that enables her to defy death. The final paragraph then makes one last, unexplained turn. A non sequitur at every level, it serves as an epilogue that not only closes the text on a lyrical note but signals the power of lyricism, just as the prologue that in many respects it repeats drew attention to the power of language:

> Viens, dit-il, allons en prison, nous deux ensemble, sans elle sans eux, moi tout seul je te ferai seule toi seule tu feras la nuit de tes lèvres sur mes yeux et je te verrai par-delà les murs et les temps. Si tu veux de moi je t'étreindrai et nous créerons les nouvelles histoires, si tu ne veux pas je te demanderai pardon. Tu seras en haut et en bas et je serai dedans. Dehors le mystère des choses s'asséchera, les générations reflueront morts sur mots sous le soleil, mais dedans nous aurons cessé de mourir. (209)

> [Come, says he, let's away to prison, we two alone, without her without them, alone I will make you alone, alone you will make the night with your lips on my eyes and I shall see you beyond walls and time. If you will have me I will hold you in my arms and we shall create new tales. If you won't I shall ask your forgiveness. You will be above and down below and I shall be inside. Outside, the mystery of things will dry up, under the sun the generations will wash up worlds over words, but inside we shall have stopped dying. (136)]

This epilogue contains nothing at the level of plot to explain the hopefulness with which the ending looks forward to the future. Rather, the way this singular 'explicit'[55] completes or 'accomplishes' the book has the effect of drawing attention to its *in*explicability. The discrepancy between the notion of a 'prison' and the vital, loving space described emphasises the excess of the narrative over the events it recounts. The impossibility of explaining the joyful, hopeful tone at the end as the result of anything internal to the diegesis suggests that *telling the story* has made a difference: a difference that it cannot *say*, cannot convert into knowledge, can only acknowledge rather than know.

The ending thus affords its own narrative satisfaction. In other words, *Dedans* too is a narrative driven by the desire for the end that at the same time it defers, as outlined in the Introduction. For Brooks, most of whose analyses deal with nineteenth-century novels, the end is a moment of recognition that contrasts with the uncertainty of the middle whose meaning it retrospectively determines:

> The desire of the text is ultimately the desire for the end, for that recognition which is the moment of the death of the reader in the text. Yet recognition cannot abolish textuality, does not annul that middle which is the place of repetitions, oscillating between blindness and recognition, between origin and ending. Repetition toward recognition constitutes the truth of the narrative text.[56]

But does it make a difference when the recognition achieved at the end is above all, as in *Dedans*, the recognition of the *illusory nature of any end*?

It makes no difference at the level of narrative structure. In fact, Brooks points out as a corollary to his argument that

> repetition speaks in the text of a return which ultimately subverts the very notion of beginning and end, suggesting that the idea of beginning presupposes the end, that the end is a time before the beginning, and hence that the interminable never can be finally bound in a plot. Any final authority claimed by narrative plots, whether of origin or end, is illusory.[57]

The satisfaction afforded by even the most traditional, definitive, clarificatory resolution is always the satisfaction of an illusion. Where a difference arises, it seems to me, is in relation to the desire for the illusion. Brooks goes on to equate psychoanalysis and literature in this respect:

> An analysis, Freud would eventually discover, is inherently interminable, since the dynamics of resistance and the transference can always generate new beginnings in relation to any possible end. It is the role of fictional plots to impose an end which yet suggests a return, a new beginning: a rereading.[58]

Yet, as my earlier discussion of Felman's work brought out, the illusory or fictional status of the authority his interpretations could claim was something Freud repeatedly had to *re*discover: psychoanalysis resists the insight that the truth it has to offer is a fiction.

Unlike literature. Here, then, is where Cixous's work most sharply points up its difference from psychoanalysis. In 'A Kind of Magic', the writer recalls that she and Derrida 'exchanged long narratives on experiences that completely escaped the possibility of narration. Which was, really without us at all realizing, a kind of invented, totally lay, piece of *miteinander* analysis.'[59] *Dedans*, too, is a narrative about an experience that appears to completely escape the possibility of narration; as such, it in turn represents 'a kind of invented analysis'. But, unlike psychoanalysis, it displays no nostalgia for the narratable, no desire to pin down or close down meaning – latent or manifest! Perhaps the crux of the difference between 'literature' and 'psychoanalysis' is a matter of attitude (that is of posture, of positioning) towards the border between narrative and the 'inside' the narrative seems to express. The blitheness with which Cixous's narrator sets about inventing 'another past' for herself in place of the one she has lost is an indication that, for her, that border is no prison. The freedom she takes in revisiting it speaks eloquently of her pleasure; she displays no resistance towards the fact that the past is *infinitely*, rather than *definitively*, to be explicated. In her practice of language, the narrator has in effect travelled very far toward a place 'où les mots n'enferment plus' ['where words no longer imprison'], a place where 'nous aurons cessé de mourir' ['we shall have stopped dying']. She is wholly taken up with exploring something that defies any attempt to know it: she is an analyst. She enjoys that defiance: she revels in fiction.

Notes

1. Hélène Cixous, 'A Kind of Magic', *Cixous, Derrida, Psychoanalysis*, ed. Mark Dawson, Mairéad Hanrahan and Eric Prenowitz, *Paragraph*, 36:2 (2013), 161–88, at 163. The conference in which the volume originated was entitled 'Hélène Cixous, Jacques Derrida: Their Psychoanalyses'; it was held at the University of Leeds on 1–3 June 2007 and organised by Martin McQuillan, Eric Prenowitz and Ashley Thompson. Cixous gave the opening keynote talk.
2. Ibid.
3. Ibid., 161 and 170.
4. 'I started reading Freud when I was eighteen. I was extremely excited and happy because from what I had heard about Freud, I was absolutely sure that he would introduce me to paradise. Of course I hurried to the text on female sexuality ... and I was expelled from paradise immediately. Not

because I disagreed, but it was simply that I wasn't there. I read, and I didn't understand anything. And I started wondering whether I existed and whether I was female or whatever, or human. It was a trauma. I dropped Freud' (ibid., 165).

5. Prime examples of this can be found in *Neutre* [*Neutral*] (Paris: Grasset, 1972), *Portrait du soleil* [*Portrait of the Sun*] (Paris: Denoël, 1973), *Partie* [*Part*] (Paris: Editions des femmes, 1976) and *Anankè* (Paris: Editions des femmes, 1979). *La* is widely interpreted as a riposte to Lacan's assertion that 'La femme n'existe pas' ['The woman does not exist']. For an exceptionally comprehensive reading of *Portrait du soleil*, see Christa Stevens, *L'Écriture solaire d'Hélène Cixous: Travail du texte et histoires du sujet dans* Portrait du soleil (Amsterdam: Rodopi (Faux Titre), 1999).

6. 'A Kind of Magic', 167.

7. Ibid., 165.

8. Ibid., 164.

9. Most of Cixous's commentators to date have had occasion to note the importance of dreaming in her writing. The most recent critical concentration on the question is the volume *Rêver croire penser. Autour d'Hélène Cixous*, ed. Marta Segarra and Bruno Clément (Paris: Hermann, 2010).

10. *Rêve je te dis* (Paris: Galilée, 2003) [*Dream I Tell You*, trans. Beverley Bie Brahic (Edinburgh: Edinburgh University Press, 2006)].

11. 'Qu'est-ce qu'un rêve nocturne? puis diurne? Qu'est-ce qu'un réveil? À quelle heure se réveille-t-elle? et fait-il jour quand elle commence à écrire? Rêve-t-elle encore quand elle note ses rêves? Commence-t-elle alors à les interpréter et à les mettre en œuvre littéraire? Qu'est-ce qu'une conscience ou une vigilance à l'œuvre dans l'écriture? Mais aussi bien: qu'est-ce que la vigilance *du* rêve, la pensée *du* rêve?', Jacques Derrida, *Genèses, généalogies, genres et le génie: les secrets de l'archive* (Paris: Galilée, 2003), 33 ['What is a nocturnal dream? A diurnal? What is waking ? What time does she wake? And is it daylight when she begins to write? Is she still dreaming when she notes her dreams? Does she then begin to interpret them and shape them into literature? What is a consciousness or vigilance at work in the writing? But also: what is the *dream's* vigilance, the *dream's* thought?', *Geneses, Genealogies, Genres and Genius: The Secrets of the Archive*, trans. Beverley Bie Brahic (Edinburgh: Edinburgh University Press, 2003), 23–4].

12. Ginette Michaud has begun the investigation of this 'as if' in her readings of Cixous's and Derrida exploitation in writing of specific dreams; see *'Comme en rêve': Lire Jacques Derrida et Hélène Cixous*, vol. 2 (Paris: Hermann, 2010).

13. See Bruno Clément, *L'Œuvre sans qualités. Rhétorique de Samuel Beckett* (Paris: Seuil, 1989).

14. Derrida's analysis of Lacan's reading of Poe was epoch-making in this respect; see 'Le Facteur de la vérité', *Poétique*, 21 (1975), 96–147, reprinted in *La Carte postale: de Socrate à Freud et au-delà* (Paris: Flammarion, 1980), 439–524 ['The Purveyor of Truth', first partially translated by Willis Domingo, James Hulbert, Moshe Ron and Marie-Rose Logan, *Yale French Studies*, 52 (1975), 31–113; a full translation by Alan Bass was published in *The Post Card: From Socrates to Freud and Beyond* (Chicago: University

of Chicago Press, 1987), 411–96]. This is not to suggest that the preference awarded to issues of content over those of form had not previously been discussed; see, for example, E. H. Gombrich's 'Freud's Æsthetics', *Encounter*, 26:1 (1966), 30–9; reprinted in *Literature and Psychoanalysis*, ed. Edith Kurzweil and William Phillips (New York: Columbia University Press, 1983), 132–45. But the 1970s as a whole saw an exponential leap in thinking about the relationship between psychoanalysis and literature. Some of its highpoints remain principal references today: *Literature and Psychoanalysis: The Question of Reading: Otherwise*, ed. Shoshana Felman, *Yale French Studies*, 55/56 (1977); *Psychanalyse et littérature*, Jean Bellemin-Noël (Paris: PUF, coll. Que sais-je?, 1978); and *La Carte postale: de Socrate à Freud et au-delà* in its entirety. More recently, Jean-Michel Rabaté's *Jacques Lacan: Psychoanalysis and the Subject of Literature* (Basingstoke: Palgrave, 2001) proves that the question continues to be fruitful thirty years later. For an excellent analysis of the evolution and implications of criticism's use of psychoanalysis, see Peter Brooks, 'The Idea of a Psychoanalytic Literary Criticism', in *Critical Inquiry*, 13:2 (1987), 334–48.

15. Shoshana Felman, 'To Open the Question', *Literature and Psychoanalysis: The Question of Reading: Otherwise*, 5–10, at 9. In other relevant discussions of psychoanalysis's 'outside', John Forrester teases out the implications of the 'rumour' that Derrida was the analyst of Lacan's analyst in 'Who Is in Analysis with Whom? Freud, Lacan, Derrida', *Economy and Society*, 13:2 (1984), 153–77; and Peggy Kamuf argues that Derrida and Cixous posit the question of compassion as the repressed of psychoanalysis in 'Outside in Analysis', *Mosaic*, 42:4 (December 2009), 19–34.

16. Felman, 'To Open the Question', 7.

17. Ibid., 8.

18. Jacques Lacan, *Le Séminaire, livre II: Le Moi dans la théorie de Freud et dans la technique psychanalytique* (Paris: Éditions du Seuil, 1978), 265, quoted in Felman's own translation in Shoshana Felman, *Jacques Lacan and the Adventure of Insight: Psychoanalysis in Contemporary Culture* (Cambridge, MA and London: Harvard University Press, 1987), 144.

19. Ibid., 147 and 149.

20. Jacques Lacan, *Écrits* (Paris: Éditions du Seuil, 1966), 449.

21. Hélène Cixous, *Dedans* (Paris: Grasset, 1969; reprinted by des femmes, 1986); *Inside*, trans. Carol Barko (New York: Schocken Books, 1986). Unless otherwise indicated, page references in this chapter are to the 1986 reprint followed by the translation, which I have modified in places.

22. 'A Kind of Magic', 166.

23. *Three Steps on the Ladder of Writing*, 8.

24. Ibid., 11–12.

25. *La Venue à l'écriture* in *Entre l'écriture* (Paris: des femmes, 1986), 13.

26. 'De la scène de l'Inconscient à la scène de l'Histoire', in *Hélène Cixous, chemins d'une écriture*, ed. Françoise van Rossum-Guyon and Myriam Diaz-Diocaretz (Paris and Amsterdam: Rodopi/Presses Universitaires de Vincennes, 1990), 19.

27. Sigmund Freud, *New Introductory Lectures on Psychoanalysis*, The Pelican Freud Library, vol. 2 (Harmondsworth: Penguin, 1973), 112.

28. Ibid., 106.
29. Freud first introduced the notion of *Nachträglichkeit* in the case history of the Wolf Man: 'This is simply another instance of *deferred action* [*Nachträglichkeit*]. At the age of one and a half the child receives an impression to which he is unable to react adequately; he is only able to understand it and to be moved by it when the impression is revived in him at the age of four; and only twenty years later, during the analysis, is he able to grasp with his conscious mental processes what was then going on in him' (Sigmund Freud, *Case Histories II*, The Pelican Freud Library, vol. 9 (Harmondsworth: Penguin, 1979), 278).
30. The archival material available for consultation indicates hesitation in relation to the choice of tense in various passages. For example, a sheet of rushed writing, suggestive of a first draft, reveals that the verbs in 'il fait jour dedans la nuit, je perds l'espoir à force de satisfaction [. . .] Le passé ne cache plus qu'il a été ma prison. [. . .] Tous les matins je suis une petite fille' (76) were all originally in the imperfect. Material relating to *Dedans* is held in Boxes 1 (which also contains archives concerning Cixous's first short stories) and 2 of the Fonds Hélène Cixous at the Bibliothèque Nationale de France in Paris.
31. Marc Augé, *Non-lieux: Introduction à une anthropologie de la surmodernité* (Paris: Seuil, 1992).
32. This is by no means to suggest that the sequence of lovers is solely to be considered a problem of the narrator. *Dedans* is in ways Cixous's most overtly 'feminist' book in its criticism of men's inability to engage with women, as seen most sharply in the narrator's reproaching her grandfather for never looking at his wife to see how she was changing (110–11).
33. See Jacques Derrida, *Spectres de Marx: l'état de la dette, le travail du deuil et la nouvelle Internationale* (Paris: Galilée, 1993); *Specters of Marx: The State of the Debt, the Work of Mourning and the New International*, trans. Peggy Kamuf, with intro. Bernd Magnus and Stephen Cullenberg (New York and London: Routledge, 1994).
34. Nicolas Abraham et Maria Torok, 'Deuil ou mélancolie: Introjecter – incorporer', *L'Ecorce et le noyau* (Paris: Champs Flammarion, 1978), 259–75.
35. Jean Laplanche and Jean-Bertrand Pontalis, *Vocabulaire de la psychanalyse* (Paris: Presses Universitaires de France, 1967); *The Language of Psychoanalysis* (London: Karnac, 1973).
36. Nicolas Abraham et Maria Torok, 'L'Ecorce et le noyau', in *L'Ecorce et le noyau*, 203–26.
37. Morag Shiach, *Hélène Cixous: A Politics of Writing* (London: Routledge, 1991), 75–6.
38. *Hélène Cixous: Authorship, Autobiography and Love*, 26.
39. Anne-Marie Picard, 'Writing Within the Secret Father', *Hélène Cixous: Critical Impressions*, ed. Lee A. Jacobus and Regina Barreca (Amsterdam: OPA, 1999), 32.
40. 'My Algeriance, in other words: to depart not to arrive from Algeria', 159.
41. Furthermore, *Dedans* is not Cixous's first published fictional text, although it is probable that parts of it predated the short stories collected in *Prénom de Dieu*, published two years before *Dedans*, in 1967.

42. While this paragraph is not distinct enough from the text to be defined as a preface, it shares a number of the prefatory functions analysed by Genette in *Seuils* (Paris: Seuil, 1987) [*Paratexts: Thresholds of Interpretation*, trans. Jane Lewin with a foreword by Richard Macksey (Cambridge: Cambridge University Press, 1997)]. In particular, the marked contrast between its discursiveness and the diegetic focus of the opening of Part I emphasises a literariness that encourages (at least retrospectively) a reading of the prologue, if not as a 'mode d'emploi' or manual giving directions on how to read it (*Seuils*, 194), at least as a signal that the book is to be read as a work of the imagination.

43. *Dedans* contains many allusions to *King Lear*, a work also primarily about a relationship between father and daughter. These are particularly obvious in the many plays on 'rien', the French word for nothing – for example: 'Je suis donc le tout qui n'est rien' (172) ['Then I am the all that is nothing'] and, especially, the final repetition of 'Viens, dit-il, allons en prison' (209) ['Come, says he, let's away to prison' (136)] echoing Lear's 'Come, let's away to prison' (5.iii.8). But whereas for Lear 'nothing will come of nothing' (1.i.89), it is because Cixous's narrator has 'plus rien à perdre, ni personne' (13) ['nothing more, nor anyone, to lose' (8)], possesses 'rien, que [s]on enfance' (27) ['nothing, but [her] childhood' (17)], that there is space for something to take shape: 'là-bas il n'y a plus rien ni personne, on peut arriver; on peut trouver; moi, non pas moi, mais qui sait, une trace' (149) ['over there there's no longer anything or anyone, it is possible to arrive; it is possible to find; me, no not me, but who knows, a trace' (97)].

44. Michel de Montaigne, 'De l'amitié', *Œuvres complètes*, ed. Albert Thibaudet and Maurice Rat (Paris: Gallimard (Bibliothèque de la Pléïade), 1962), 187; 'On Friendship', consulted online at http://www.gutenberg.org/files/3600/3600-h/3600-h.htm#link2HCH0027, 4 November 2013. Martine Motard-Noar was the first to comment on the Montaigne allusion; see *Les Fictions d'Hélène Cixous: Une autre langue de femme*, 27.

45. 'De l'amitié', 186.

46. Many years later, Cixous adopts this position explicitly: 'I am on the side of Moses, *the one who does not enter*' ('My Algeriance', 170).

47. Cixous thus goes even further than Benveniste, who had recently shown that the first- and second-person pronouns were shifters; that is, the identity of their referents shifts with the speaking person (see Emile Benveniste, 'De la subjectivité dans le langage', *Problèmes de linguistique générale I* (Paris: Gallimard (coll. Tel), 1966), 258–66). Cixous also deploys the third person in other ways to destabilise the reference. In particular, numerous chapters open with a third-person pronoun with no obvious antecedent: 'JE LE SUIVIS PARTOUT' (32) ['I FOLLOWED HIM EVERYWHERE' (20)], 'JE L'AI CONNU' (43) ['I KNEW HIM' (27)], 'IL regarde droit devant' (93) ['HE is looking straight ahead' (61)], 'IL EST REVENU' (193) ['HE HAS RETURNED' (126)]. This obliges the reader to register a hiatus between the words on the page and their possible referent.

48. Sellers explicitly refers to the narrator's 'fantasy of a pre-Œdipal union with the father' (*Hélène Cixous: Authorship, Autobiography and Love*, 34), although she does not explore the theoretical twist such a description involves.

49. *Dedans* could thus be argued to anticipate a number of the points Deleuze and Guattari's *L'Anti-Œdipe* (Paris: Galilée, 1972) would make a few years later.

50. I do not have the space here to discuss the specifically Jewish dimension to this scene of remembering but it is clearly crucial. The narrator's identity later swells to accommodate much of the Jewish diaspora: 'Je suis née il y a deux cents ans en Westphalie et il y a trois cents ans en Espagne, il y a six cents ans en Palestine, il y a cent ans en Afrique, et depuis, une ou deux fois ici et là' (149) ['I was born two hundred years ago in Westphalia and three hundred years ago in Spain, six hundred years ago in Palestine, a hundred years ago in Africa, and since then, once or twice here and there' (97)].

51. Antonin Artaud, 'Ci-Gît', *Œuvres complètes*, vol. 12 (Paris: Gallimard, 1974), 77.

52. The word 'contraction' and its various forms recur many times throughout *Dedans*, as does 'distraction' ('distraire', 'distrait', etc.), which inscribes another link with *King Lear*: 'Better I were distract; / So should my thoughts be sever'd from my griefs, / And woes by wrong imaginations lose / The knowledge of themselves' (4.vi.281–4). But whereas for Lear language offers a distraction, in *Dedans* the use of these signifiers (whose etymology, from the Latin *con-trahere*, *dis-trahere*, means draw together/apart, unite/separate) reminds us that language is in *traction*, constantly pulling in different directions. And different times: 'distraite' by the future, the mother is detached from her children whereas the narrator and her brother remain in the present (14/9). Moreover, it is the narrator's rage on realising that her mother is distracted by the future rather than the past that decides her to go out each day (15/9), to cross the line between inside and outside.

53. See, for example, Shiach's *Hélène Cixous: A Politics of Writing*, 73, and Picard's 'Writing Within the Secret Father', 50.

54. See page 35 above.

55. The term 'explicit' to designate the last words of a book is more arcane in English than in French. According to the *OED*, the term is probably shortened from *explicitus est liber* (the book is unfolded, or complete), by analogy with 'incipit'.

56. *Reading for the Plot*, 108.

57. Ibid., 109.

58. Ibid.

59. 'A Kind of Magic', 185.

Chapter 3

An Elementary Deconstruction:
Les Commencements

'J'ai une très grande proximité avec Derrida que je considère depuis toujours comme mon autre' ['I have a very great proximity with Derrida whom I have always considered to be my "other"']:[1] Jacques Derrida has occupied a unique, privileged place for Hélène Cixous throughout her writing life. It was to him she showed her earliest writings following their initial encounter in the Café Balzar – an encounter which took place after their now legendary 'non-encounter' at his *Agrégation* oral in whose unilaterality (she could see his back; he could not see her) he found the inspiration for his reading of her texts, many decades later, in *H. C. Pour la vie, c'est-à-dire* . . . Her first book, the published version of her doctoral thesis, already paid tribute to his thinking. While the body of her thesis makes no reference to him, in a note to an appendix Cixous recognises having 'surtout' [especially] made use of 'la remarquable étude de Jacques Derrida' ['Jacques Derrida's remarkable study'] of Plato's *Phædrus* in 'La Pharmacie de Platon' and gives a full bibliographical citation, although the bibliography proper specifies the details of only a small fraction of the more than two thousand works consulted in the course of her research.[2] The two remained in constant exchange until Derrida's death in 2004, reading each other's books as soon as they appeared and talking frequently on the telephone. As Geoffrey Bennington has pointed out, the rhythm of their relationship was similar to that of a psychoanalysis; each appears to have found in the other a source of both wisdom and support.[3] Latterly, beginning with their contributions to the 1990 colloquium *Lectures de la différence sexuelle*, their friendship flowered very visibly in the extraordinary series of texts they mutually devoted to each other's work.[4] It would be difficult to overemphasise the importance of their intellectual dialogue for the evolution of their thinking, or to overestimate the influence reciprocally exerted by each corpus on the other, ever since that first encounter in the Balzar.

It is thus no surprise that critical reception of Cixous's work has always tended to privilege her proximity to Derrida. In the first monograph ever devoted to her writing, Verena Conley described Derrida as the principal figure 'with whom Cixous from her specifically (*féminine*) literary border, maintains an ongoing dialogue',[5] while, more recently, Mireille Calle-Gruber considers the links between Cixous's and Derrida's texts as so close as to situate them 'vers les deux versants de la même crête' ['on the two slopes of the same ridge'].[6] Nevertheless, given the synchrony of their trajectories, there is a significant dissymmetry in the critical use which has been made of their proximity. In her presentation of *L'événement comme écriture*, Marta Segarra explains that several contributors had asked her 's'il s'agissait de lire Cixous à la lumière de Derrida, ou inversement' ['if it was a matter of reading Cixous in the light of Derrida, or inversely'] (8). It is noteworthy that the inverse remains, precisely, a relatively rare occurrence; few commentators on Derrida invoke Cixous,[7] whereas there is a frequent tendency (including on my part) to read her work via his, using the insights generated by his writings as a way to approach the dense textuality of her books. Thus, for example, Morag Shiach describes Derrida as one of the philosophers and theorists who 'shaped' Cixous's writing;[8] for Christa Stevens, Derrida's texts form part of the theoretical background 'à partir duquel l'écriture cixousienne demande à être lue' ['from which Cixous's writing calls to be read'].[9] Quite apart from the weight attributed in the most recent scholarship to his critical works dealing specifically with her texts, notably *H. C. pour la vie, c'est à dire . . .*, commentary often uses Derrida's *theory* to elucidate Cixous's *practice*. For example, in 'To Give Place', Peggy Kamuf in effect presents Cixous's thinking about the gift as a specific case of a more general model elaborated by Derrida. In response to the question: 'What would be a gift that returns [. . .] to no subject, to no instance of appropriation?', a page and a half is devoted to explaining Derrida's notion of the impossible gift before the article returns to Cixous: 'It is to this possibility of the impossible, to the movement of thought, desire, and naming in the absence of an apparent phenomenon of gift, that Cixous's writing is given over.'[10]

This is emphatically not to suggest that the difference between Cixous and Derrida has been read as a simple opposition between practice and theory. Many of the commentators mentioned above – Kamuf, Calle-Gruber, Michaud – are also among the finest readers of Derrida and, as such, profoundly sensitive to the ways he himself 'practised' what he theorised. From the outset, deconstruction forcefully challenged the theory-praxis opposition; *De la grammatologie* already stressed that deconstruction – like the metaphysics it seeks to displace – was as much a practice as it was a theory. Or, to borrow the linguistic terminology he often favoured, Derrida repeatedly highlighted the performative dimension to every constative act. For example, when analysing the academic institution, he maintains:

> en chacune des opérations que nous tentons ensemble (une lecture, une interprétation, la construction d'un modèle théorique, la rhétorique d'une argumentation, le traitement d'un matériau historique et même une formalisation mathématique), un concept institutionnel est en jeu, un type de contrat signé, une image du séminaire idéal construite, un *socius* impliqué, répété ou déplacé, inventé, transformé, menacé ou détruit. L'institution, [. . .] c'est aussi et déjà la structure de notre interprétation. Dès lors, si elle prétend à quelque conséquence, ce qu'on appelle très vite *la* déconstruction n'est jamais un ensemble technique de procédures discursives, encore moins une nouvelle méthode herméneutique travaillant sur des archives ou des énoncés à l'abri d'une institution donnée et stable; c'est aussi, et au moins, une prise de position, dans le travail même, à l'égard de structures politico-institutionnelles qui constituent et règlent notre pratique, nos compétences et nos performances.

> [in every operation we pursue together (a reading, an interpretation, the construction of a theoretical model, the rhetoric of an argumentation, the treatment of historical material, and even of mathematical formalization), we argue or acknowledge that an institutional concept is at play, a type of contract signed, an image of the ideal seminar constructed, a *socius* implied, repeated or displaced, invented, transformed, menaced or destroyed. An institution [. . .] is also and already the structure of our interpretation. If, then, it lays claim to any consequence, what is hastily called Deconstruction is never a technical set of discursive procedures, still less a new hermeneutic method working on archives or utterances in the shelter of a given and stable institution; it is also, and at the least, the taking of a position, in the work itself, towards the politico-institutional structures that constitute and regulate our practice, our competences and our performances.][11]

Any theoretical, epistemological or hermeneutic activity (or 'opération') is necessarily performative in that it entails a specific relation, either of consolidation or of transformation, to the institution in which it takes place. Derrida further considers that a challenge to institutional authority at this performative level is more troubling politically than a 'purely' constative one:

> La force reproductive de l'autorité s'accommode plus facilement de déclarations ou de thèses soi-disant révolutionnaires dans leur contenu codé pourvu que soient respectés les rites de légitimation, la rhétorique et la symbolique institutionnelle qui désamorcent et neutralisent tout ce qui vient d'ailleurs. L'irrecevable, c'est ce qui, par-dessous les positions ou les thèses, vient déranger ce contrat profond, l'ordre de ces normes, et qui le fait déjà dans la *forme* du travail, de l'enseignement ou de l'écriture.[12]

[The reproductive force of authority can get along more comfortably with declarations or theses whose encoded content presents itself as revolutionary, provided that they respect the rites of legitimation, the rhetoric and the institutional symbolism that defuses and neutralizes everything that comes from outside the system. What is unacceptable is what, underlying positions or theses, upsets this deeply entrenched contract, the order of these norms, and that does so in the very *form* of the work, of teaching or of writing.]

Indeed, the virulent resistance his Derrida's work encountered (as exemplified in the 'Derrida affair', the controversy over whether he should be awarded an honorary doctorate by the University of Cambridge) can be attributed to the fact that he practised what he preached, that his texts are intimately linked to a reflection on their politico-institutional conditions, a reflection that 'n'est plus un complément *extérieur* de l'enseignement et de la recherche, elle doit en traverser, voire en affecter les objets mêmes, les normes, les procédures, les visées' ['is no longer an *external* complement to teaching and research; it must make its way through the very objects we work with, shaping them as it goes, along with our norms, procedures, and aims'].[13] Similarly, the reductive way in which Cixous became known internationally as a 'theorist' and indeed the criticisms levelled at her for not being theoretical 'enough' (or 'semi-theoretical', as analysed by Kamuf) point to a correlation between the dominance of the constative in a text and its receivability.

Derrida and Cixous are therefore more alike than they are different in that the unsettling force of their texts relates as much, if indeed not more, to the (unconventional) way they write as to the message conveyed.[14] The difference between them is a difference between writing practices, not an opposition between a theory and a practice. One of the most obvious manifestations of that difference nevertheless remains the fact that Derrida's practice is *more* theoretical than Cixous's.

Cixous has recourse to a telling image relative to this dissymmetry in an early interview where she discusses the difference between Derrida's work and her own as a matter of disciplinary constraints. Derrida's concern to make sense arises from his positioning with respect to philosophical discourse:

Philosophical discourse [. . .] is not free, since it must obey imperatives of signification. A philosopher is obligated to hold on to logic – even Derrida, for example, who pushes his work to the limit where logic vacillates. [. . .] [T]he moment you name the undecidable, you already, in a certain way, arrest it. Derrida knows this. That is why he always says that each time he arrests, each time he coins a concept, he hurries to put it into that general movement of oscillation in order not to make of it a master concept. But it is like a ford of a river, if you like: he must jump from concept to concept, or from rock to rock, whereas I allow myself to say, since I do not have any obligation toward philosophy, I really do prefer swimming. I prefer being in the water and openly in the water [. . .] [A] philosopher [. . .] wants to transmit as much meaning as possible. That is the writing of Derrida, who condenses in a way that is a polysemy. He transmits an intensity, a richness of condensation, of meaning. Philosophy is demonstrative. [. . .] I let myself be carried off by the poetic word. Is it a mad word? Does it say something? I must say that my steed or my barge and my poetic body never do forget philosophical rigor [. . .] but I have no obligation toward that kind of thinking, toward this kind of rigor. I take it into account but precisely as that from which I can take my distance. And I would even say that it is my mission, my calling, to be able to distance myself from it.[15]

In later years, Cixous has moved away from painting the difference between herself and Derrida in terms of the difference between a philosophical discourse (albeit one that stretched the boundaries of philosophy) and a poetic one. Since 'Circonfession', she increasingly discusses his work simply as a writing; indeed, her texts on him focus very much on him *as writer*.[16] But this early image of Derrida's work as stepping stones in contrast with Cixous's swimming conveys compellingly the notion that the work of conceptualising, creating a theoretical construct (albeit one in movement) that *stands out* from the language used to convey it, is integral to his practice in a way that is not the case for her, and helps to foreground the singularity of these two very different challenges to the 'solid' ground of metaphysical thinking. The quotation makes clear furthermore that, for Cixous, philosophical rigour is not just an incidental difference between them but specifically 'that from which [she] can take [her] distance'.

More broadly, Cixous develops her thinking about the politics of different modes of discourse in 'Une maîtresse femme' ['A Woman Mistress'], the first part of the exchange with Catherine Clément at the end of *La Jeune née*. Dealing with the question of women's assumption of the position of 'master' in a teaching environment, she states that 'le savoir, à part exception, est constamment pris, capté par une volonté de puissance' ['with few exceptions, knowledge is constantly caught up in, is entrapped by a will for power'].[17] In her opinion, in addition to being historically denied access to positions of mastery, women often do not enjoy the discourse required in such positions: a 'discours qui ne met pas en jeu un sujet de l'énonciation repérable, qui parle à ce moment-là, non pas au nom, mais au titre d'un savoir universel' ['discourse that does not involve a locatable subject of enunciation, that speaks at that particular moment not just in the name of but as universal knowledge itself'] is generally 'plus agréable à la masculinité qu'à la féminité' ['more appealing to masculinity than to femininity'].[18] Nevertheless, her response to this situation is markedly different from that of Duras, for instance, another (woman) writer who equally found theoretical discourses unpalatable.[19] Cixous is willing to adopt a more theoretical discourse in oral situations for strategic reasons, as a refusal to yield 'organized discourse' solely to those who embrace a 'discourse of mastery', unconcerned by the irrevocable association between knowledge and power (252/136). Elsewhere, she makes clear that she is in no way anti-theoretical:

> Like most women of my generation, I believe, I had inhibitions, faced with the rigid, defining, and decisive side of most theoretical discourses. True, I did have resistances. I had to work through them in order to be able to approach the spaces containing a certain amount of useful and necessary knowledge in order to carry out another type of work which would be on the side of femininity. I am not and do not feel like being ignorant.[20]

The 'spaces' she wishes to approach are thus neither outside nor opposed to the sphere of knowledge; she is concerned not to valorise a position of ignorance, as might an 'anti-theory', but rather to displace the relation between knowledge and power.

To my knowledge, Derrida left no written trace of his thoughts concerning the preponderance of the theoretical in his discourse relative to hers.[21] However, the idea of her relative irreceivability dominates his evocation in *H. C. Pour la vie . . .* of his response on first reading her work. He recalls his initial reaction twice, in strikingly similar terms, once at the beginning of the text and once towards the end:

> Qu'est-ce que c'est que ça? me suis-je à peu près demandé. Qu'est-ce qui arrive là? Qu'est-ce qui m'arrive? Quel genre? Qui pourra jamais lire ça? Moi? (HC, 18)

> [What *is* this? I asked myself more or less. What is happening here? What is happening to me? What genre? Who could ever read this? Me? (HCE, 7)]

> un mélange de révélation et d'incompréhension, une lecture avide mais incapable de reconnaître ce qu'elle lisait là. Qu'est-ce qui arrive là, me suis-je dit sans m'entendre le dire, sans m'entendre à entendre si je sous-entends: mais qu'est-ce qui arrive là? qu'est-ce qui se met au monde et dans la littérature, etc. Ou 'qu'est-ce qui m'arrive là?'; 'Qu'est-ce que je vais faire, moi, avec ça?' 'Qu'est-ce que c'est que ce type? ce type nouveau d'autobiographie délirante et sublime?'; 'Qui est-ce?'; 'Qu'est-ce qu'elle veut, celle-là?' (HC, 130)

> [a mixture of revelation and incomprehension, an avid reading but one unable to recognize what it was reading here. What is happening here, I said to myself without hearing myself say so, without knowing whether I was

hearing myself or implying it [*sans m'entendre à entendre si je sous-entends*]: What on earth is happening here? What is brought into the world and into literature, etc.? Or 'What is happening to me here?'; 'What am I going to do with this?'; 'What on earth is this type, this new type of raving and sublime autobiography?'; 'Who is this?'; 'What is it that she wants?' (HCE, 146)]

The series of questions conveys a sense of total bewilderment caused by the unprecedented, unclassifiable quality of Cixous's text. The uncertainty relates as much to gender as to genre; the break after the first use of 'type' – 'Qu'est-ce que c'est que ce type? ce type nouveau d'autobiographie . . .' – invites us to read the word in its French meaning of 'guy' as well as 'type', especially given the abrupt specification of (the author's? or the autobiography's?) femininity immediately afterwards in the final 'celle-là'. The subject who produced 'that', 'ça', defies any attempt at identification as much as the strange thing it produced.

Yet the most disconcerting aspect to Derrida's claim to have been disconcerted is perhaps his repeated use of the question 'Qu'est-ce . . .' to express it. This ties in with his argument throughout the book that Cixous's work exceeds any attempt to ascertain an identity in answer to such a question, as exemplified in the homonymic play of his title which immediately and unavoidably complicates any 'c'est' which might be ventured in response with its homynym 'C', the initial of Cixous's surname.[22] Nevertheless, the frequent repetition insists above all on the *form* of the question, the ontological question par excellence and for that reason typically eschewed by Derrida in his writing. In the first series of questions, the apparently straightforward use of such metaphysical terms to query what was 'happening' in this strange event (both senses of the French verb *arriver* – to arrive and to happen – are evidently at work) suggests that he was at a loss to engage with the comprehensive challenge Cixous's text posed to metaphysical modes of enquiry; it is as though he found himself without the language with which to frame a different approach. Her text places *him* in question also. When he repeats the questions near the end of his text, it is, as always, with a difference. This time, the ontological questioning is interrupted – and complicated – by a series of reporting/comment clauses: 'Qu'est-ce qui arrive là, *me suis-je dit sans m'entendre le dire, sans m'entendre à entendre si je sous-entends*: mais qu'est-ce qui arrive là ?' These clauses inscribe a difference between 'dire' (saying), 'entendre' (which means both hearing and understanding) and 'sous-entendre' (which can mean both understanding what is *not* said . . . and *meaning* what is not said, implying without saying). What one says is not necessarily what one hears, understands or implies. 'Sans m'entendre le dire': he recalls asking the ontological question without hearing or grasping what he's saying. In the next clause, the same words mean something entirely different. Coming just after the previous clause, 'sans m'entendre à entendre' first invites the reader to understand 'without hearing myself hearing/understanding'. But 's'entendre à' means to have competence in something; 'sans m'entendre à entendre' thus means without having the requisite expertise in hearing/understanding. He asks the question, then, without being in a position to understand what question he is asking. For the question he discovers he has asked contains (or implies: 'si je sous-entends') a whole series of questions. 'Qu'est-ce qui arrive là?' can imply . . . 'qu'est-ce qui arrive là?'; that is, it can imply what it says. But it can also imply the string of other questions he lists, including 'qu'est-ce qui *m*'arrive là?' What is happening *to me* there? What strange event is this that places *me* in the position of the ontologist?

In contrast with readings of Cixous in the light of Derrida, *after* Derrida,[23] then, his own text suggests that she is as much the precursor as the inheritor of his 'deconstruction'. Indeed, the first of their many texts relating to the other's work highlights from the outset the impossibility of positioning either as more originary than the other: '– Tu me précèdes . . . – Non, c'est toi qui m'as toujours . . . – Toi aussi tu me précèdes . . .' ['"You precede me . . ." "No, *you* have always . . ." "You too precede me . . ."'].[24] As Anne Berger notes, the question of 'qui commence, qui précède, qui "vient" d'abord' ['who begins, who precedes, who "comes" first'] is a subject that arises frequently between them.[25] As chance was, they met when each was beginning to write, before either had published anything; both of them wrote – have always written – *having already read* the other. In the beginning was . . . beginnings. Joint beginnings. Beginnings together. The endless incipience of *H. C. Pour la vie . . .*, its constant rebeginning, can thus be read not just as yet another example of Derrida's long-standing interest in demonstrating the impossibility of ever accessing the original beginning, the beginning beginning.[26] It also invites reading as a trace of the impossibility of ever extricating his beginning from hers. From the beginning, her text has occupied an exceptional place in his writing:

> Depuis que je la connais, je la lis et j'oublie qu'elle écrit, j'oublie ce qu'elle écrit. Cet oubli n'est pas un oubli comme un autre, il est élémentaire, il est probable que j'en vis. Son œuvre pour moi restera pour la vie comme ce que j'ai déjà oublié *a priori*: je l'oublie comme je respire. (HC, 135)

> [Ever since I have known her, I have read her and I keep forgetting that she writes, and I forget what she writes. This forgetting is not a forgetting like any other; it is elemental, I probably live on it. Her work for me will remain

for life like what I have already forgotten a priori: I forget it as naturally as I breathe. (HCE, 152)]

Cixous figures as the textual other Derrida both read and forgot, needed to read and needed to forget. We can note that 'j'en vis' is a homophone of 'j'envie', I envy; in addition to the list at the end of his book of the resistances that he, like other readers of Cixous, encounters in the challenge of engaging with her writing, he here subtly and generously acknowledges one specific to him personally. His forgetting is 'élémentaire': fundamental, irreducible. Cixous's work is what he has a priori forgotten, forgotten at the beginning, forgotten in order to begin.

Cixous's uniqueness for Derrida in this respect appears to lie above all in her proximity. Notwithstanding the patent differences between their texts,[27] he says, it is sometimes as though he no longer knows 'qui a écrit cela la première' (HC, 135) ['who wrote that first' (HCE, 153)]. She alone of those he reads, it seems, might have said what he has to say before him. Possibly for that reason, Derrida focuses in *H. C. for Life . . .* on the principal way he considers Cixous fundamentally different from him, the vital impulse which makes her stand 'for' life:

> Il semble au premier abord que pour elle [. . .] il n'y ait qu'un seul côté et non pas deux, et ce côté est celui de la vie. [. . .] C'est pourquoi moi, et c'est sans doute plus qu'une différence, un grand différend entre nous dont je reparlerai peut-être tout à l'heure, moi, qui me sens toujours tourné du côté de la mort, je ne suis pas de son côté, alors qu'elle voudrait tout tourner et faire venir du côté de la vie. (HC, 40)

> [It seems at first that for her [. . .] there is only one side and not two, and this side is that of life. [. . .] This is why I – and this is probably more than a difference, a big disagreement between us, of which I may speak again later – I, who always feel turned toward death, I am not on her side, while she would like to turn everything and to make it come around to the side of life. (HCE, 36)]

In this chapter, however, I want to probe further the difference at work in the way they say the 'same' things. Given Derrida's argument as outlined earlier that the discourse one adopts always involves a 'taking of a position, in the work itself, towards the politico-institutional structures that constitute and regulate our practice, our competences and our performances', what difference does it make that his discourse and hers conceptualise to very different degrees? Derrida claimed, 'en homme des Lumières' (HC, 90) ['as a man of the Enlightenment' (HCE, 97),[28] to recognise in Cixous's work a 'pensée des Lumières au-delà des Lumières' (HC, 108) ['a thought of the Enlightenment beyond the Enlightenment'

(HCE, 120)]. In what way might Cixous's writing go *beyond* the Enlightenment, *beyond* Derrida's? Might it be precisely in relation to the *beyond* of the text? Exploring the fictive moment at the genesis of scientific knowledge, Shoshana Felman argues at the end of *Jacques Lacan and the Adventure of Insight* that

> Science is the drive to *go beyond.* The scientist's commitment is at once to acknowledge myth and to attempt to go beyond the myth. Only when this mythical, narrative movement of 'going beyond' stops does science stop. Only when the myth is not acknowledged, and is believed to be science, does the myth prevail at the expense of science. It is precisely when we believe we are beyond the myth that we indulge in fiction.[29]

Could it be the case that Cixous's work goes 'beyond' Derrida's precisely, paradoxically, in never halting the movement of 'going beyond', never arresting the *emergence* of truth, never stopping to provide 'stepping stones' that reify the process of knowing into an object of knowledge? Her writing certainly cannot be said to clarify or to elucidate, the verbs involving light most commonly used to describe thinking inherited from the Age of Reason. But I want to suggest that it can be said to *illustrate* supremely the pursuit of truth precisely because the thinking in which it is engaged never ends in any object of knowledge. It is because it goes further than Derrida in never stopping going beyond itself that it can be considered an 'elementary' form of deconstruction: one that doesn't develop even elementary concepts.

The rest of this chapter will explore this idea in a reading of one of Cixous's beginnings, the early text itself entitled *Les Commencements* [*Beginnings*].[30] The title already affords an indication that what is at stake is a new beginning in thinking. In French, the plural 'les commencements' refers especially to the first lessons of a science or art, its elements or rudiments. The book thus presents itself as a kind of 'textbook', a (textured) book containing elementary knowledge. Elementary in the sense of basic, fundamental, essential to know, but also elementary in the sense of incipient, undeveloped: the essential text would be one where knowledge remains *in movement*. The difficulty of reading Cixous's text relates less to its erudition (from the same Latin root, *rudis*, as rudimentary), less to the extent or complexity of the knowledge it displays, than to the particular way it challenges the link between knowledge and authority. It pushes Enlightenment thinking still further by extending the challenge to knowledge as doctrine into its own practice of language. The challenge facing us is to understand how *Les Commencements*, one of Cixous's most unreadable texts, can represent a singular 'espèce de catéchisme' (16), to borrow the text's own formulation, a 'kind of catechism' like no other. Far from proposing a knowledge deemed to contain universally applicable fundamental truths, meaning here is determined by the circumstances. In this catechism, the etymological meaning of 'teaching by sound' (from the Greek *katêkheo*, 'make echo') is operative: this is a body of knowledge whose body matters.

The Beginnings of Life

Les Commencements is Cixous's third book, dated '2 février [1970]', and therefore written while Cixous, appointed in the wake of the 1968 riots to organise academic structure for the Experimental University of Paris, later to become the University of Paris 8-Vincennes, was grappling at a practical level with institutional issues of intellectual and pedagogical convention. The book is a prime example of the early texts that were just as perplexing for their author as for the outside reader. Cixous recalls being bewildered by her own writings:

> Aux commencements de mon autobibliographie, je n'écrivais pas de livres, je n'écrivais pas, il arrivait, de nuit, des choses. D'autres auraient dit 'livres' peut-être. Mais j'appelais ces rejetons de séismes et convulsions nocturnes *des choses*. Des choses vivantes parlantes, effrayantes. Sans titre. Des coulées de lave; épanchées par des cassures d'âme.

> [At the beginnings of my autobibliography, I didn't write books, I didn't write, things, by night, happened. Others might have perhaps said 'books'. But I called these progenies of earthquakes and nocturnal convulsions *things*. Living, speaking, frightening things. Without a title. Flows of lava; pouring out of breaks in the soul.][31]

The eruption of these strange, unclassifiable forms does not merely put into question the kind, or genre, of book they might be; it problematises the very category of 'books'. The idea of writing as an eruption, an explosion of an inner, obscure force overwhelming the writer's conscious agency, is further motivated in French by the paronomastic link between the words *livre* (book) and *lave* (lava) which, a little later, extends to *larve* (larva):

> Ce n'était pas des lettres: des laves. En se déposant, cependant, sous la plume qui note elles s'augmentent d'une lettre. Les voilà *larves*. Elles ne croient pas si bien dire. Les larves nous causent une légère répulsion injuste comme toute répulsion légèrement justifiée: il s'agit de notre défaut d'âme, notre goût acquis pour le défini, le situé.

[They weren't letters: lava. In being deposited, however, under the noting pen they added a letter to themselves. Then they were *larva*. They didn't know how well that put it. Larvæ cause us a slight repulsion as unjust as any slightly justified repulsion: it's a matter of our failure of soul, our acquired taste for the definite, the locatable.][32]

These texts are 'larval' not only because of the repugnance their unclassifiability may occasion (similar in certain respects to the Kristevan 'abject'[33]), but also in the sense suggested in the previous quotation of being a specifically *living* uncertainty: they represent a new, rudimentary entity, life at its beginning.

Les Commencements certainly challenges those with a taste for the 'definite' in that, while a diegetic universe is instituted from the outset, the reference points of plot and character provide even less help than in *Dedans* in the task of orienting the reader of the fiction. The plot is constantly rebeginning, the characters constantly redefining themselves. I shall begin with an analysis of the opening paragraphs which among other questions deal, obscurely, with the beginning of light:

Je fis le rêve, mais c'était Saint-Georges qui le portait puisque j'étais dans les bras de Saint-Georges et que le rêve était dans moi. Qu'il ait fait alors son apparition dans le rêve sans relâcher son étreinte m'encourageait à persévérer. Mais sa façon d'apparaître mettait en question le lieu d'où je le voyais si fortement que je dus me demander si ce rêve n'était pas déjà l'apparence d'un rêve, et s'il n'annonçait pas sa propre fin.

Je le vis. Déjà je ne travaillais plus: en effet je ne le vis que parce qu'il m'apparut. Il était debout, de profil, c'était bien lui, tel que nous aimons qu'il soit, haut et fin, la poitrine bombée, le dos creusé, la tête levée, avec cette torsion du tronc qui m'appelait par son creusement même à me joindre à lui comme la noix à sa coquille et comme la flèche à l'arc. Je n'étais pas dans ses bras. Il se trouvait debout devant une porte informe, un passage sans épaisseur: la lumière commençait là où il commençait, tout ce qui précédait me semblait obscur, et j'étais pétrie de cette obscurité. Je n'avais aucun contact avec lui, sinon je n'aurais pas été l'obscurité, ni l'œil invisible et obscur à lui-même. Je ne me voyais pas, il ne me voyait pas. Il était ruisselant d'une lumière blanche laiteuse. Le blanc qui le faisait paraître n'était ni un tissu ni autre chose qu'un tissu, c'était une substance éblouissante qui le couvrait: on aurait pu dire qu'elle le baignait à cause de cette blancheur lactée, mais elle n'était pas liquide, elle cernait les lignes de son corps. Debout, face à un ouest auquel je n'avais aucun accès, il était comme un danseur. Je devinais que cet ouest était un est renversé, car tout allait venir de là. Une infinie nostalgie me cristallisait en seuil noir et exclu. Comme j'étais hors! Tout l'amour que j'avais pour lui, donc l'amour qui était mon fait, mon art, battait dans ce blanc où je n'étais pas, et le corps noir abandonné écoulait sa couleur *avant*, devant cet objet de Beauté, ce Saint blanc laiteux tourné vers un est qui me crachait en bas de l'ouest. Même l'amour que j'avais eu était avec lui, flottait dans ses cheveux étincelants. J'aurais voulu qu'il me vînt un doigt noir pour lui toucher le front et l'épaule. Il ne bougeait pas mais il semblait être brandi par on ne sait quelle force, et cependant il ne s'éloignait pas Saint-Georges blanc tourné vers ce qui allait sortir. Il n'y avait que lui. Aucun autre objet, pas de matière, pas de présence, ni cheval, ni dragon, ni moi, donc il n'y avait pas encore d'histoire ce qui me faisait désirer qu'elle commence pour que je puisse entrer.

Cette lumière: ce n'était pas une lumière comme il y en a dans le temps, dans la réalité. C'était une émulsion, un mélange d'absence de couleur et de vent. J'appris par là qu'avant le commencement il y avait le Vent. Et après la fin. (7–8)

[I had the dream, but Saint-Georges was carrying it since I was in Saint-Georges's arms and the dream was in me. That he made his appearance in the dream without relaxing his embrace encouraged me to persevere. But his way of appearing so strongly put in question the place I was seeing him from that I had to wonder if the dream wasn't already the appearance of a dream, and if it didn't announce its own end.

I saw him. Already I was no longer working: in fact I only saw him because he appeared to me. He was standing, in profile, it was certainly him, the way we like him to be, tall and slim, his chest curving out, his back arched, his head up, with that twist of his torso whose very curve called me to join myself to him like the nut to its shell and the arrow to the bow. I wasn't in his arms. He was standing before a formless door, a passage with no depth: the light began where he began, everything that preceded seemed obscure to me, and I was steeped in its obscurity. I had no contact with him, otherwise I wouldn't have been the darkness, or the eye invisible and obscure to itself. I didn't see myself, he didn't see me. He was streaming with a white, milky light. The white that made him appear was neither a fabric nor something other than a fabric, it was a dazzling substance covering him: you could say it was bathing him because of that milky whiteness, but it wasn't liquid, it surrounded the lines of his body. Standing, facing a west to which I had no access, he was like a dancer. I guessed that that west was a reversed east, for everything was going to come from there. An infinite nostalgia crystallized me in a black, excluded threshold. I was so outside! All the love I had for him, the love that was my doing, my art, beat in the blank gap where I was not, and the black abandoned body poured its colour *before*, before this object of Beauty, this white milky Saint turned towards an east spitting me out below the west. Even the love I had had was with him, floating in his sparkling hair. I so wanted to have a black finger to touch his forehead and shoulder. He wasn't moving but he seemed to be brandished by who knows what force, and yet he wasn't going away Saint-Georges white turned toward what was going to emerge. There was only him. No other object, no matter, no presence, no horse, no dragon, no me, so there was as yet no story which made me want it to begin so that I could enter.

That light: it wasn't a light such as there are in time, in reality. It was an emulsion, a mixture of absence of colour and of wind. I learned there that before the beginning there was the Wind. And after the end.]

'Je fis le rêve': the text opens manifestly not at the beginning but *in medias res*, the definite article referring to a specific dream it posits the reader as already able to identify.[34] The beginning is not the beginning, the beginning is already *inside*, just as the oneiric quality of the continuation suggests that, from the outset, the narrator is inside her own dream. 'Saint-Georges was carrying the dream since I was in his arms and the dream was in me': the ostensibly logical sequence calls attention to the use of the preposition 'dans' (in) on which it hinges; it suggests a clear distinction between inside and outside that the passage in fact thoroughly calls into question. For we read next that Saint-Georges is 'in' the dream he carries: the dream is not neatly contained, is not merely a matter of content, but affects the person – and the writing – that contains it.

In the beginning, then, is a dream which is also not a dream, which is already 'the appearance of a dream', and which puts into question 'le lieu d'où je le voyais' ['the place I was seeing him from'], the origin of the narrator's seeing. The 'Je fis' of the first paragraph calls up 'Je le vis' at the beginning of the second;[35] a certain vision, that is a certain way of seeing (or more accurately, as we shall see, an *uncertain* way of seeing) becomes possible in this dream. The seer remains unseen – 'œil invisible et obscur à lui-même. Je ne me voyais pas, il ne me voyait pas' – but the light that is the condition of seeing is visible: 'la lumière commençait là où il commençait, tout ce qui précédait me semblait obscur [. . .] J'appris par là qu'avant le commencement il y avait le Vent.' The intertextual echoes of this sentence signal that *Les Commencements*, too, begins before it begins. The creation of light from a preceding obscurity and wind beckons compellingly towards the most famous beginning of all, the opening verses of the Book of Genesis:

> In the beginning of creation, when God made heaven and earth, the earth was without form and void, with darkness over the face of the abyss, and a mighty wind that swept over the surface of the waters. God said, 'Let there be light', and there was light; and God saw that the light was good, and he separated light from darkness.[36]

Indeed, the word *fis* evokes the Biblical *fiat lux* from the very outset. At issue, then, is a rewriting of the Book of Genesis: *Les Commencements* presents as Cixous's own creation myth. The manuscript indicates that initially Saint-Georges was simply 'Georges'; his elevation to sainthood took place during the writing of the text.[37] The fact that Georges was the name of Cixous's father invites a reading of the text as a mythological exploration of her own origins as much as a story to explain how the world began, especially since the narrator's mother will share the same (overdetermined) name as the author's 'real' mother: Ève.

I shall return later to the question of identity. First, bearing in mind that the link between the words *voir* and *savoir* strongly overdetermines the link between seeing and knowing in French, let us examine how this text creates a light that does not clarify. One of the most obvious differences between Cixous's version of creation and the original Biblical scene is that, in the place of a clear-cut separation between light and darkness, Cixous's light rather mixes things up. It is specifically an 'émulsion': a liquid mixture sensitive to light, deriving from the Latin *emulgere*, to milk. The light bathing Saint-Georges is repeatedly described as milky: 'lumière blanche laiteuse', 'blancheur lactée', 'Saint blanc laiteux'. Furthermore, the French word *saint* is a homonym of *sein*, breast (the second paragraph specifies that he has a 'poitrine bombée'); this (paternal) Saint has the makings of a maternal figure. From the beginning sexual roles are fluid. 'Je fis le rêve': the narrator is in the position of both God (as Creator) and man, since the verb *faire* is widely used in the sense of engendering a child, whereas the masculine Saint-Georges is in the role of the woman 'carrying' it. And not just any woman: as someone who makes an 'apparition', he plays the Virgin Mary to the narrator's God.[38] If he is 'carrying' the dream (within her), is the narrator in his arms as a lover or as a child? And, 'brandi' or brandished, is he not himself an erection? The scene becomes still more complicated if we take into account that the word *rêve* (like pers*é*v*é*rer, le*v*ée, ch*ev*al, d*ev*ant and even le *V*ent . . .) contains Ève; the mother is (also) in the place of the child. The contradictions become manifest in the second paragraph with the clashing statements that the narrator was *not* in Saint-Georges's arms, that the west was a 'reversed east', and that the light was 'ni un tissu ni autre chose qu'un tissu' ['neither a fabric nor something other than a fabric'].

In this universe, then, there is *mingling* at the beginning of the beginning. 'Je n'avais aucun contact avec lui [. . .] Il n'y avait que lui' ['I had no contact with him [. . .] There was only him']: in the pre-beginning, there is a gap, a blank, between the narrator and Saint-Georges, between her and him, between *lui* and anything else. 'Aucun autre objet, [. . .] donc il n'y avait pas encore d'histoire ce qui me faisait désirer qu'elle commence pour que je puisse entrer' ['No other object, [. . .] so there was as yet no story which made me want it to begin so that I could enter']: for the story to start, there has to be a con-tact, a co-touching: there has to be an *other*. Any commencement is a joint beginning, *a commencement* (from the Latin com-, *inire init*, go in), a co-entering. 'Lui' is the past participle of the verb *luire*, to shine, as well as a masculine pronoun. It seems that this hi/story only begins when *l-u-i* comes into contact with something else to become *l-u-m-i-è-r-e*, when *lui* and *mère* are in contact. In the Book of Genesis, creation is a matter of dividing one into two (light/darkness, day/night, heaven/earth, land/water, etc.); in Cixous's story, it is impossible to isolate a single origin because the condition for the story is that the other begins.

As the above analysis shows, it is above all the writing, as a body made of letters, that becomes visible at the beginning of *Les Commencements*. From the outset it highlights that words are not discrete entities but rather letters endlessly recombining, rebeginning in different forms. Thus, for example, the antanaclastic use of *fin* first as 'end', then as 'slim' (*haut et fin*), or of *blanc* in both senses of white and gap, undermines the possibility of considering the different meanings of the words as safely separable from each other.[39] At an even more elementary level, the opening *fis* echoes in *vis* (and *vie*), *profil*, *infinie* and is visibly displaced in *fin*, emphasised by its final position in two of the first three paragraphs. Similarly, *rêve* not only echoes in *persévérer*, *levée*, *cheval*, *devant* and even *le Vent* as well as in *Ève* but also, reversed from left to right like the east reversed in the west, can be heard in *vers* (towards) – and will later be heard in its its homonym *ver* (worm), a form of elementary life similar in shape to the serpent that is as tightly entangled with the figure of *Ève* as the dragon is with Saint-Georges. The proliferation of connections formed by the tight weave of the writing is a constant reminder that the word text shares the etymology of *tissu*; the text is a weave of letters. Absent and present: the signifier does not need to 'appear' in order to generate meaning; the description of Saint-Georges as an 'objet de Beauté [...] laiteux' plays implicitly on the homophony between *lait* (milk) and *laid* (ugly). This is a recurrent pattern in Cixous's work: juxtaposing a term not with its direct opposite but with something in its place, something which recognisably displaces it, opens up a space in which a new relationship can emerge. The last section of the book, entitled 'Le Beau et le Lait', invites the reader to 'reconnaître qu'il y a et n'y a pas de différence entre le beau et le lait et que c'est cette différence qui n'est pas qui joue entre Saint-Georges et moi le rôle de Dieu' ['recognize that there is and is not any difference between the beautiful and milk and that this difference which is not plays the role of God between Saint-Georges and me'] (205). The principal challenge of reading *Les Commencements* is that of being sensitive to a 'difference which is not'. The 'difference which is not' is the difference that makes all the difference.

We can note that the opening passage of *Les Commencements* features a door, a passage: in the beginning is an *already-different* space, just as the narrator will later arrive into a house without 'aucun franchissement, aucune relation de passage, de précédence, car l'arrivée consiste en un état absolu' ['any crossing, any relation of passing, of precedence, for the arrival consists of an absolute state'] (165). Beginning means *having already* moved into a space which both is and is not the space left behind, for example a dream-world which is not simply external to reality. How can we understand the difference between a dream and 'the appearance of a dream'? Is an 'apparent' dream a reality? Is it more or less dreamlike than a dream, more or less realistic than reality? Just as the 'blanc' allowing Saint-Georges to appear is 'ni un tissu ni autre chose qu'un tissu', so the dream-like universe of *Les Commencements* problematises the distinction between a dream and its others, discursive as well as non-discursive. At the end of the opening passage, a few paragraphs after those quoted above, Cixous quotes Leonardo da Vinci's line: 'La natura è piena d'infinite ragioni.' The usual translation in English is 'Nature is full of infinite causes' but in this context it is noteworthy that the word for causes in the usual French translation, like the Italian original, is *raisons*, reasons. The beginning of *Les Commencements* affirms, indeed, that nature is full of infinite *reasons* that never occurred in experience, new ways of thinking that expand our horizons of understanding:

> Tout ceci expliquait ce que l'expérience ne connaît pas: que le rêve, qui était dans moi accueillant Saint-Georges et me refusant, était porté par Saint-Georges qui m'étreignait [. . .] Le soleil était dans le soleil, et la lune était dans le soleil qu'elle reflétait et la lune était dans le soleil qui était dans le soleil. (9)

> [All this explained what experience doesn't know: that the dream, which was in me welcoming Saint-Georges and refusing me, was carried by Saint-Georges who embraced me [. . .] The sun was in the sun, and the moon was in the sun it reflected and the moon was in the sun which was in the sun.]

Dreaming helps to explain what might previously have seemed inexplicable but is no longer unprecedented: it dreams a new reality into being by dreaming into being the discourse that reflects it.

Making Heads or Tails of Words

The adoption of the quotation from da Vinci (an artist known also for his scientific innovations) argues strongly against a reading of Cixous as anti-theoretical. While the poetic tone of the opening passage dominates throughout the text, other discourses also make their voices heard. Unlike *Dedans* but like many of Cixous's subsequent texts, *Les Commencements* at times deploys a theoretical vocabulary, especially from the fields of psychoanalysis and linguistics; the distinction between theory and other discourses is one of the 'differences which are not' the book explores. The claim by theory to articulate a transcendent truth is undermined by the juxtaposition of the theoretical and the non-theoretical, as in the following example: 'cette stase narcissique où vous pourrez regarder votre regard sans avoir recours à quelque objet médiateur, et découvrir l'insondable bestial qui opacifie le deuxième fond de l'œil humain' ['this narcissistic stasis when you can look at your gaze without having recourse to any mediating object, and discover the unfathomable bestiality that opacifies the second bottom of the human eye'] (98). The poetic final clause obliges the reader to question whether the preceding description, with its unmistakable allusion to Lacan's mirror stage, has any greater claim to objectivity or whether it similarly derives from a particular, personal point of view. (Freud is implicated as much as Lacan in that the only other time a form of the word 'narcissique' occurs is in a reference to *Zur Einführung des Narzissmus* [*On Narcissism: An Introduction*], one of only three book-titles mentioned in the text (27).) In the same way, Cixous makes an incongruous use of the word 'signifier': 'c'est parce que le signifiant allaite naturellement la bouche qui s'y attache, que je m'élève au sein' ['it's because the signifier naturally breastfeeds the mouth attached to it that I raise myself on the breast'] (206); and again:

> cet art ne serait rien à côté du travail de ses lèvres sur les miennes et du travail du mot lèvres sur le mot lèvres, et de chacune de ces lettres sur les autres lettres et sur elle-même, et, de développer le signifiant en tous sens et tous arts, éprouvant son élasticité, son extension, sa peau (210)

> [this art would be nothing beside the work of his lips on mine and the work of the word lips on the word lips, and of each of these letters on the other letters and on itself, and, from developing the signifier in every direction and every art, testing its elasticity, its stretch, its skin]

The text thus obliges the reader to consider theoretical words such as signifier precisely *as signifiers*, that is as bodies liable to be cut, displaced, reassembled in exactly the same way as other words.

It is significant that the passage in *Les Commencements* in which Cixous most explicitly articulates the plasticity of linguistic matter also offers the most direct critique of the repressive aspect of theoretical discourse. Again, the scene takes place in one of the narrator's dreams (a singularly untranslatable one):

> Je suis à V., lieu de malaise professionnel, où je suis tenue de répandre un discours fondamental, à intervalles réguliers. [. . .] Je viens de verser à V. un

de ces discours obligatoires que je pratique fort mal. [. . .] Une jeune personne militante, dure, insinuante me retient par perversité. Ses questions tendent à me faire avouer une culpabilité, elle m'interroge avec un discours qui cherche à faire rendre gorge au mien, à l'aide d'une terminologie de ces écoles que je redoute parce qu'elle ne m'est pas assez familière. Je me sens acculée jusqu'en zone d'ignorance, par un persiflage inaudible qui se joue sur l'implication de la maison, dans ce que j'ai dit. Je cherche à me dégager car mon propre réel est de faire l'amour avec Saint-Georges, je suis pressée de m'esquiver; est-ce qui V? rebondit comme je cherche à me dégager. Je ne veux pas répéter. La militante me coince, d'autres surgissent, je suis d'ailleurs pieds nus, je suis aussi de plus en plus nue ce qui accroît ma gêne; elle me dit alors que ce que j'ai dit lui paraît très *mornitif*. Embarrassée jusqu'à l'accablement par ce mot qui relève des écoles où je n'ai pas accès, je me refuse à tout commentaire. (186–7)

[I am in V., a place of professional malaise, where I am bound to spread a fundamental discourse, at regular intervals. [. . .] I have just delivered at V. one of the obligatory discourses I practise so badly. [. . .] A militant, hard, insinuating young lady keeps me back out of perversity. Her questions aim at getting me to admit guilt, she questions me with a discourse trying to get me to give back mine, with the aid of a learned terminology I dread because it is not familiar enough to me. I feel pushed back right to the zone of ignorance, by an inaudible mockery concerning the implication of the house in what I said. I try to free myself because my own real is to make love with Saint-Georges, I am in a hurry to dodge away; do d ge? bounces back as I try to get away. I do not want to repeat. The militant corners me, others come up, besides I am barefoot, I am also more and more naked, which increases my embarrassment; she tells me then that what I said seems very *mornitive* to her. Embarrassed to the point of collapsing by this word coming from the schools to which I've no access, I refuse to comment.]

The association in this dream between epistemic and moral failure, between being wrong and being in the wrong, is patent: the narrator feels under pressure to 'avouer une culpabilité', admit her guilt.[40] 'V' unmistakably evokes a university, especially as the latter word is inscribed, cut in two, its head in the word immediately preceding the passage quoted, '*uni*ple' (a mixture of 'unique' and 'multiple'), its tail in 'per*versité*'. The focus is firmly on the repressive aspect of the communication of knowledge. An inaccessible terminology associated with the Law ('discours obligatoires') and with might (the person using it is 'militante') is used to mystificatory effect to make the narrator feel intimidated ('je redoute'), defensive ('je me sens acculée', 'coincée'), vulnerable ('nue'), embarrassed ('embarrassée jusqu'à l'accablement'). This is manifestly a scene of knowledge used as a tool of domination.

The narrator participates in the scene, delivers (*verser*) a speech as expected of her, or perhaps *not* as expected of her. The choice of verb merits comment; *verser*, like *répandre*, can mean to pour (a liquid); in addition, etymologically it means to turn around or overturn. The narrator in effect subverts the usual discourse, the turning point coming at the moment where she seeks to free herself: 'Je cherche à me dégager car mon propre réel est de faire l'amour avec Saint-Georges' ['I try to free myself because my own real is to make love with Saint-Georges']. The jargonistic phrase 'mon propre réel' would not be incongruous in any 'school' that encouraged the use of a masterful discourse, an obvious example alluded to here being that of Lacan, whose substantivation of 'Réel' was a notable feature of his theory.[41] But that makes all the more striking both the application of the phrase to an activity which would, precisely, be out of place in such a context, and its contrast with the following linguistic play: 'je suis pressée de m'esquiver; est-ce qui V? rebondit'. Cixous's response to the tyranny of masterful discourses is neither to ignore nor to replicate but rather to *an-atomize* them, that is to treat them as bodies, cut them into their constituent parts, and then reassemble them. Cut into pieces, the word 'esquiver' rebounds, picks up, starts up again, acquires new life; this cutting is life-giving rather than lethal.[42] On the next page, the oppressive aspect of the word *mornitif*, a fabricated word (and one therefore that nobody could understand) and endowed by its first syllable with a deathly connotation (*mort* means death), is neutralised when it, too, is subjected to similar treatment: 'Saint-Georges me montre que mornitif s'est fabriqué en coupant la tête à génitif ou prenant le bout de définitif' ['Saint-Georges shows me that mornitive was made by cutting the head from genitive or taking the end of definitive'] (188). In a later (and if anything even more untranslatable!) passage,[43] the cuts proliferate still further:

> Encore ce vertige: un mot que j'aime bien pour la rime: tige, ge. En fait ge revient ainsi par le geste de tomber, à partir de la phrase qui me précipite. On aurait dit que le mot générateur de toute l'espèce, et qui avait été 'mornitif', était un serpent que l'on aurait coupé en plusieurs morceaux, puis recousu sur une autre tête, la tête première (*génitif*) resurgissant au bout des mots, là où elle pouvait s'agripper, en bref une monstrueuse évolution. Gêne, coupée, mort, coupée, verti, coupé, je, coup, able. En outre, Saint Ge, or, ges, avait changé de visage (197)

> [Still this vertigo: a word I like a lot for the rhyme: below, ego. In fact ego comes back eagerly in falling, following the sentence precipitating me on. You could say that the word generating the entire species, that had been 'mornitive', was a serpent that had been cut into several pieces, then sewn back onto another head, the first head (*genitive*) re-emerging at the end of words, wherever it could get a hold, briefly a monstrous evolution. Gen, cut, mor, cut, vert, cut, ego, cut, able. In addition, Saint Ge, or, ges, had changed his image]

The isolation of the origin is patently impossible: 'mornitif', which the preceding quotation had asserted was a derivative of 'génitif' (or 'définitif') is now presented (albeit in the conditional past, a tense which virtualises what it proffers) as the 'mot générateur', the word which generates the others. The cutting challenges all hierarchies, all attempts to privilege one word, one section of a word, over another. The 'mor' that is left behind while attention is focused on the 'nitif' reappears in '*mor*ceaux'; the 'ge' that, cut from 'nitif', resurfaces at the end not only of 'tige' and 'vertige' but also of 'visage', moreover comes back at the beginning, in 'geste', 'générateur' and 'gêne', not to mention its climactic reinscription at both beginning *and* end of the *je*'s mirror ima-ge, Ge-or-ges. It effectively thus becomes impossible to identify a 'tête première', a first head, starting with that of the narrator herself, the object of the verb 'précipite' (from the Latin *præceps*, *præcipitis*, falls head first, from *præ* + *caput*, head). Far from abolishing the difference between head and tail, Cixous's decapitation enables the position of head – or tail – to circulate, promotes the *multiplication* of heads and tails. This economy has no place for a chief head, a head head, just as the couple formed by the narrator and Saint-Georges constitutes 'un monstre multiple et sans chef, se désirant, moi la queue lui la tête nous la morsure, ses dents les miennes, en notre sublime économie' ['a multiple monster without a chief, desiring itself, me the tail him the head, us the bite, his teeth mine, in our sublime economy'] (102).

The 'mot générateur de toute l'espèce' in the passage could thus equally be said to be the fallen head of the word 'vertige' (and silent tail of the word 'esquiver'), the reverse of the French for dream, the *ver* or worm whose shape is similar both to a stem ('tige') and to a snake and whose distinguishing characteristics include its lack of eyes and its ability to regenerate itself when cut. The narrator felt under pressure to 'avouer une culpabilité' in the examination dream: the fault of what she produces in the face of an aggressive knowledge is specifically that it is 'coup-able', guilty but also *cuttable*, like the 'animaux coupables en trois comme les longues bêtes tordues, d'un vert étincelant' ['animals cutable into three like the long, twisted beasts, of a shining green'] (31) she imagines. In fact, *Les Commencements* epitomises Cixous's early, monstrous, 'larval' texts in that it resembles the 'morceaux d'un ver coupé' ['pieces of a cut worm'] (35) that it invokes, especially given the homophony in French between *ver* (worm) and *vers* (line of verse). The book can be said to teem with (rudimentary) life insofar as it comprises a mass of tiny wriggling, squirming creatures, none of which can be considered more important than any other but all of which are essential, fundamental, *elementary*.[44] This lack of privilege is reflected at the level of the book's macrostructure: the narrator declares her desire to 'commencer le livre ailleurs qu'au début du livre, afin qu'il jouisse d'une deuxième tête et d'une deuxième bouche et qu'il ne soit point cette gueule d'angoisse qui veut se mordre et se tord' ['begin the book other than at the start of the book, so that it will enjoy a second head and a second mouth and not be this anguished face trying to bite itself and twisting'] (19). Its non-linearity and the absence of a clear narrative progression emphasise that other sections could equally constitute the beginning.[45] Indeed, the lack of hierarchy extends to Cixous's *œuvre* as a whole. For such a prolific and respected author, it is noteworthy that no one text has dominated either the critical or the popular reception of her work: none is considered more a 'masterpiece' than any other.

The book's thorough-going refusal of hierarchy could also be argued to represent a metaphorical can of worms in that it is problematic to handle, threatening like Pandora's box to infect or destabilise the world outside it when opened. One particularly visceral sequence where the narrator expounds the relationship between a tapeworm and its host invites consideration as a reflection on the troubling relationship between the book itself and its reader, suddenly interpellated by the pronoun 'vous':

> imaginez que vous avez le ténia – que le ténia vous voit, qu'il y a cet œil de ténia qui vous regarde passer et ruminer, qui sourit, qui sait tout ce que vous avez dans le ventre, mais qui ne sait rien d'autre, qui est à vous, dans vous, c'est vous le maître, vous le nourrissez, il vous dépouille, il bouge peu, il frôle les parois, il vous mordille le colon, imaginez son long silence morcellé, sa vigilance. (191)

> [imagine that you have a tapeworm – that the tapeworm sees you, that there is this tapeworm's eye that watches you pass by and ruminate, that smiles, knows what you have in your stomach, but doesn't know anything else, that belongs to you, in you, you are the master, you nourish it, it fleeces you, it scarcely moves, it grazes the walls, it nibbles at your colon, imagine its long divided silence, its vigilance.]

At the beginning of the dynamic, 'vous' is the master, occupying the position of control in that it has ('avez'), owns ('à vous'), contains ('dans vous') the worm. Yet the chiasmic construction of 'que vous avez le ténia – que le ténia vous voit' already adumbrates the possibility that the roles may be reversed, and indeed the worm is already the one who sees and knows ('qui sait tout ce que vous avez dans le ventre'). This last expression comically reanimates the cliché in French meaning to know what stuff someone is made of: the tapeworm alone knows what is literally in its host's stomach. On the one hand, then, there is a knowledge that is specifically limited to the body ('ne sait rien d'autre'), and on the other a master in effect nourishing what should be food for his thought.

In an attempt to dislodge the worm (also termed a 'ver solitaire' or solitary worm in French), 'vous' eats marrow-seeds that break it apart into pieces, making it excretable, that is separable from its host:

S'il n'est pas déjà mort en chaque morceau, comment résisterait-il, si blanc et mou à la lumière cribleuse, alors imaginez l'effroi du ténia lorsqu'il s'est précipité dans le brasier d'air activé où la lumière l'embroche aussitôt, s'il n'avait pas d'yeux il en aurait partout maintenant tout le long du corps et de part en part, et comment symboliserait-il le seuleil sinon par ce foudroiement où il échoue en bouts de serpent de mer pitoyable, haï, embroché mort-né: vous le prenez pour un ténia – (vous êtes-vous demandé en quoi pourquoi le ver est solitaire) – lorsqu'il s'effondre – (c'est une solitude 'naturelle': la plus immédiate et sans issue que son redoublement par l'expulsion) – et vous prenez le ténia pour un ver solitaire et vous le condamnez avec fureur, vous le reniez, vous le prenez pour quelque effet de rhétorique dégoûtant en tout indépendant de votre organisme – puis vous le prenez pour un serpent, aucun rapport avec vous, (vous ne vous prenez pas pour un serpent, ni pour un lieu à serpent) et vous pouvez vous ré-jouir, vous pouvez commencer, de cette séparation; il se peut même qu'enfin différents, vous puissiez regarder ces bouts blancs tranchés, laminés, mats, avec satisfaction. (191–2)

[If it isn't already dead in each bit, so white and soft, how would it resist the sorting light, so imagine the tapeworm's fright when it's precipitated into the inferno of activated air where the light skewers it immediately, if it didn't have eyes it would now have them everywhere along its body and throughout, and how would it symbolize the sun's-eye if not by the lightning strike where he falls apart into bits of a pitiful, hated, skewered, still-born sea serpent: you take it for a tapeworm – (did you ever wonder why the worm lives alone) – when it collapses – (it's a 'natural' solitude: the most immediate, with no way out other than its repetition by the expulsion) – and you take the tapeworm for a solitary worm and you condemn it with fury, you disown it, you take it for some entirely disgusting rhetorical effect independent of your organism – then you take it for a serpent, no relation with you, (you don't take yourself for a serpent, or a serpent's place) and you can re-joice, you can begin, from this separation; it may even be that, finally different, you can look at the white, chopped, rolled-over, dull ends with satisfaction.]

The roles are now reversed in that the tapeworm is the one penetrated in its interior, 'embroché', skewered by light. Passing through the host's body opens up bodily orifices throughout its own body, each equivalent to an eye; it loses its head ('s'est précipité') but *gains* body. The worm – previously described as 'cette bouche suceuse, cette tête-bouche, cette bouche têteuse, cette tête-queue coupée en morceaux' ['this sucking mouth, this head-mouth, this suckling mouth, this head-tail cut into pieces'] (191) – figures a body whose parts are in constant exchange. The 'foudroiement' – being struck by lightning or pierced by a sharp look – that breaks it apart paradoxically enables it to symbolise a 'seuleil', both 'soleil' (sun) and 'seul œil' (single eye), single in form yet irreducibly plural in meaning; the worm's fragmentation is echoed linguistically in the sudden proliferation of synonyms or equivalents: 'ténia', 'ver solitaire', 'serpent de mer'. In French, 'serpent de mer' means a hackneyed subject as well as a mythological animal;[46] the multiplication of terms also atomises ready-made, conventional language, the fragmentation signifying a new form of symbolisation, one where the single or sole or solitary is inseparable from the multiple. The referential function of language is further problematised by the repeated expression *prendre pour*, meaning to (mis)take something for something else. 'Vous le prenez pour un ténia [. . .] vous prenez le ténia pour un ver solitaire [. . .] puis vous le prenez pour un serpent': used in relation to a term generally considered a synonym, the expression shows how words make the difference. An identity is something named as such, separated from other things by words; the distinction in perception between the 'ténia' and its others is an 'effet de rhétorique', a rhetorical effect, disgusting or otherwise. A linguistic construct which, therefore, can be reformulated infinitely, unendingly, beginning again and again.

In pride of place among the worm's others sits 'you'. The relationship between 'vous' and the worm can be read as a figure of the relationship between reader and book; just as the 'solitary' worm depends for its existence on co-existence, so a book depends on its reader. What, then, are the implications of this scene for the reader of *Les Commencements*? 'Vous pouvez vous ré-jouir, vous pouvez commencer, de cette séparation': those wishful of putting an end to the link between them and the occasion of their disgust can begin another existence, one in which they are 'enfin différents', finally apart. Doing so may even generate the satisfaction of seeing the dull white pieces forced into the light. However, the 'genius' of this elementary form of life is that the process of differentiation is unexpectedly pleasurable; differences need to be continually generated for the pleasure to continue:

C'est parce qu'il est perdu, pensez-vous, si vous poussez, il ne ré siste plus. C'est là qu'est son génie: vous le prenez pour un serpent, que vous prenez pour un ver, dont la nature est absolument autre que vous, vous êtes séparé, il y a ces morceaux percés par terre autour du siège, morts de lumière, visibles blancs opaques, sans yeux, c'est vous maintenant qui avez l'œil sur le ténia, mais il y a le génie du ténia: c'est le plaisir que le moment de la séparation vous a donné, un plaisir très doux, une caresse qui vous surprend, mais qui n'est pas invraisemblable, si l'on songe à la douceur de la peau du ténia. Après tout, ce qui vous surprend c'est qu'un serpent aveugle et mutilé vous fasse plaisir, c'est son génie, mais vous ne seriez pas surpris si le ténia était une langue ou un doigt amoureux. (192)

[It's because he's lost, you think, if you push, it won't re sist any longer. That's its genius: you take it for a serpent, that you take for a worm, whose nature is absolutely other than yours, you are separated, there are these pierced bits on the ground around the seat, dead from light, visible white opaque, without eyes, it's now you who have your eye on the tapeworm, but there's the tapeworm's genius: it's the pleasure that the moment of separation gave you, a very sweet pleasure, a caress that surprises you, but is not unlikely, if you consider the softness of the tapeworm's skin. After all, what surprises you is that a blind, mutilated serpent should give you pleasure, that's its genius, but you wouldn't be surprised if the tapeworm was a lover's tongue or finger.]

The eroticised pleasure caused by the creature evokes the illicit pleasure enjoyed in the Garden of Eden when Adam and Eve are tempted by the serpent to eat the fruit of the Tree of Knowledge. The roles are now reversed in that 'c'est vous maintenant qui avez l'œil sur le ténia', who is reduced to a mass of dead white segments around the seat. The worm is 'perdu', but it is not alone in having lost. The economy of knowledge in which it is believed that identities can be defined is an economy of taking: 'You take . . . you take . . . you take . . .'. However, the desire to define the other puts an end to the unexpected pleasure the other can give, the pleasure *only* the other can give, the pleasure of being surprised, that is *surpris*, surprised, literally sur*taken*: 'un plaisir très doux, une caresse qui vous surprend'. Taking any identity as definitive is a mis-take insofar as the definition necessarily excludes the surprising, the as yet unknown. At issue in *Les Commencements* is thus a *knowledge in progress*, a knowledge in movement: 'Il n'est pas question d'identification. C'est une autre question dont il est question' ['It's not a question of identification. Another question is under question here'] (186). It is more a question of bringing to light a relation which cannot be brought to light as such, for example finding the

nom d'espèce sous lequel la maison et ce chat se trouvent dans un système de relations telles qu'à la limite on peut réellement prendre l'un pour l'autre, compte tenu de la difficulté plus grande éprouvée à prendre la maison plutôt que le chat. Il n'y a pas, dans ce système, de couple dehors-dedans (186)

[name of the species covering the system of relations between the house and this cat whereby at the limit one can really be taken for the other, taking into account the greater difficulty involved in taking the house rather than the cat. In this system, there is no couple outside-inside]

The infinity of relational possibilities means that any finite definition of an identity is necessarily unsatisfactory. Intellectual inquiry is more a process of exploring or exceeding limits than of setting them; knowledge is endlessly *processual*.[47] *Les Commencements* already shows in an unprecedented way that, because of the impossibility of ever containing knowledge, knowledge is always more than a matter of content. The difference between a 'faux savoir', or false knowing, and a 'savoir spectral', or spectral knowing, is that the latter takes into account the fact that knowledge is always haunted by an outside, an as-yet unknown:

> car on ne sait jamais et ensuite on ne sait plus ce qu'on aurait su si on avait cru pouvoir savoir. Donc on ne sait pas, puisqu'on n'avait pas prévu le faux savoir, où coucher ce qui arriverait d'imprévu, on manque du savoir spectral dans lequel, ou par-dessus, on aurait pu mettre ce que l'on croit savoir maintenant après coup (140)

> [for you never know and then you no longer know what you would have known if you had believed that you could know. So, since you hadn't foreseen false knowing, you don't know where to lay the unforeseen that will happen, you lack the spectral knowing in which, or above which you could afterwards have put what you now think you know]

'Où coucher ce qui arriverait d'impré-*vu*': what might a knowledge be that made space for the unknown, the unforeseen?

Emergent Knowledge

Les Commencements's answer to that question appears to be: *a fiction.* 'Parce que quand je sais que je ne sais pas, alors il faut que je me raconte une autre histoire / Et c'est la nôtre' ['Because when I know that I don't know, then I have to tell myself another story / And it's ours'] (24): the narrator's response to not knowing is to tell a story. Cixous's approach to the epistemic questions which contemporaneously dominated the beginnings of deconstruction is distinctive not only in its elementary form, in the form it gives to the elementary, but in its investigation of the link between the unknowable and the fictional, between imagining and knowing. As the place where what doesn't yet exist *nevertheless exists*, 'existe comme tout ce qui est imaginable et pas plus' ['exists like all that is imaginable and no more'] (26), fiction can inaugurate a new, unprecedented way of thinking.

At one point, Ève asks the narrator if the book is a 'roman policier', a detective novel, the genre whose narrative drive and emphasis on solving a mystery perhaps place it furthest from the relentless uncertainties and opacities of Cixous's text. The narrator replies: 'C'est une énigme: Où trouve-t-on le serpent?' ['It's a riddle: Where can the serpent be found ?]

(77). Her reply more displaces the question than answers it; it is not clear if the riddle is an alternative genre to a detective novel, or the plot of a detective story revolving around the whereabouts of the serpent. Moreover, the place of the serpent turns out to be displacement itself, according to Saint-Georges who replies to the same question: 'sous une autre forme que la sienne, et on le trouve quand il n'est plus là, parce qu'il est ce qui n'existe pas' ['in a different form from its own, and you find it when it is no longer there, because it is what doesn't exist'] (77). As the nonexistent, with no place of its own, the serpent finds a place in displacing other forms. We can note the structural resemblance with the narrator herself, whose anonymity is the condition of possibility of a generalised polynymy. Having only the beginning of her name opens up a whole host of names to her:

> J'ai oublié mon nom; il n'est pas perdu bien sûr, je l'ai toujours; je n'en ai gardé que l'entrée, un son hybride, intéressant, oscillatoire: entre le J et le H, exactement un son d'essai, si bien que toute effusion sans le savoir est sur le point de me nommer. (43)

> [I've forgotten my name; it isn't lost of course, I still have it; I've only kept the entry, a hybrid, interesting, oscillatory sound: between J and H, precisely a trial sound, such that every effusion without knowing is on the point of naming me.]

The beginning is already 'hybrid'; as we saw before, the origin is plural from the beginning. The initial is paradoxically a mix of letters, the H and J suggesting that the name begins as both name and pronoun ('je'), that is a word that can take the place of another name. It makes a 'son d'essai',[48] a trial or provisional sound, one liable to change in the future, to be replaced by any 'effusion', outpouring or flow. 'Toute effusion sans le savoir est sur le point de me nommer': because the sound is just a beginning, it generates a flow of possible names, of names in flow, names which can potentially name her as long as they remain potential, 'on the point' of naming. The names are valid 'sans le savoir': a naming that spoke from a position of knowledge would fail as a name. The point, indeed, is that the narrator's name *never concludes*.

Les Commencements is a fiction whose texture is as intensely characterised by its lack of conclusion as its overall structure. Contradictions, discrepancies, incompatibilities abound at every level without ever reaching a dialectical resolution. The text takes place on the 'plane of Contradiction':

> Le plan de la Contradiction est l'englobement de plans – on peut les voir avec plusieurs yeux, ou l'œil général – libérés des exigences de la vision humaine

qui n'admet pas que les angles se combinent sans crier à l'énucléation. C'est un ensemble en mouvement non-représentable sauf de profil-face, où dehors < que dedans, perceptible seulement à l'œil de dieu, qui peut voir en même temps le jour et la nuit (86)

[The plane of Contradiction is the encompassing of planes – you can see them with several eyes, or the general eye – freed from the exigencies of human vision that can't admit that angles combine without protesting about enucleation. It's a whole in movement, non-representable except in profile-fullface, where outside < than inside, perceptible only to the eye of God, who can see day and night at the same time]

Unlike conventional vision which eliminates binocular disparity (the parallax or difference between what the right and left eye separately see), this 'œil général' or 'œil de dieu' (or 'œil d'yeux', to pick up on yet another divergent chain of signification . . .) is not threatened by logical or spatial incompatibility. Like the earlier 'seuleil', this eye is both singular and plural. 'Enucleation' means the extraction of the kernel from a nut and has a figurative meaning of elucidation, in the sense of abstracting the core or central part of the whole; the term is used in surgery to refer to the removal of a whole from its enveloping cover, notably an eye. Ironically, then, conventional vision perceives the partial vision resulting from discarding some of the whole as more entire and illuminating than the greater but disparate whole whose non-coincidence with itself defies conventional modes of perception. This 'ensemble en mouvement', perceptible to those alone with the sensitivity to see it, can only be represented 'de profil-face'. Two divergent perspectives cannot be given at exactly the same time. But juxtaposing them can create an image of 'ce point où tout était possible parce qu'on n'y avait pas encore introduit la succession' ['the point where everything was possible because succession had not yet been introduced there'] and where the narrator could 'tout penser sans [s]e soucier de ce qui se produirait' ['think anything without worrying about what would happen'] (17–18).

The narrator's solution to the problem of representing an 'ensemble en mouvement' is to invent a serpentine style, that is to speak with a 'langue qui fourche', the French expression for a slip of the tongue, literally a forking tongue. As the preceding analyses showed, this is manifest at the level of writing. Indeed, the way the text snakes or winds along from signifier to signifier is explicitly figured as a forking of the 'langue française':

Et je peux lancer mes trois langues contre sa langue française, pour la circonvenir et la séduire, et même la fourcher. Fourcher son nom aussi; qu'est-ce qu'il y a dans Saint-Georges: il y a sang et gorges, geint, sage, singe, or, sein, gain, tain, et bien d'autres écailles de miroir encore, et de serpent. (108)

[And I can cast my three languages against his French language, to get around and seduce it, and even to make slip or split. Split his name also; what is there in Saint-Georges: there is *sang* [blood] and gorges, *geint* [groan], sage, *singe* [monkey], *or* [gold], *sein* [breast], gain, tain, and many other shards of a mirror, and of a serpent.]

Les Commencements itself moves in the least linear or teleological fashion possible, serpentinely, sinuously (a word which shares the etymology of *sein*), sliding along from letter to letter, as epitomised in the very form of the letter S. Musing over the difference between languages evident in a series of 'noms noués des SSSS' ['names knotted with SSSS'] (108), the narrator adds: 'Quelque chose serpente de Papness à Bosslé, qui est étranger à ma langue maternelle' ['Something that is foreign to my maternal tongue winds along from Papness to Bosslé'] (108). Her writ(h)ing marks her as different from her mother, whose answer to the query about where the serpent can be found is to define it, pin it down to a place: 'Dans le dictionnaire sous S' ['In the dictionary under S'] (78). Yet this difference is no more an opposition than any other in the book: at issue is a *transformation* of the 'langue maternelle'.

In fictional terms, the text's inconclusivity deploys its effects most manifestly at the level of the characters. Thus, while Saint-Georges's name inscribes a clear association with the father from the outset, elsewhere we read: 'Un délicat inceste brode nos peaux. Certains jours où je suis fils de mon amant je suis allaité à son sein, au cours de certaines nuits quand Saint-Georges est né de ma chair, tantôt cygne émergeant, il me semble que j'ai mis au monde mon propre père' ['A delicate incest embroiders our skin. Some days when I am the son of my lover I am suckled at his breast, some nights when Saint-Georges is born of my flesh, sometimes an emerging swan, it seems to me that I've given birth to my own father'] (126). All possible sexual and generational relations are in circulation: Saint-Georges is mother to the narrator-as-son, who is also mother to Saint-Georges-as-her-own father. The characters are in constant exchange, endlessly passing their limits without the change ever becoming definitive; the narrator elsewhere describes the transformation produced in her relationship with Saint-Georges as

un retour d'Ève en Adam à la fin des temps, avec le trésor de connaissances des différences, donc chair agitée, émouvante, en fusion et extraordinairement sensible à la moindre excitation, car elle est la chair marquée de l'Histoire depuis notre origine, sa matière est mémoire et sa peau est oreille. (159)

[Eve's return in Adam at the end of time, with the treasure of the knowledge of differences, so turbulent flesh, moving, in fusion and extraordinarily sensitive to the slightest excitement, for it is flesh marked with History since our origin, its matter is memory and its skin is ear.]

A body 'in fusion', with a heightened sensitivity to the differences that make it what it is, a body 'marked with History': inventing such a body takes fiction beyond the limits of fiction. This emulsive, effusive story (*histoire*) is both fiction and history: it's a place where History gives up its capital H, loses its head but tells a tale in which, as announced in the book's final pages, 'il y a une autre Histoire qui commence: elle est imaginaire, c'est pourtant une histoire vraie' ['another History begins: an imaginary one, yet a true story'] (224). In the logic of *Les Commencements*, that History has already begun in the book that announces it: not just because imagining its possibility is enough for it to exist,[49] but because the text's endless incipience supports the narrator's final extravagant claim to undermine the bedrock of 'la civilisation occidentale' ['Western civilisation'] (224), one whose founding myth is that of a unique, homogeneous origin.

This reaching of fiction beyond itself returns us to the overall problematic of this chapter. *Les Commencements* suggests that Western civilisation has laid obstacles in the path of its own pursuit of truth by privileging the object of knowledge over the process in which it emerges. Lacan similarly warns against the danger of confusing 'more or less predigested' forms of knowledge with the truth:

> This mistake exists in every form of knowledge, insofar as knowledge is nothing other than the crystallization of symbolical activity that it forgets, once constituted. In every knowledge already constituted there is thus a dimension of error, which consists in the forgetting of the creative function of truth in its nascent form.[50]

Derrida's insistence on the importance of historicising the concepts he works with approaches this insight from a different angle. Cixous's fiction can be said to represent an 'elementary' deconstruction, one that goes not better than Derrida's but *further*, in integrating it into her practice of writing. Her narrator explicitly links the text's incessant movement to the process of thinking: 'il n'y a pas la moindre place pour une pensée, je suis mobilisée en totalité par le mouvement' ['there is not the slightest place for a thought, I am entirely mobilized by movement'] (152). Her text is an ongoing *thinking*, a thinking in movement, rather than a place in which 'thoughts' are fixed. A thinking which insistently, consistently, defers the moment at which the uncertain, the unknown, the as-yet-unheard-of, gets crystallised in knowledge:

Il y avait quelque chose de tremblant entre ces noms et d'insaisissable, [. . .]
qui ne se laisse pas captiver, qu'il faudrait pourtant saisir, mais je n'en vois
pas la nécessité, je me demande si je veux la saisir, [. . . je temporise, ne
retardant, je le sais, que le moment de dire ce que je saurai dès que je l'aurai
dit, ce qui se sait déjà mais que je peux encore ne pas savoir, tant que ça ne
s'entend pas, et que ça reste en Inouï, le seul lieu sans histoire et sans géogra-
phie, là où les habitants parlent des langues pas encore vivantes, et sans soleil
encore, c'est là que tremble la chose, présolaire, qui ne se voit pas encore.
(202)

[There was something tremulous and elusive between those names [. . .] that
won't let itself be captured, but that has to be grasped, but I don't see the
need, I wonder if I want to grasp it, [. . .] I play for time, delaying only, I
know, the moment of saying what I will know once I'll have said it, what is
already known but that I can still not know, as long as it isn't heard, and it
stays in Unheard-of, the only place without a history and without a geogra-
phy, where the inhabitants speak languages not yet alive, and still without a
sun, that is where the presolar thing that can't yet be seen trembles.]

By deferring the moment of knowing, the narrator prolongs the time
during which knowledge is *in process*. Her thinking reflects its tremulous, elusive, 'presolar' object, trembling itself between knowing ('I
know') and not knowing ('I can still not know'). 'Ce que je saurai
dès que je l'aurai dit': knowing comes after saying, writing is a space
of *not yet* knowing. Conversely, for Cixous knowing signals the end
of writing. Significantly, the only time the narrator is unambiguously
in a position of knowledge is in the book's final lines where, also for
the first time, the link between *voir* and *savoir* comes clearly into
view:

Saint-Georges descend ou monte à côté de moi, sans que je le voie. Sans le
voir je sais qu'il est mon double sans être mon reflet ou moi le sien. [. . .]
Comment l'œil gauche regarderait-il l'œil droit? Je sais ce qu'il voit: je sais
aussi ce qu'il ne faut pas encore savoir. Et je sais aussi que nous ne savons pas
encore ce que nous verrons lorsque tous nos yeux arriveront à cet endroit de
l'infini où commence une autre Histoire très différente. Parce qu'il sait que je
sais comment l'Histoire sans parallèle commence, Saint-Georges rit. Le plaisir
est très haut dans le ciel maintenant. Et je me mets à rire. (231–2)

[Saint-Georges descends or climbs beside me, without my seeing him.
Without seeing him I know that he is my double without being my reflection
or me his. [. . .] How might the left eye look at the right eye? I know what
he sees: I also know what must not yet be known. And I know also that we
do not yet know what we will see when all our eyes get to the infinite place
where another, very different, History begins. Because he knows that I know
how the History without parallel begins, Saint-Georges laughs. The pleasure
is very high in the sky now. And I begin to laugh.]

The book culminates in a knowledge that opens onto 'another, very different, History' in which knowing does not exclude *not* knowing. Especially, it does not presume to know the other. In this vision of a new beginning, the difference between what the left and right eyes see is central. The nascent (hi)story is 'without parallel', unprecedented, unmatched; unprecedented, above all, as a place in which lines of sight are different and can intersect, meet each other, enter into contact with each other. Without a parallel, but with parallax. In astronomy, the principle of parallax is used to determine the position of a celestial body as measured from different angles along the earth's orbit. A new line of sight has allowed an unanticipated heavenly body to emerge; the book ends with pleasure 'very high in the sky'.

In the future heralded by *Les Commencements*, pleasure takes the place of the sun. Reason, then, is not the only source of light. With its displacements and contradictions, Cixous's writing not only exposes the limitations of logic in thinking about certain kinds of questions, but already illustrates – that is invents – an effusive, trembling, 'presolar' body of knowledge in which thinking admits its body, in which no limits to what can be thought are prescribed for the sake of clarity and where the pleasure of thinking outweighs the rules.

Notes

1. *Photos de racines*, 89; *Rootprints*, 80.
2. Hélène Cixous, *L'Exil de James Joyce ou l'art du remplacement* (Paris: Grasset, 1968), 841; *The Exile of James Joyce*, trans. Sally Purcell (New York: David Lewis, 1972), 744.
3. Geoffrey Bennington, 'Teleanalysis', in *Cixous, Derrida, Psychoanalysis*, ed. Mark Dawson, Mairéad Hanrahan and Eric Prenowitz, *Paragraph*, 36:2 (2013), 270–85, at 278.
4. See Hélène Cixous, 'Contes de la différence sexuelle' ['Tales of Sexual Difference']; and Jacques Derrida, 'Fourmis', in *Lectures de la Différence Sexuelle*, 69–102. In addition to *H. C. pour la vie, c'est à dire . . .*, Derrida's other writings on Cixous include 'Un Ver à soie: Points de vue piqués sur l'autre voile', in Hélène Cixous and Jacques Derrida, *Voiles* (Paris: Galilée, 1998), 23–85 ['A Silkworm of One's Own', in *Veils*, trans. Geoffrey Bennington (Stanford: Stanford University Press, 2001), 17–92]; and *Genèses, généalogies, genres et le génie: Les secrets de l'archive* (Paris: Galilée, 2003) [*Geneses, Genealogies, Genres and Genius: The Secrets of the Archive*, trans. Beverly Bie Brahic (Edinburgh: Edinburgh University Press, 2006)]. Cixous's texts on Derrida include 'Quelle heure est-il, ou La porte (celle qu'on ne passe pas)', in *Le Passage des frontières: Autour du travail de Jacques Derrida*, ed. Marie-Louise Mallet (Paris: Galilée, 1994), 83–98 ['What is it o'clock? or The door (we never enter)', trans. Catherine A. F. MacGillivray, *Stigmata: Escaping Texts* (London: Routledge, 1998),

57–83]; *Portrait de Jacques Derrida en Jeune Saint Juif* (Paris: Galilée, 2001) [*Portrait of Jacques Derrida as a Young Jewish Saint*, trans. Beverly Bie Brahic (New York: Columbia University Press, 2003)]; 'Ce corps étranjuif', in *Judéités: Questions pour Jacques Derrida*, ed. Joseph Cohen and Raphael Zagury-Orly (Paris: Galilée, 2003), 59–83 ['This Stranjew Body', in *Judeities: Questions for Jacques Derrida*, trans. Bettina Bergo and Michael B. Smith (New York: Fordham University Press, 2007), 52–77]; 'De la démoncratie en littérature ou Le Diable sans Confession', in *La Démocratie à venir: Autour de Jacques Derrida*, ed. Marie-Louise Mallet (Paris: Galilée, 2004), 189–223 ['The Devil Without Confessing Him', trans. Beverly Bie Brahic, available online at http://escholarship.org/uc/item/0cs123x8]; 'Fichus et caleçons', in *Derrida: Cahier Derrida, Cahiers de l'Herne*, 83, ed. Marie-Louise Mallet and Ginette Michaud (Paris: Éditions de l'Herne, 2004), 56–61; *Insister: A Jacques Derrida* (Paris: Galilée, 2006) [*Insister of Jacques Derrida*, trans. Peggy Kamuf (Edinburgh: Edinburgh University Press, 2007)]; 'Ce qui a l'air de quoi', in *L'Événement comme écriture: Cixous et Derrida se lisant*, ed. Marta Segarra (Paris: Campagne Première, 2007), 11–71; and 'Jacques Derrida as a Proteus Unbound', trans. Peggy Kamuf, *Critical Inquiry* 33 (2007), 389–423. The links between the two writers have also been the specific focus of a number of publications; see, for example, Laurent Milesi, 'Portraits of H. C. as J. D. and Back', *New Literary History*, 37:1 (2006), 65–84; *L'événement comme écriture: Cixous et Derrida se lisant*, ed. Marta Segarra (Paris: Éditions Campagne Première, 2007); Ginette Michaud, *Battements du secret littéraire: Lire Jacques Derrida et Hélène Cixous 1* and *'Comme en rêve': Lire Jacques Derrida et Hélène Cixous 2*; and *Cixous, Derrida, Psychoanalysis*, ed. Mark Dawson, Mairéad Hanrahan and Eric Prenowitz, Special Number, *Paragraph*, 36:2 (2013).

5. *Hélène Cixous: Writing the Feminine*, 5.
6. *Photos de racines*, 89; *Rootprints*, 79.
7. Notable exceptions are the two volumes of Ginette Michaud's *Lire Jacques Derrida and Hélène Cixous* and Judith Still's *Derrida and Hospitality: Theory and Practice* (Edinburgh: Edinburgh University Press, 2010).
8. *Hélène Cixous: A Politics of Writing*, 3.
9. *L'Ecriture solaire d'Hélène Cixous*, 18.
10. 'To Give Place', 74, 79 and 85–7.
11. Jacques Derrida, 'Mochlos ou le conflit des facultés', *Du droit à la philosophie* (Paris: Galilée, 1990), 397–438, at 423–4; 'Mochlos or the Conflict of the Faculties', in *Eyes of the University: Right to Philosophy 2*, trans. Jan Plug and others (Stanford: Stanford University Press, 2004), 83–112, at 102.
12. Jacques Derrida, 'Ponctuations: le temps de la thèse, *Du droit à la philosophie*, 439–59, at 451–2; 'Punctuations: The Time of a Thesis', in *Eyes of the University: Right to Philosophy 2*, trans. Jan Plug and others (Stanford: Stanford University Press, 2004), 113–28, at 123.
13. Jacques Derrida, 'Les Pupilles de l'Université: Le principe de raison et l'idée de l'Université', *Du droit à la philosophie*, 461–98, at 462; 'The Principle of Reason: The University in the Eyes of Its Pupils', *Eyes of the University*, 129–55, at 129.

14. When detailing the resistances encountered by Cixous's work, Derrida places 'en premier lieu' ['in first place'] its poetic force, that is 'la chose de l'écriture et de la langue' (HC, 122) ['the business of writing, and language' (HCE, 136)].

15. *Hélène Cixous: Writing the Feminine*, 151–2.

16. For example: 'Toi et moi, lui et moi, nous "écrivons"' ('Contes de la difference sexuelle', 58) ['You and I, he and I, we "write"' ('Tales of Sexual Difference'), 58].

17. *La Jeune née*, 264; *The Newly Born Woman*, 144.

18. *La Jeune née*, 253 and 269; *The Newly Born Woman*, 137 and 146 (translation modified).

19. In Duras's *Détruire dit-elle*, for example, 'la théorie de Rosenfeld', the only theory in which the main character Alissa believes, turns out to be that of a child who died at the age of eight.

20. *Hélène Cixous: Writing the Feminine*, 147.

21. In a conversation reported or invented in *Insister*, however, Cixous ascribes to Derrida the view that his relative clarity is pedagogically superior: 'J'ai un concept pédagogique conventionnel. Quand je vois la différence entre ton texte et le mien! Dans le genre conférence, pour les gens un peu plus attardés, moi je les repêche parce que je suis pédagogue, toi, tu les largues' ['I have a conventional pedagogical concept. When I see the difference between your text and mine! In the lecture mode, for the ones who are a little slow, I fish them out because I'm a pedagogue, whereas you, you cut them loose'] (*Insister*, 63; *Insister of Jacques Derrida*, 84). In context, 'ton texte et le mien' ['your text and mine'] could mean either all of their writings or only those destined to be delivered orally, the latter category representing a considerably higher proportion in Derrida's case than in Cixous's (see Anne Berger, 'Appels', in *L'événement comme écriture: Cixous et Derrida se lisant*, 85–107, at 100). Either way, Derrida's comment as relayed here by Cixous implies that she has gone too far in her textual invention. That is, she has gone too far *for others*: the pedagogical issue appears to be more a matter of ethics (of concern for the reader/audience, as expressed in the verb 'repêcher': to fish out or rescue) than of efficiency in transmitting a message. Clearly, the fact that this is Cixous's representation of Derrida's point of view makes all the difference; whereas a similar judgment signed by Derrida himself (if indeed that represented his opinion) could only be read as a criticism, no such strategic or political danger arises from Cixous's attributing such a view about herself to him. Bearing this in mind, it is nonetheless interesting to consider Derrida's reported valorisation of pedagogical conventionality in relation to his argument, as developed above with specific regard to academia, that one's practice performs the institution, constructs a model of one's 'ideal' institution/seminar/socius. It would suggest he was of the view that Cixous's challenge to the institution they both sought to transform was more uncompromising than his own.

22. See HC, 27; HCE, 19.

23. Nicholas Royle has explored some of the complexities of what reading (in his case, Derrida) 'after Derrida' might mean in the Introduction to *After Derrida* (Manchester and New York: Manchester University Press, 1995), especially 2–5.

24. 'Contes', 31. The opening section of Cixous's text was not translated in the piece included in *The Portable Cixous*. Similarly, discussing her initial encounter with Derrida twenty years after that first text, she muses: 'it all begins with a postcard. [. . .] The other thing that I would like to underline is the mystery of the beginning, that is: what or who starts the letter? Of course the letter is not a letter, there is a postcard that is not a postcard: it is the usual supplementary structure. But who begins? I shouldn't say who begins *ever*, but who begins first, who first begins, who second begins, who re-begins?' ('A Kind of Magic', in *Cixous, Derrida, Psychoanalysis*, 177).
25. 'Appels', 88.
26. Derrida's problematisation of the origin is reflected in the multiple beginnings of many texts; see, for example, *Mal d'Archive* (Paris: Galilée, 1995) [*Archive Fever*, trans. Eric Prenowitz (Chicago: University of Chicago Press, 1998)] and *États d'âme de la psychanalyse* (Paris: Galilée, 2000) ['Psychoanalysis Searches the States of Its Soul', in *Without Alibi*, trans. Peggy Kamuf (Stanford: Stanford University Press, 2002), 238–80].
27. 'Combien peu se ressemblent les choses que nous écrivons, l'une et l'autre [. . .] difficile d'imaginer des écritures, des façons, des manières, des gestes, des rythmes, des langues, des vies d'écriture, et des vies tout court, plus hétérogènes et dissemblables, plus éloignées l'une de l'autre et des deux côtés' (HC, 135) ['how little the things the two of us write resemble one another [. . .] it is difficult to imagine anything more different, difficult to imagine writings, ways, manners, gestures, rhythms, languages, lives of writing and simply lives that are more heterogeneous, more dissimilar, more distant from each other and on both sides' (HCE, 153)].
28. Rather than citing the various refutations of Habermas's claim that deconstruction was a rejection of the Enlightenment, I shall content myself with quoting the words with which Ginette Michaud ends her tribute to Derrida's memory. She concludes her book with an extract from an interview in which Derrida explains that he always turns on a light when writing: 'il faut une lumière artificielle supplémentaire [. . .] j'ai toujours l'impression que la lumière manque' ['I need an additional artificial light [. . .] I always have the impression that light is missing'] (*Veilleuses: Autour de trois images de Jacques Derrida* (Québec: Éditions Nota bene, 2009), 113).
29. *Jacques Lacan and the Adventure of Insight*, 158.
30. Hélène Cixous, *Les Commencements* (Paris: Grasset, 1970); reprinted by des femmes in 1999. Page references to the later edition will be given in the text.
31. Hélène Cixous, 'Die Ursache – La Chose', *L'Amour du loup et autres remords* (Paris: Éditions des femmes, 2003), 111.
32. 'Die Ursache – La Chose', 113.
33. See Julia Kristeva, *Pouvoirs de l'horreur: Essai sur l'abjection* (Paris: Éditions du Seuil, 1980).
34. Significantly, the published beginning was not the first one. The material relating to *Les Commencements* in the Fonds Hélène Cixous consists of two notebooks in Box 5 containing a manuscript version of the text. This begins more conventionally at the beginning, with a beginning: 'Ça commence par une date: 2 x 9   9bre 1969' ['That begins with a date: 2 x 9   9ber 1969']. The section which opens the published text originally

came later, starting on page 11 of the notebook: 'Je fis un rêve, mais c'était Saint-Georges qui le portait . . .' ['I had a dream, but it was Saint-George who carried it']. When this section was placed at the entrance to the text, the substitution of a definite for the indefinite article stresses all the more emphatically that the beginning is in the middle.

35. As well as the preterite of *voir* (to see), *vis* is the present of *vivre* (to live) and a homophone of 'Vie' (life), the last word of the opening section (9). This vision is, indeed, a creation vision: a vision of creating life. The antecedent of the pronoun *le* is similarly uncertain: while what follows would indicate that it refers to Saint-Georges, the sentence's structural similarity with the text's incipit suggests that it refers to the dream.

36. Genesis 1: 1–4, *The New English Bible*, The Bible Societies in association with Oxford University Press and Cambridge University Press (Oxford: Oxford University Press, 1972).

37. The first place where the 'Saint' is not a belated addition is on page 45 of the manuscript, at the beginning of some larger pages which themselves were inserted later. Towards the end of the manuscript notebooks, 'Saint' and 'Georges' appear to have been written together, suggesting that the change of name was not a last-minute decision but took place during the writing of the book.

38. These roles will be reversed later in the text. The simile in the opening quotation joining the narrator to Saint-Georges 'comme la noix à sa coquille' ['like the nut to its shell'] anticipates the first sentence of the book's final paragraph where 'le lien qui m'attache à Saint-Georges était analogue ou identique au lien du fruit à son noyau' ['the link attaching me to Saint-George was analogous or identical to the link of the nut to its kernel'] (231). The Marian connotation of fruit is made explicit elsewhere with an allusion to the *Ave Maria* when the narrator talks of her pleasure in the 'fruit de mon unique entraille' ['fruit of my single womb'] (144). The text also attributes to Saint-Georges a resemblance to the 'maire' or mayor, a word which is both a homophone of 'mère' (mother) and an anagram of Marie (134).

39. For a first discussion of Cixous's writing in terms of a 'generalized homonymization', see Eric Prenowitz, 'Make Believe: *Manhattan*'s *Folittérature*', *New Literary History*, 37 (2006), 147–67.

40. This recalls Freud's classic analysis according to which we dream we are in an examination situation 'whenever, having done something wrong or failed to do something properly, we expect to be punished by the event – whenever, in short, we feel the burden of responsibility' (*The Interpretation of Dreams*, Pelican Freud Library 4 (London: Penguin, 1975), 378). Cixous has often discussed writing as a *felix culpa*, most recently in 'De la démoncratie en littérature ou Le Diable sans Confession'.

41. For the most comprehensive discussion to date of the status of the reference to Lacan in Cixous's writing, see *L'Ecriture solaire d'Hélène Cixous*, 73–6.

42. I have discussed the life-giving aspect of the cut for Cixous in 'Long Cuts', *parallax* 44, 13:3 (2007), 37–48.

43. The play on the French signifier makes a literal translation meaningless. My analysis will focus only on the original; my main priority in the translation is to give a sense of how the French works.

44. 'Ver', in turn, is not unique in this respect; another image which functions as a metafictional representation of the whole which contains it is that of the 'sol de mosaïque dont le dessin m'échappait tant il était morcelé' ['mosaic floor which was in so many pieces that its design escaped me'] (110). The importance of the text's *aliveness* can be read in the fact that the mosaic, like the worms, is animate: 'je sens le sang couler dans chaque petit bout de mosaïque' ['I sense the blood flowing in every little bit of mosaic'] (111) can be read as suggesting that the mosaic, as well as the narrator, is bleeding.

45. As noted above, the published beginning is not, in fact, the beginning of the manuscript version.

46. The manuscript contains 'serpents de merde' ['shit serpents']; the change thus loses the scatological allusion but gains by evoking an earlier passage where, playing on the fact that 'Loch' means both 'lake' in (Scottish-) English and 'hole' in German, Cixous's narrator evokes the Loch Ness monster (74) in relation to her mother's 'simplicité intolérable, agressive à force d'innocence' ['intolerable simplicity, so innocent it was aggressive'], figured by a 'monde sans murs, sans fonds, sans résistances, sans nuits, sans traces, sans soleil sans inquiétude sans force autre que son absolue sim-plicité [. . .] Sans commencement [. . .] monde qui vous suce les yeux pour boucher ses propre trous' ['world without walls, without bottoms, without resistances, without nights, without traces, without sun without worry without any strength other than its absolute simplicity [. . .] Without a beginning [. . .] a world that sucks your eyes to plug its own holes'] (68–9).

47. There lies the tapeworm's 'génie', a word that Derrida examined at length in relation to Cixous's work in *Genèses, généalogies, genres et le génie: Les secrets de l'archive*. Note, however, that in addition to its meanings of genius, genie, engineering, the word is also itself the tail of a word, the suffix *-génie* meaning production or development. In other words, what is exceptional about the tapeworm is its capacity for production, for process, for differentiation, a capacity that indeed, making its identity hard to define, facilitates its being 'taken' for something else.

48. *Les Commencements* thus anticipates Derrida's work on the difference between Hegel's aspiration to an 'Absolute Knowledge' and Genet's under-mining of categoriality in *Glas* (Paris: Galilée, 1974).

49. This quotation is part of another chain in which Cixous sets her name insistently to work. In particular, the 'son d'essai' (which is also the 'son d'S') echoes in several languages, the English *son* being the translation of the French *fils*. In one of the most directly autobiographical moments, the narrator recalls having clung to life by a thread when faced with the horrors of History: 'je suis vomie sur une terre absurde, indéterminée, casuelle, à laquelle je ne tiens que par un fil et je ne sais lequel, et c'est seulement peut-être le fil sans S, le fil unique soudain tendu entre deux histoires, deux axes, deux langues, et sur lequel j'ai trébuché, tandis que j'errais en précursion' ['I'm thrown up on an absurd, indeterminate, casual land, clinging to it only by a thread and I don't know which one, and it's perhaps the thread without an S, the only thread suddenly stretched between two stories, two axes, two languages, onto which I stumbled, while I was wandering precur-sively'] (103). The X of Cixous's name, like the H (pronounced *hache* or

axe in French) and the S, could take us down another, chiasmic, route of relation; elsewhere, for example, the narrator claims to have 'pour but une immobilisation des deux parties en un point X' ['as an aim the immobilisation of the two parts at a point X'] (85) and, seated on a couch, her body and that of Saint-Georges 'dessinaient de superbes lettres inconnues, qui faisaient penser à un mélange de S et de X' ['drew superb unknown letters, that evoked a mixture of S and X'] (20). Letters enable her to invent for herself a superb new SeX, in which all kinds of relation become possible.

50. This is also the gist of Derrida's extraordinary reading of the performative power of Cixous's *puisse*; see HC, 14–16, HCE, 2–5.

51. Jacques Lacan, *Le Séminaire, livre II*, 29, quoted in *Jacques Lacan and the Adventure of Insight*, 157.

Chapter 4

The Illegitimate Mother: *Souffles*

In 2010, Cixous agreed for the first time to republish in French the two texts for which, still today, she remains best known internationally. 'Le Rire de la Méduse'[1] and 'Sorties',[2] her individual contribution to *La Jeune née*, the joint initiative with Cathérine Clément which by then had been out of print for decades, appeared together in a volume entitled *Le Rire de la Méduse et autres ironies* [*The Laugh of the Medusa and Other Ironies*]. In her introduction to the new edition, the writer muses over the irony that a text in many ways unique in her œuvre should have played the greatest part in defining her reputation. She describes it as the only time she had 'crié', or screamed, in writing: 'Il m'arrive encore de crier, mais pas en littérature. On ne crie qu'une fois en littérature. J'ai crié. Allons. Une bonne fois' ['It still happens that I scream, but not in literature. One only screams once in literature. I screamed. Go for it. One good scream'].[3] For Cixous, 'Le Rire' differs from her other literary texts not as a non-literary text but as a literary text that 'screams'; her 'cri' is an 'é-crit', as much a piece of writing as any other text bearing her signature. But a piece that uses writing as a call to action, indeed as a call to arms: 'Le Rire, et autres sorties, est un appel. Un coup de téléphone au monde. On a dit: un manifeste' ['Le Rire, and other sorties, is a call. A telephone call to the world. It's been said: a manifesto'].[4] The substitution of 'sorties' for the 'ironies' of the volume's title calls attention to the various meanings of the word Cixous had selected as the title of her part of *La Jeune née*, including the military sense of a sortie or foray. Literature here ventures beyond its usual limits to engage a different, manifestly political, relationship with the world.

Cixous nevertheless takes her distance from those who consider 'Le Rire' a manifesto, defined by her beloved *Oxford English Dictionary* as a public declaration of policy and aims. In particular, she notes that, whereas in France 'Le Rire de la Méduse' and *La Jeune née* were 'books', everywhere else in the world they are perceived as 'acts' (29). Her patent annoyance at this is clearly not a matter of renouncing the political dimension of the two texts, or of writing in general; not only does 'Le Rire' exhort women to take specific action that will produce political change – that is to write – but she ends her introduction speculating whether the text may not still be timely in 2010, contrary to her hopes at the original time of writing. What, then, motivates her dissatisfaction?

Cixous's reticence with regard to the reception of 'Le Rire de la Méduse' and *La Jeune née* appears to be largely a question of translation. These texts won their author international renown especially in English, and they continue to be taught throughout the non-Francophone world 'presque toujours en anglais, ou en traductions à partir de l'anglais!' ['nearly always in English, or in translations from the English!'] (31). This inevitably means that much of the text's plays on language are lost, notably that of 'vol': 'C'est comme si ma Méduse ne volait que d'une aile, elle qui en a tant' ['It's as if my Medusa flew on only one wing, she who has so many'] (30). The homonymy in French between theft and flight is, indeed, central to Cixous's notion of femininity as she develops it in 'Le Rire de la Méduse':

> Voler, c'est le geste de la femme, voler dans la langue, la faire voler. Du vol, nous avons toutes appris l'art aux maintes techniques, depuis des siècles que nous n'avons accès à l'avoir qu'en volant; que nous avons vécu dans un vol, de voler, trouvant au désir des passages étroits, dérobés, traversants. Ce n'est pas un hasard si 'voler' se joue entre deux vols, jouissant de l'un et l'autre et déroutant les agents du sens. Ce n'est pas un hasard: la femme tient de l'oiseau et du voleur comme le voleur tient de la femme et de l'oiseau: illes passent, illes filent, illes jouissent de brouiller l'ordre de l'espace, de le désorienter, de changer de place les meubles, les choses, les valeurs, de faire des casses, de vider les structures, de chambouler le propre.[5]

> [Flying is woman's gesture – flying in language and making it fly. We have all learned the art of flying and its numerous techniques; for centuries we've been able to possess anything only by flying; we've lived in flight, stealing away, finding, when desired, narrow passageways, hidden crossovers. It's no accident that *voler* has a double meaning, that it plays on each of them and thus throws off the agents of sense. It's no accident: women take after birds and robbers just as robbers take after women and birds. They (*illes*)[n] go by, fly the coop, take pleasure in jumbling the order of space, in disorienting it, in changing around the furniture, dislocating things and values, breaking them all up, emptying structures, and turning propriety upside down.][6]

The central point that women found in flight and in theft a displaced relation to the property from which they were historically excluded passes into the English translation. But the radical impossibility in

French of separating the two meanings of the same word from each other is rendered only by a footnote after the first use of the word 'fly': 'Also, "to steal." Both meanings of the verb *voler* are played on, as the text itself explains in the following paragraph (translator's note).'[7] Although the idea that flight and theft are inextricably related to each other is conveyed constatively in this way, the experience of reading the translation is wholly different from that of reading the original. The English separates the two meanings whose inextricability in French exemplifies the troubling of property being described. (In addition, it privileges one meaning over the other: in the English, the idea of theft is subordinate to that of flight.)

Other aspects of the writing of this quotation similarly lose some of their force in translation: the coinage of 'illes' (also commented on in a footnote), the 'agents du sens', etc. My concern here not being, however, to deplore the losses inevitably incurred in translation, I want to highlight two particular shifts created in the translation. Firstly, Cixous does not consider a special relation to displacement as exclusive to women, but just as much a property of birds and robbers; I shall return to this later in relation to Genet. Note in particular the word 'dérobés', with its connotations of both stealing and stealing away, evading or fleeing, which shares the same etymology as 'robe' or dress. Secondly, there is an amphibology in the sentence beginning 'Du vol, nous avons toutes appris l'art aux maintes techniques'. In addition to clipping the wings of 'vol' by rendering it unequivocally as 'flying',[8] the translation eliminates the ambiguity of the connection between 'vol' and 'art': 'We have all learned the art of flying and its numerous techniques'. By reading the positioning of 'Du vol' at the beginning of the sentence as a poetic detachment for reasons of emphasis, the English version reads loses sight of another possible translation: 'From flying/stealing, we all learned about art ...'. This alternative reading posits a broader association between flight/theft and art; woman's relation to displacement is excellent preparation for the demands of art. The French original thus signifies more strongly than the translation both that the feminine quality of flying/stealing is not exclusive to women and that the inventiveness it develops provides them with an escape route. Yet, circulating in translation, 'Le Rire' ironically became best known in a form that reduced (and often obscured) its own inventiveness, the quality it most sought to support and promote. The text does not call on women to write in order merely to claim their equal share of the symbolic universe. It calls on them to write because (as we've just seen in *Les Commencements*) writing is the sphere of inventing the new: 'En littérature, ça existe, ce qui n'existe pas encore en réalité' ['In literature, what doesn't yet exist in reality exists'] (28). The reception of the two texts as 'acts' rather than 'books' paradoxically signals an inability, or an unwillingness, to recognise the act that creative writing (to be understood in the broadest possible sense as all writing that is creative, inventive) itself constitutes.

Moreover, a further translation also operated. The enormous success of 'The Laugh of the Medusa' led to Cixous herself being translated into an 'auteur de manifestes' ['author of manifestos'] (30). Medusa defined Cixous more than Cixous created Medusa: 'Elle m'a joué un sacré tour: moi qui croyais l'avoir inventée, délivrée du mythe, voilà qu'elle m'avait prise dans ses lacs: je devins l'auteur du Rire de la Méduse, dans l'univers, autrement dit son père, ou sa servante !' ['She played a hell of a trick on me: I thought I had invented her, rescued her from the myth, only to find that she had caught me in her toils: I became the author of The Laugh of the Medusa, throughout the universe, in other words her father, or her servant!'] (29). This very Cixousian reversal of roles where the author becomes the creature of her creation, the creation the author of her author, raises two questions which will frame the reading of *Souffles* proposed in this chapter. It suggests that the text creates its origin as much as the reverse. And Cixous's sense of transformation into Medusa's 'father, or her servant', rather than her mother, emphasises that gender roles are social constructs.

The reception of 'Le Rire de la Méduse' and 'Sorties' in the years following their initial publication was dominated by this second question. The two texts are first and foremost concerned with the introduction of a sexual, and especially feminine, difference where none had previously been recognised. The notion of *écriture féminine* expounded there quickly catapulted Cixous to international recognition – and to international controversy. Accusations went flying, mainly that Cixous essentialised women but also that she did not essentialise them enough. There is little to be gained from rehearsing these arguments which retain little purchase on Cixous's work today.[9] From a current vantage point, the idea of an essentialist Cixous is difficult to reconcile not only with 'Le Rire de la Méduse' but with 'The Laugh of the Medusa', given that one of the piece's most polemical aspects concerned an assertion which translated relatively straightforwardly into English. In a much-quoted footnote, Cixous included Jean Genet, a male writer, among the rare few French authors whose texts she considered 'feminine':

Alors quelles sont les écritures dont on pourrait dire qu'elles sont 'féminines'? Je ne ferai ici que désigner des exemples: il faudrait en produire des lectures qui fassent surgir dans leur signifiance ce qui s'y répand de féminité. Ce que je ferai ailleurs. En France [. . .] pour feuilleter ce que le XXᵉ siècle a jusqu'à présent [1974] laissé s'écrire, et c'est bien peu, je n'ai vu inscrire de la féminité que par Colette, Marguerite Duras . . . et Jean Genet.

[Which works, then, might be called feminine? I'll just point out some examples: one would have to give them full readings to bring out what is pervasively feminine in their significance. Which I shall do elsewhere. In France [. . .], leafing through what's come out of the twentieth century – and it's not much – the only inscriptions of femininity that I have seen were by Colette, Marguerite Duras, . . . and Jean Genêt [sic].][10]

Genet's presence on this list was in and of itself enough to invalidate the idea that Cixous was a proponent of an essentialism that would imprison women in roles, behaviour and desires determined by biology. The femininity in question here is manifestly not a matter of femaleness. Moreover, in another book in which Genet looms large, Cixous carries her deconstruction of sexual positions even further, exploring how not only femininity but *motherhood* is a metaphorical position. This was already posited in 'Le Rire de la Méduse'; one of the elements which generated the debate about essentialism was the link it proposed between femininity and the mother. Woman 'écrit à l'encre blanche' ['writes in white ink']; for Cixous, she is more likely than man to have kept the voice of the mother alive in her: 'Dans la femme il y a toujours plus ou moins de la mère qui répare et alimente, et résiste à la séparation, une force qui ne se laisse pas couper, mais qui essouffle les codes' ['In women there is always more or less of the mother who makes everything all right, who nourishes, and who stands up against separation; a force that will not be cut off but will knock the wind out of the codes'].[11] This is for cultural reasons; women's exclusion from power means they have less to lose, and are thus more likely to perceive the other as something to nourish rather than a threat. A child is the perfect example of a relationship to an other that need not entail violence; precisely, however, it is an *example*, an image or figure of a possible mode of relation open to all: 'La *mère* aussi est une métaphore' ['The mother, too, is a metaphor'].[12]

Souffles [*Breaths*], one of Cixous's densest, most lyrical texts, explores the mother as metaphor.[13] Written at the same time as 'Le Rire de la Méduse' and 'Sorties', it shares many of the themes and figures of those better-known texts, but it has absolutely nothing of the manifesto about it. Presented on the back cover as a 'méditation et psaume sur la passion d'une femme' ['meditation and psalm on the passion of a woman'], it is far removed from the 'clear and distinct ideas' Descartes recommended in his *Meditations*. On the contrary, it constitutes a space of exuberant, voluptuous generosity in which the ability to hear the mother's voice bears fruit in an intense eroticism. 'Texte pour la première Voix. Celle de la "mère": celle qui t'a touchée jadis. [. . .] A la fois texte-mère et texte-enfant, texte-amour: espace des genèses' ['Text for the first Voice. That of the "mother": the one that touched you long ago. [. . .] Both text-mother and text-child, text-love: a space of geneses']: the mother's legacy is far removed from a linear transmission. The child in whom the mother's voice echoes continues the mother, creates the mother. The child produces the mother as much as the mother produces the child.

Souffles is especially a hymn of praise to those in whom the mother's voice echoes. In pride of place are the poets Cixous calls her 'anges' or angels, including Milton, Rimbaud and Rilke but above all Genet ('ange' is even an anaphone of 'Jean'). It is unlikely this text represents one of the readings Cixous had in mind in her footnote to 'Le Rire de la Méduse' since it contains little actual commentary on his text and his name – spelled 'Genêt', as in the footnote discussed above – features only a few times (82, 121, 122, 166).[14] Genet figures nevertheless prominently, mainly as a lover, under the name 'Jenais'.[15] Examination of the archival documents available for consultation reveals that the other writer's presence was considerably more visible in earlier versions of the book.[16] In addition to the passages in the definitive text concerning Jenais, many of those where either a third-person pronoun or 'J'' is deployed originally inscribed his proper name.[17] In addition, substantial passages relating to his works were cut from the published version. In fact, *Souffles* is exceptional among the books whose archives I have had the opportunity to study in that the manuscript contains large swathes of text of which little or no trace remains in the final version. Other than Genet, the principal figure the cut sections deal with is Saint Theresa of Avila, whose presence has nearly totally disappeared from the book. In other words, the two main figures *Souffles* originally celebrated are Genet and Saint Theresa of Avila, a male homosexual and a celibate nun. The mother in question here is manifestly a *metaphorical* mother.[18]

It is particularly significant that so many passages dealing with the text's literary forebears were cut. The genetic material thus shows that the birth of the book involved the creation of an origin from which to separate; again, child-text and mother-text come into being together. At every level, *Souffles* suggests that the ability to enjoy the other's difference without seeking to appropriate it, to care for the other as other, is available to anyone at all who can invent it. And it is not only the maternal metaphor that extends and parallels the metaphor of femininity privileged in 'Le Rire'. The 'capacité de se dé-proprier sans calcul' ['capacity to depropriate unselfishly'] which in that text was figured as the 'propre' or property of woman[19] is here a characteristic not only of the 'mother' but of the 'nègre'. Already in 1974, *Souffles* proposed a visionary harnessing of sexual and postcolonial politics.

Writing Gene(t)sis

Souffles pants. If Cixous had written it in English, she would doubt-less have played on the homonymy between the verb denoting excited breathing and the item of apparel once restricted to men but now worn by both sexes. The French puts its own homonymy to work: Halètement Allaitement [panting breastfeeding]. This adds a connotation of child-birth to the suggestion of an orgasmic eroticism created by the rhythm of the text which, at both macro and micro levels, strongly evokes an accel-erating breathing. The book's 223 pages are increasingly cut in various ways as it progresses. Occasional small gaps between paragraphs give way to longer ones of up to a page or more. From the beginning, the text is punctuated by short paragraphs in a smaller font, most of which are either literal or obviously displaced quotations from other literary and biblical texts; the second half contains a number of sections in italics. Most unusually, four of these are introduced by the same subtitle, 'Une nouvelle genèse' ['A new genesis']; these pauses stress beginnings rather than completions. As the end approaches, births proliferate. Inhalation, exhalation: the increasingly close-spaced alternation creates a growing feeling of being out of breath. 'On aura commandé que *Souffles* soit coupé' (198): towards the end of the text, the text's progressive panting is associated with the cutting of an umbilical cord.

An impression of breathlessness is immediately created in the rapid sequence of short paragraphs, brief sentences and emphatic punctuation with which *Souffles* opens.[20] The book begins with the birth of a 'je', called forth by an unnamed and unidentifiable voice:

> Voici l'énigme: de la force est née la douceur.
> Et maintenant, qui naître?
> La voix dit: 'Je suis là.' Et tout est là. Si j'avais une pareille voix, je n'écrirais pas, je rirais. Et pas besoin de plumes alors de corps en plus. Je ne craindrais pas l'essoufflement. Je ne viendrais pas à mon secours m'agrandir d'un texte. Fort!
> Voix! Un jet, – une telle voix, et j'irais droit, je vivrais. J'écris. Je suis l'écho de sa voix son ombre-enfant, son amante.
> 'Toi!' La voix dit: 'toi'. Et je nais! – 'Vois' dit-elle, et je vois tout! – 'Touche!' Et je suis touchée.
> Là! c'est la voix qui m'ouvre les yeux, sa lumière m'ouvre la bouche, me fait crier. Et j'en nais. (9)

[This is the enigma: from strength is born softness.

And now, to be born as whom?

The voice says: 'I am there.' And everything is there. If I had a similar voice, I wouldn't write, I would laugh. And no need for pens then for a body as well. I wouldn't be afraid of running out of breath. I wouldn't come to help myself by extending myself with a text. Fort!

Voice! A jet, – a voice like that, and I would go straight on, I would live. I write. I am the echo of the voice its shadow-child, its feminine lover.

'You!' The voice says: 'you'. And I am born! – 'See' it says, and I see everything! – 'Touch!' And I am touched.

There! It's the voice that opens my eyes, its light opens my mouth, makes me cry out. And I am born of it.]

The opening enigma is above all an enigma of the voice, which echoes literally from the beginning in the text's first syllable, voi-ci. The nameless voice is what makes this birth possible, makes it possible for an uncertain, unnamed identity to be born. 'Et maintenant, qui naître?': in writing, there is no limit to the identities one may assume, including 'je'. 'J'écris. Je suis l'écho de sa voix son ombre-enfant, son amante': to write is to echo the original voice (and indeed 'je' is called into being an echo of 'voix', as 'toi'), to continue it from a point of difference, as child and/ or lover. This response troubles sexual as well as generational boundaries: 'je nais', 'j'en nais', 'je' is born as an echo of Jean Genet. Later on the same page in a note, a quotation from Goethe[21] is attributed to 'Hélène', the only direct inscription of Cixous's own first name in the book. *Souffles* thus opens not only with a loss of breath (another word for which is 'haleine') but with a visible dethroning of the author's proper name that allows the nascent subject to explore her affinities with others.

This echoing voice already has unmistakably maternal associations. 'Fort' (followed by 'Da' on the next page) recalls Freud's interpretation in *Beyond the Pleasure Principle* of his grandson's game with a reel as an attempt to compensate for his mother's absence by symbolising her disappearance and subsequent return. Writing echoes the mother's voice, creates a replacement mother. In turn, 'fort' echoes the opening enigma: 'de la force est née la douceur', a version of Samson's riddle in the Book of Judges. A mother's voice, already linked with paradox, with contradiction, can echo in (male) figures such as Genet or Samson. In particular, it troubles the distinction between subject and object. '"Vois" dit-elle, et je vois tout! – "Touche!" Et je suis touchée': the mother's speech has a truly extraordinary illocutionary force in that even its commands are performatives, effecting action by a subject other than itself!

The question of an alternative mother or mother-substitute that may contrast sharply with conventional figures of the mother arises as early as the text's two epigraphs, conventionally a privileged site for marking a text's indebtedness to its literary sources. The first, 'Nun hast du mir den ersten Schmerz getan' (translated when the epigraphs return in reverse order at the end of the book in a form of epilogue as 'Maintenant tu m'as fait la première douleur' ['Now you have given me my first pain']), the beginning of a song from a cycle by Schumann setting Chamisso's *Frauenliebe und Leben* to music, announces the association between mother and voice that the text's opening develops. The second comes from the opening section or 'Attunement' of Kierkegaard's *Fear and Trembling*: 'Quand l'enfant doit être sevré, sa mère recourt à une nourriture plus forte pour l'empêcher de périr . . .' ['When the child must be weaned, its mother has recourse to a stronger food to prevent it from perishing . . .']. In Kierkegaard's 'Attunement', four different versions of Abraham's sacrifice of Isaac on Mount Moriah alternate with four short paragraphs dealing with the separation of mother and child, each beginning with the words 'When the child is to be weaned' and ending, in a manner reminiscent of the Beatitudes delivered on the Sermon on the Mount, with 'Lucky the one . . .' Kierkegaard's text thus already associates a paternal figure par excellence with a mother (and reinscribes the mother in the shift from Old to New Testaments, whose respective focus on God-the-Father and God-the-Son traditionally excluded her) in a move that Cixous carries still further in her subsequent displacements of this quotation. At six points throughout *Souffles*, she introduces variants of Kierkegaard's versions of the maternal separation:

> Quand l'enfant devenu grand, doit être réveillé, son rêve se noircit le sein. Et l'enfant croit que sa mère a changé. Mais l'amour est le même. (25)

> Renonce: reçois. Quand la mère doit être réveillée, l'enfant aussi est triste de penser qu'ils seront de plus en plus séparés. Mais leur tristesse est la même. (35)

> Et elle aussi s'était noirci le sein, pour nous faire croire que la mère n'est plus. Heureuse, celle qui n'a pas perdu sa mère autrement. (45)

> Lorsque la femme devenue grande doit être sevrée, sa mère cache prudemment son sein. Et la femme n'a plus de mère. Heureuse la femme qui n'a pas perdu sa mère autrement. Mais son amour est le même. Et son regard est toujours plein de lait. (206)

> Sa bonté. Quand elle doit être sevrée, sa mère recourt à une faim plus forte pour l'empêcher de faiblir. Heureuse la femme qui jouit de la plus forte nourriture! (207)

> Quand son texte doit être sevré, elle part sans se retourner. (217)

[When the child grown big must be woken, his dream blackens its breast. And the child believes that his mother has changed. But the love is the same. (25)

Renounce: receive. When the mother must be woken, the child too is sad to think that they will be increasingly separated. But their sadness is the same. (35)

And she too had blackened her breast, to make us believe that the mother is no longer.
    Happy the one who has not lost her mother otherwise. (45)

When the woman grown big must be weaned, her mother prudently hides her breast. And the woman no longer has a mother. Happy the woman who has not lost her mother otherwise. But her love is the same. And her gaze is still full of milk. (206)

Her goodness. When she must be weaned, her mother has recourse to a stronger hunger to save her from weakening. Happy the woman who enjoys the strongest food! (207)

When her text must be weaned, she leaves without looking back. (217)]

The striking point about these variations is how the various positions circulate. 'L'enfant', 'la mère', 'la femme', 'son texte' succeed each other as subject of the opening subordinate clause; the subject of the main clause varies between 'son rêve', 'l'enfant', 'sa mère' and 'elle'. Comparison of the first example with the Kierkegaard passage it rewrites is illuminating:

When the child is to be weaned the mother blackens her breast, for it would be a shame were the breast to look pleasing when the child is not to have it. So the child believes that the breast has changed but the mother is the same, her look loving and tender as ever. Lucky the one who needed no more terrible means to wean the child![22]

The issue at stake here is the difference between mother and breast, between the mother and her body: already for Kierkegaard, the 'bad' breast is proof of the 'good' mother. Cixous goes still further in detaching breast from mother. In her version, 'son rêve se noircit le sein' : the breast is blackened by a dream rather than the mother, a substitution overdetermined not only by the name Ève, as previously seen, but by the paronomasia between 'rêve' and 'sévrer' (to wean), which in turn is replaced by the verb 'réveillé(r)'. 'Mais l'amour est le même': this image of maternal love, in the form of a dream refusing its breast by deliberately making it ugly,[23] is so far removed from conventional figures of the mother as to be virtually unrecognisable. Moreover, in the penultimate variant offering a different version of the epigraph, Cixous replaces 'food' with 'hunger': instead of milk, the mother gives the child 'une faim plus forte', a stronger hunger. The 'good' mother is the one who encourages the child's desire rather than quenching its thirst, provides it with a 'soif' which itself 'donne à boire sans jamais assouvir' ['provides something to drink without ever satisfying'] (190). Or, to invoke a signifier Cixous exploits throughout the text, the good mother is not the one who 'désaltère' (quenches one's thirst) but the one who 'altère' in both senses: makes thirsty and makes other.

Black Milk

'C'est l'heure maintenant de la textée' (ms. 297bis): as this play on the word 'tétée' (breastfeed) in the manuscript encapsulates, the replacement for mother's milk with which *Souffles* is most concerned is clearly the poetic text itself. In 'Le Rire de la Méduse', Cixous borrowed the metaphor of 'white ink' to describe feminine writing; Souffles invites reading as a celebration of 'black milk', that is writing from sources whose maternity is manifestly metaphorical, a 'mother-text' that appears patently as the imaginative invention it is. Writing is metaphorised as milk most obviously in relation to Milton:

> La nuit Milton était ainsi travaillé: ce qui dans son corps s'altérait, se dissociait, se regroupait, insistait tant au matin pour être exposé séant qu'il 'lui fallait être trait'. Il lui semblait en avoir plein les pis. Pour la dictée (ayant difficulté à se tirer lui-même l'écriture il se donnait à traire à ses filles) il avait une posture favorite, propice à l'opération, perché plutôt qu'assis, sur un fauteuil, une jambe passée sur le bras de son siège. (71)

> [At night Milton was thus labouring: what was changing in his body, undoing itself, gathering together again, was so insistent on being suitably exposed that he 'had to be milked'. He seemed to have his udders full. To dictate (having difficulty milking his own writing he got his daughters to milk him) he had a favorite posture, one propitious to the operation, perched rather than seated, on an armchair, with one leg over the arm of his seat.]

Milton is the host of an otherness ('ce qui dans son corps s'altérait') by which he himself is changed and which clamours to be expressed: the French plays implicitly on the fact that, as in English, the same verb is used for both milk and words. 'Trait' means line or stroke as well as the past participle of the verb 'traire': the words within inverted commas can be translated as both 'it needed to be sign' and 'he needed to be milked'. The poet, then, is the one in whom otherness flows as milk. Addressing the 'mère absolue', the narrator muses that the idea that her 'aides' (the poets in whose work she finds sustenance) could 'faire gicler tes pis' ['make your udders spurt'] would not have left them 'inaltérables' ('unalterable') (66). The poet is the one who, milking the mother, needs in turn to be milked.

Since relatively few of the authors thematise the mother directly in the works Cixous invokes in *Souffles*, it is clearly not theme that indicates that a specifically maternal voice echoes in a text, situating a writer in the 'région natale des écritures' ['birth region of writings'] (29). Rimbaud is the exception: in his poem 'Being Beauteous', the eponymous 'Être de Beauté' ['Being of Beauty'], also described as a 'mère de beauté' ['mother of beauty'], is linked with the creation of a 'nouveau corps amoureux' ['new loving body']. This poem is quoted in its near entirety in phrases scattered throughout a long sequence of text similarly dealing with a vision of an as-yet-unnamed being (38–52). Yet the sequence culminates in an expression of the impossibility of designating the mother directly: 'elle sort d'elle-même, la mère de beauté et me regarde: ah je vois! que si sans l'abîmer je ne puis d'un nom la faire retentir, je puis au prix d'un certain sacrifice la faire éclater au jour!' ['she emerges from herself, the mother of beauty and looks at me: ah, I see! that if I cannot make her resound with a name without injuring her, at the price of some sacrifice I can bring her to light'] (52).[24] The mother cannot be named directly but her presence can be revealed indirectly, brought to light – or brought into being: the expression 'la faire éclater au jour' forcefully suggests a birth, the narrator can give birth to her own mother – under her various guises. Samson represents the most obvious example: on the one hand he is the strongest and most masculine of men. Yet, as the narrator recognises, the hair at the source of his strength (another link with Medusa) is also what makes him vulnerable: 'J'ai vu ça dès l'enfance: l'extrême force et l'extrême faiblesse nouées dans ces fils virils' ['I've seen that since my childhood: extreme strength and extreme weakness knotted together in those virile threads'] (13). Samson's 'fils virils' make him a special kind of 'fils viril' or virile *son*, give him access to a 'nouvelle puissance', 'une autre façon d'être mâle' ['new power', 'new way of being male'] (14), a strength that derives explicitly from contact with the source: 'Que la source soit coupée, je dépéris' ['If the source is cut, I waste away'] (14). Hair, however, grows again; what distinguishes Samson is that when cut, his source regenerates.

For Cixous, then, Samson figures the ultimate paradox: a man who recreates his source, gives birth to his own mother. The parallel is obvious between Samson and Œdipus, eternally associated with the riddle of the Sphinx; furthermore, Milton's focus in *Samson Agonistes* on Samson's last days, blind and cut off from his people, famously highlights the similarities with Sophocles's *Œdipus at Colonus*. But Cixous's Samson is as much a maternal as an œdipal figure. Just before the first explicit quotation from Samson Agonistes, a one-line paragraph reads: 'La mer la voit et s'enfuit. Sa tempête sans son' ['The sea sees her and flees. Her storm without sound'] (53). In French, not only is 'mer' a homophone of 'mère' but 'sans son' is a homophone of Samson: Samson is one incarnation of 'la mère sans son', the mother without sound, the mother in the least superficially maternal form possible.

The question, then, is how to recognise the mother. Far from an intrinsic capacity, the ability to discern 'the mother' in her innumerable appearances is the fruit of a particular process of sensitisation:

> Combien d'histoires se seront déstructurées, restructurées, combien de guerres déclarées, menées, de populations soulevées déplacées, renversées, avant que je commence à voir luire un rayon dans mon aveuglement! Naguère l'idée que Samson n'était peut-être personne d'autre que ma mère, m'eût effrayée.
> Combien de mers et gouffres et ravins, de rêves et textes, ai-je dû ouvrir pour qu'une mère réelle n'affecte plus la vraie mère aux mille noms qui est en moi. A J'en-sans-mère riche en toutes les mères qu'il se donne, ou à lui mon amant ma mère, je dois de n'être plus l'enfant d'un seul et tyrannique désir,
> et toutes les mères qui s'ouvrent en moi (73–4)

> [How many stories will have been destructured, restructured, how many wars declared, prosecuted, how many populations stirred up, displaced, reversed, before I'll begin to see a ray shining in my blindness! Formerly the idea that Samson was perhaps no other than my mother would have frightened me.
> How many seas and chasms and ravines, dreams and texts, have I had to open so that a real mother will no longer affect the true mother with a thousand names in me. It's to J'en-without-a-mother, rich in all the mothers he gives himself, that I owe the fact that I am no longer the child of a single, tyrannical desire,
> and all the mothers who are opening in me]

The difference between a 'mère réelle' and the 'vraie mère' overlaps with that between the visible and the invisible. The narrator's blindness was less that she could not see than that she thought the mother was recognisable by sight; it gives way not to seeing, but to 'voir luire'. Fifteen years before Jacques Derrida was to argue that sexual difference 'reste à interpreter, à déchiffrer, à désencrypter, à lire et non à voir' ['is to be interpreted, to be deciphered, to be decoded, to be read and not to be seen'],[25] Cixous's writing suggests here that the 'vraie mère' is something to be read, deciphered, rather than seen. Or, from an alternative angle, the 'vraie mère' is the mother that one creates – 'gives oneself' – rather than inherits. The first sentence of the second paragraph of the above quotation continues as follows in the manuscript version: 'pour que la mère légale, donc fictive, n'aille point se rabattre sur l'immense et variable figure-de-mère aux mille figures, et la confinant au rôle classique, la décimer, interdire, stériliser. A Jean-sans-mère . . .' ['so that the legal, thus fictive, mother should not be pulled down over the immense and variable figure-of-the-mother with a thousand faces, confining her to the classical role, decimating, forbidding, sterilizing her. To Jean-without-a-mother . . .'] (ms. 205). If, as Joyce says in *Ulysses*, paternity is a 'legal fiction', the *amor matris* with which Cixous is concerned in *Souffles* is not the (legal) reality that he opposed to it as possibly the 'only true thing in life' but rather an *illegitimate fiction*, the illegitimate invention of a mother whose truth lies paradoxically in its very illegitimacy.

'Jean-sans-mère': Genet, the illegitimate thief who was motherless from infancy, is for Cixous the prime example of a writer whose reinvention of the mother in writing makes him a mother. In a well-known passage from *Journal du voleur*, Genet imagines that a 'vieille voleuse' ['old thief'] with a 'visage plat et rond comme la lune' ['a face as flat and round as the moon'] who begs from him is his mother, and proposes that dribbling or vomiting over her could be as meaningful a sign of tenderness as the more conventional gift of flowers or kisses.[26] *Souffles* alludes explicitly to this passage: 'Une vieille pocharde au visage plat et lunaire qui pourrait être ma mère si j'étais Jean d'Espagne' ['An old drunk with a flat, lunar face who could be my mother if I was Jean of Spain'] (44). As the reference to 'all the mothers' that Genet gives himself recognises, however, the 'mother' in Genet's writing extends far beyond this one figure. At the time Cixous was writing *Souffles*, Derrida's *Glas* had just proposed a reading of Genet's writing as an attempt to write the mother's 'seing', an arcane term for signature that is a homophone both of 'sein' (breast), and of 'saint'.[27] Genet's aspiration to sainthood had long dominated discussion of his work, notably featuring in the title of Sartre's *Saint Genet: comédien et martyr*.[28] As an illegitimate child, Genet bore the name of his mother, Gabrielle Genet. Derrida read the mother's signature, however, not in her proper name or in a naming that respects the proper, property, appropriateness, but rather in the dissemination of her proper name throughout the web of words – regardless of the distinction between proper and common nouns – that form the fabric of the text:

Genet, par un de ces mouvements en *ana*, aurait, le sachant ou non – j'ai mon avis là-dessus mais qu'importe – silencieusement, laborieusement, minutieusement, obsessionnellement, compulsivement, avec les gestes d'un voleur dans la nuit, disposé ses signatures à la place de tous les objets manquants. Le matin, vous attendant à reconnaître les choses familières, vous retrouvez son nom partout, en grosses lettres, en petites lettres, en entier ou en morceaux, déformé ou recomposé. [. . .] Il a tout affecté de sa signature. Il a affecté sa signature. Il l'a affectée de tout. Il s'en est affecté (il se sera même, plus tard, attifé d'un accent circonflexe). Il a essayé d'écrire, lui, proprement, ce qui se passe entre l'affect et le seing.

[Genet, in one of the movements in *ana*, knowingly or not – I have my own opinion about that but never mind – silently, laboriously, meticulously, obsessively, compulsively, with the gestures of a thief in the night, would have arranged his signatures in the place of all the missing objects. In the morning, when you expect to recognise familiar things, you find his name everywhere, in large letters, small letters, whole or in bits, deformed or recomposed. [. . .] He affected everything with his signature. He affected his signature. He affected it with everything. He affected himself with it (later, he will even put on a circumflex accent). He tried to write, properly, what happens between affect and the signature.][29]

As an example, he traces the endless inscription in Genet's writing of 'gl', formed of the phonemes with which the name Gabrielle begins and ends: from 'glaïeul' (gladiolus) conjuring up 'glaviaux' (spit) in the scene with the mother mentioned above, to 'glaive', 'aigle', 'seigle', opening up in an infinite list onto 'algues', 'galère', 'galaxie', 'galalithe', etc., not to mention the 'glas' which gives his own text its name. Every word in Genet's text would eventually be included in the disseminatory web; for instance, 'glas' shares the same etymology as 'classe', 'classification', etc. Indeed, if, for Derrida, Genet's writing sounds the 'glas du nom propre' ['deathknell of the proper name'] (*Glas*, 27), it is because it profoundly destabilises all categorisations, troubles the boundaries between words, things, words as things. Notably, gl itself is unclassifiable: neither masculine nor feminine, neither word nor merely element of a word, it bears witness to a process of signification from which no transcendental signified ever finally emerges,[30] yet which heralds meaning: 'Ce n'est pas un mot – gl hisse la langue mais n'y tient pas et la laisse toujours retomber, ne lui appartient pas – encore moins un nom, à peine un proprénom. / Mais peut-être le sujet de l'annonciation' ['It is not a word – gl hoists language but doesn't hold on and always lets it fall down again, doesn't belong to it – still less a name, scarcely a propronoun. / But perhaps the subject of annunciation'] (*Glas*, 329). Gl is the angel of meaning, a sign of both Gabrielle and Gabriel.

In Derrida's analysis, in other words, the mother signs not with a 'nom propre' or proper name but by inscribing her 'non-propre', her non-properness, her excess over the proper. An inkling of how *Glas* inspired Cixous's exploration in *Souffles* of the 'true mother with a thousand names' is already visible above in her somewhat surprising use of the verb 'affecter' ('pour qu'une mère réelle n'affecte plus la vraie mère'), which recalls Derrida's ('Il a tout affecté de sa signature'). The influence of *Glas* appears even more evident in the earlier versions than in the published text. Derrida's text was written in two columns, one dealing with Hegel (in whose name echoes the 'aigle' of Genet's text), the other concerning Genet. As stated earlier, much of Cixous's manuscript concerns St Teresa of Avila.[31] Whereas *Glas* investigated the differences between Genet and Hegel, Cixous's text initially offered a 'meditation' on the differences between a saint and a sainte. There are surprising similarities between these two members of the 'chevalerie de la plume et du sein' ['knighthood of the feather and the breast'] (ms. 100): both write of living in 'cells', the one in a convent, the other in prison; Teresa's insistent use of metaphors of the flight of birds – especially of doves[32] – or butterflies makes her in French a 'voleuse' like Genet; most importantly, the writing of both is an intensely desirous 'chant de la chair' ['song of the flesh'] (ms. 109), where the physical and the spiritual are inseparable from each other. Thus for example, Cixous's Teresa likens the host, her beloved's body, to a cake that becomes more desirable the more it is eaten: 'loin d'assouvir, il relance l'appétit [. . .] Les saints et les prisonniers des Centrales connaissent ce bien vital' ['far from satisfying, it relaunches one's appetite [. . .] Saints and prisoners know this vital good'] (ms. 98). Genet's desire in *Pompes funèbres* for his lover, Jean D., whose body he compared to a 'flacon de Venise' or Venetian flask and fervently imagined consuming, is similarly represented as confusing body and soul:

> son corps était une langue qu'il maîtrisait, caressait, – ou sa langue ce corps qu'il enculait – et puis merde, parfois son corps comme celui d'une cantatrice était en effet l'épais flacon d'une âme, mais parfois son âme était cette langue (pas celle de sa bouche mais celle de sa vie) qui travaillait les chairs, baisait les organes, orchestrait ces forces fabuleuses, les sources de souffles qu'il trouvait quand le dernier avait été rendu. Ainsi à ses mystères lui-même a mis un terme? Cela le met hors de portée; je ne suis pas dans son flacon. (83)

> [his body was a language he mastered, caressed, – or his language the body he buggered – and then shit, sometimes his body like that of a singer was in fact the thick flask of a soul, but sometimes his soul was the language (not of his mouth but of his life) that worked on the flesh, fucked the organs, orchestrated the fabulous force, the source of breath he found when the last one has been given. So he himself put an end to his mysteries? That puts him out of reach; I am not in his flask.]

Just as Genet's language troubles the distinction between body and soul, so does Cixous's own use here of 'langue'. Unlike in antanaclasis, it is impossible to assume which meaning of the word is foregrounded: part of the body or verbal system. As the end of the quotation obliquely reminds us, a 'flacon' can also contain a 'génie' or genie. If Genet is Cixous's 'bon génie', it is also because his genius lies in refusing a separation between container and contained, in escaping from the dichotomy of flesh and word so fundamental to Christianity. But here too is the main point of difference Cixous develops between these particular 'saint' and 'sainte'. Recalling the passage in Teresa's *Life* where the saint remembers her acceptance of mortification when St John of the Cross divided a host between her and another nun, Cixous comments: 'Ce qui nous sépare la sainte et moi, ce n'est ni l'appétit, ni l'objet de l'appétit, c'est notre rapport au symbolique, à l'idéalisation, à la médiation' ['Saint Teresa and I are separated not by appetite, nor the object of our appetite, but by our relationship to the symbolic, idealization, mediation'] (ms. 103). In contrast with her distaste at the priest's intervention between Teresa and God, it is because Genet – or 'Jean saint sans croix', Saint John *without* the Cross (ms. 107) – accepts no limits to his desire, refuses all external authority that would dictate to him what and how he should worship, that she finds in him a palatable form of Christian: 'Jean l'hostie, s'introduisant de nuit dans son assassin, le chrétien qui s'introduit comme autre dans mon corps, l'autre langue dans ma bouche, enfin! je peux dire rire sucer mon saint sans m'en vomir! Un livre s'ouvre comme notre cellule, notre con' ['Jean the host, letting himself at night into his assassin, the Christian who as other lets himself into my body, the other tongue in my mouth, at last! I can say laugh suck my saint without vomiting ! A book opens like our cell, our cunt'] (ms. 107).

The archival documents contain other signs that *Glas*'s role was significant in the elaboration of *Souffles*. The manuscript comprises two long sections, one numbered 20–207, the other numbered 188bis–303bis; two surviving sequences of the typescript of the latter section are numbered 214b Duinô–263b Duinô, and 300bis–341bis. Taken with the fact that the word 'colonnes' (columns) features at least seven times in the published text, this suggests that, like *Glas*, the text was originally going to be presented in columns. In his text, Derrida had glossed the (sexual) implications of writing in columns: 'Si j'écris deux textes à la fois, vous ne pourrez pas me châtrer. Si je délinéarise, j'érige. Mais en même temps, je divise mon acte et mon désir' ['If I write two texts at once, you cannot castrate me. If I delinearize, I erect. But at the same time, I divide my act and my desire'] (*Glas*, 91).[33] By introducing a division or differential, writing in columns is emblematic of a doubled and therefore uncentred erection, or one centred only on a gap, a space, one whose non-privileged position means that it cannot itself be lost, 'castrated'. Furthermore, it promises to destabilise the entire symbolic edifice built on phallocentric privilege. In *Souffles* the 'colonnes', often associated with 'piliers' and with 'colosse', recall the columns Samson used to pull down the temple of his enemies around them: 'je suis ces chaînes, ces piliers, je me prépare à être ces colonnes. A ébranler. L'équivoque colosse que je deviens a pris ma place' ['I am these chains, these pillars, I am ready to be these columns. To shake down. The equivocal colossus I am becoming has taken my place'] (13). This equivalence between Samson and the columns he brought down in vengeance around the Philistines is echoed in another passage where the 'mère absolue', 'la tête penchée, les yeux fixes, raide comme un saint en extase' ['her head bent, her eyes fixed, rigid like a saint in ecstasy'], is metaphorised in similar terms:

> Jusqu'à ce que tu aies obtenu la certitude qu'ayant compris les piliers, ayant fait tienne leur moelle, t'étant pénétré de leur essence singulière, tu n'auras tout à l'heure aucun mal à faire passer ta volonté par leurs colonnes. Toi-même pilier, tu t'es frayé dans la pierre de tes semblables un passage inaccessible aux humains. (66)

> [Until you have reached the certainty that having understood the pillars, having made their marrow yours, having imbibed their singular essence, you will shortly have no difficulty in having your will pass by their columns. Yourself a pillar, you frayed a path inaccessible to humans for yourself in the stone of your kind.]

This quotation is reminiscent of the extraordinary sequence of miracles that Genet's narrator effects by dint of similar concentration at the end of *Miracle de la rose*, in one of which Harcamone, the condemned man whose imminent execution is what incites Genet to produce the miracles, passes through the closed door of his cell, and in another of which 'un vol de plus de cent colombes' ['a flight of more than one hundred doves'] is released from the flies of his trousers.[34] That the destruction created by the columns is at the same time constructive, serving to open up a hitherto unimagined space, becomes still clearer in another passage where the 'mother of beauty' assumes an unmistakably Samsonian form:

> le coup qu'elle me porte –
> éventre le toit arqué de l'édifice que boutent deux hauts piliers, – et il y avait sous ce toit deux ou trois cent mille hommes et femmes qui attendaient prêts à lacérer l'air d'une seule clameur, maintenant convulsés, – leur propre ruine –
> me donne accès à d'immenses et tumultueuses zones qui depuis ma première heure m'étaient restées inconnues. (54)

[the blow she deals me –
   rips apart the arched roof of the edifice buttressed by two tall pillars, – and under the roof there were two or three hundred thousand men and women who were waiting ready to slash the air with a single clamour, now convulsed, – their own ruin –
   gives me access to immense, tumultuous zones that had remained unknown to me from my first hour.]

Shattering the edifice shored up by the pillars and bringing about the 'propre ruine' of the people assembled there – or the ruin of the proper – opens up these 'immenses et tumultueuses zones' whose sexual difference calls for investigation. These unknown zones strongly evoke the 'contrée de la féminité' ['country of femininity'] (148) or 'continent noir', to borrow, as she says, the 'nom par lequel l'oncle Freud dé-nomme – la contrée, par lui redoutée, du con' ['name by which uncle Freud calls – the country, feared by him, of the cunt'] (147). *Contrée, continent, flacon, colombes, colonnes, colons*: the unexplored temple the mother's columns make available for contemplation echoes that of the female sex itself: 'O, con! Temple subitement visité . . .' (18). Cixous's own decision finally not to write in columns may reflect a desire to emphasise the audible over the visible,[35] to focus on how a sexually different figure resounds in writing. In the most striking example, the 'con' resonates like the 'gong' to which it is explicitly (and paronomastically) compared:

L'air résonne des **on**des émises par un **con** de bronze: après sept mille détours, le grand battant horiz**on**tal a frappé **son gong**. L**on**gtemps, l**on**gtemps gr**on**de, et g**on**fle l'air immense de ses **on**des, le **con** du monde. Nous pelot**on**nés au sein de sa voix géante. Le dais céleste est dilaté, ses quatre col**on**nes cons**on**nent. Un **son** ne succède pas à un **son** mais le doublant, l'étoffe et le porte plus loin, **on**de sur **on**de chante le grand **con con**quérant. (17; my emphasis)

[The air resounds with the waves emitted by a cunt of bronze: after seven thousand detours, the great horizontal hammer banged its gong. For a long, long time roars and swells the cunt of the world roars and swells the immense air with its waves. Us huddled up to the breast of its giant voice. The heavenly canopy is dilated, its four columns sound together. A sound does not succeed another sound but, echoing it, expands and carries it further, wave on wave sings the great conquering cunt.]

Writing as a 'Nègre'

Sexual difference echoes, then, wherever the pillars of property are undermined, wherever something serves to 'troubler les rapports de propriété' ['trouble property relations'] (162). Like 'voler', the French verb 'souffler' has a number of meanings; as well as 'to breathe', it too signifies 'to steal'. *Souffles* in effect extends more widely the link proposed in 'Le Rire' between 'le vol' and femininity, reflecting at length on the implications of Freud's metaphorisation of femininity as the 'dark continent'.[36] 'Le Rire' approaches this comparison from one angle, signalling that Freud's metaphor turns woman's sexuality into an unrepresentable enigma, dangerous to any who seek to penetrate it. In his preface to *Le Rire et autres ironies*, Frédéric Regard admires the fact that in 1975 Cixous could already foresee the junction between gender studies and postcolonial studies that would emerge so powerfully some decades later.[37] Yet *Souffles* already elaborates in depth on the links between sexual and postcolonial politics. Cixous's pæan to 'le vol' in this text associates it just as much with Africa as it does with women. The long sequence she devotes to it (163–81) opens with a (stolen) quotation from an African, St Augustine: 'Non de la chose mais de son vol j'ai le désir' (163) ['It was not the thing I wanted to enjoy but the theft and the sin itself'].[38] Moreover, as a thief whose pleasure lies in the challenge to property rather than its accumulation, Genet is associated primarily with 'nègres' (blacks):

> Le vol mène Genêt au continent premier, parmi les nègres où il se fait reconnaître pour semblable [. . .] Quel rapport entre le vol et la féminité? (Et quel entre le vol, la femme et le nègre?) Nous, nègres, femmes, volants, nous sommes du visible les enchanteurs, en plein jour nous lâchons la nuit, nous sommes les chanteurs de l'inaudible, les éclaireurs des sens. (166)

> [Theft leads Genêt to the first continent, among the blacks where he is recognized as a fellow creature [. . .] What relationship between theft and femininity? (And between theft, woman and the black?) We, blacks, women, fliers, we are the enchanters of the visible, in full daylight we let loose the night, we are the singers of the inaudible, those who light up the senses.]

The association derives not only from the solidarity Genet showed in his play, *Les Nègres* [*The Blacks*], but also from his identification with the 'hommes d'un continent noir' ['men of a dark continent'] in the final scene of *Pompes funèbres*.[39] Yet Cixous's words also indicate her own sympathy with the colonised of her native Africa.[40] This sympathy is manifest in an autobiographical sequence cut from the published text where, discussing her lack of desire for or curiosity about religions, she attributes her freedom from their power to their

> complicité avec un système que je méprisai toujours totalement. Elles m'apparaissaient comme le plus grotesque, le plus servile, le plus puant des appareils idéologiques. En période d'administration colonialiste aucune force n'est plus solide et insinuante: c'est elle qui gère les immenses sources du crime. (ts. 220b Duinô)

[complicity with a system I always totally scorned. To me they seemed the most grotesque, the most servile, the most stinking ideological apparatus. During the colonialist administration period, no force was more solid and insinuating: it organized the immense sources of crime.]

While this explicit criticism of the colonial regime does not figure in the published text, there remains a two-page account of 'un détail isolé, un seul' ['a sole, isolated detail'], the single aspect of religious apparatus by which she claims to have been affected and which for her encapsulated the power of the Catholic Church: the white drapery of the priests' and altar-boys' vestments, in contrast to which she felt the difference of the 'noirceur' or blackness of her heart (108). 'Nous, nègres, femmes, volants': her linking of herself to the 'nègres' thus has a strong autobiographical determinant. It reads both as an expression of solidarity with an oppressed community to which she did *not* belong, and as a sign of the intense affinity she felt with them.[41] It is therefore not only as woman but as 'nègre' that 'le vol' offers her a means of liberation, of regaining control over a colonised territory: 'J'évacuai le bien, le blanc, le défendu, et à la place des blêmes troupes qui naguère me colonisaient, je montai de toutes parts, moi-même m'occupant, me réincorporant, me rendant à moi' ['I evacuated the good, the white, the forbidden, and in the place of the pallid troups that previously colonized me, I rose up everywhere, occupying myself, re-enlisting myself, surrendering to myself'] (178).

'*J'évacuai* . . . *des blêmes troupes qui me colonisaient*': the process of decolonisation is linked with that of excretion. In particular, just as the two meanings of 'le vol' can never be detached from each other,[42] so the word 'colon' hovers undecidably between two senses, colonist (itself a term that Genet had much exploited in his subversion of hierarchical relationships: in the 'colonie pénitentiaire' or reform school where he was imprisoned as a child, the prisoner was the colonist) and colon. Whereas the few inscriptions of Genet's 'proper' name in *Souffles* sport a supernumerary circumflex, 'colon' takes the place one might rather expect 'côlon' [the colon that is part of the body] to occupy: 'Ce qui fut reste est plus que tout. Ce qui fut tout est moins qu'un reste du reste. Je comprends le continent sauvage, ses forêts, ses fêtes quelque part dans mes entrailles, du côté du colon' ['What was a remainder is more than all. What was all is less than the remainder of a remainder. I understand the wild continent, its forests, its feasts somewhere in my entrails, on the side of the colon'] (183). Following 'forêts', 'fêtes', 'côté', the manifest absence of the circumflex signals the association between 'côlon' and 'colon', making the one effectively a 'reste' or remainder of the other.[43] More importantly, if the colonist is reduced to the occupier of the colon, the colon – a disparaged part of the body – is promoted to entire continent. All the colonial relationships are displaced: at issue is a new kind of colonization where the colonies colonize the 'colon' rather than vice versa (elsewhere Cixous writes: 'un dragon se tord dans mes entrailles, c'est la jungle qui me colonise' ['a dragon twists in my entrails, the jungle is colonizing me'] (197)), and where all terms and places circulate. The 'continent sauvage' is '*du côté* du colon', which can mean both *towards* and *in* the colon; rather than a localisable entity, it manifests itself, for example, where 'mon con [. . .] se tourne en trou de ton cul' ['where my cunt [. . .] turns into the hole of your ass'] (23).

This lability of colonial identities suggests that the profound challenge to the 'Empire du propre' that Cixous characterises as 'feminine' in 'Le Rire de la Méduse' and associates with the 'vraie mère' in *Souffles*, can also be metaphorised as the fruit of a 'black' or postcolonial experience. Because it *unsettles*, in every sense of the word, 'voler' can be considered a decolonising gesture, one as proper to 'nègres' as it is to women. This is not to assimilate the two; on the contrary, it is to suggest that the singular – and irreducible – experience of woman finds an *echo* in that of the colonised – as in that of the thief – without eliding the differences between them; like Genet, woman can be the blacks' 'semblable' without being identical to them. 'Identification, vieille histoire' ['Identification, an old story'] (134), the narrator exclaims in horror at the idea of her mirror-image; similarly, in the manuscript, Cixous specifies that the most difficult relationship is an exchange that does not involve the sacrifice of either's uniqueness: 'Le miracle ce n'est ni la substitution, ni la rédemption, c'est que l'unique puisse habiter l'unique sans s'altérer. C'est ça le travail de l'amour, la révolution corporelle' ['The miracle isn't substitution, nor redemption, it's that the unique can inhabit the unique without altering. That is the work of love, bodily revolution'] (ms. 108). In *Souffles* Cixous is concerned to celebrate not her doubles but her *others*,[44] as is unmistakable in the joy she feels on reading Genet's *Pompes funèbres*: 'Délivrée! Si je le veux, pouvoir être gênée sans être gênée. Preuve que je ne suis plus à la merci des règles d'unité, de non-contradiction, et autres formalités policières. Genre: en jeu' ['Freed! If I want it, the ability to be embarrassed without being embarrassed. Proof that I'm no longer at the mercy of the rules of unity, non-contradiction, and other police formalities. Genre: in play'] (28). Freed from the principle of non-contradiction, she can find herself not only 'gênée sans être gênée', embarrassed without being embarrassed, but 'Genet sans être Genet'. Or indeed 'nègre sans être nègre': 'genre' being an anagram of 'nègre', the 'nègre' is literally but *indirectly* evoked wherever genre is put into play.

Souffles, then, is an exploration of a metaphorical blackness as much as of a metaphorical motherhood. This mixing of metaphors itself serves to highlight that the poetic text is unsettling – and maternal – *because* of its metaphoricity, because of words' ability to establish a relationship between irreducibly different terms. This metaphoricity becomes particularly apparent in Cixous's treatment of the proper name, the verbal form most usually considered a guarantor of identity.[45] Significantly, in French 'nègre' also means a ghost writer, one whose writings appear under another name. While clearly both Genet and Cixous sign their texts, in each case the signature can be argued to problematise the onomastic referentiality it invokes. Building on Derrida's analysis of the way Genet's proper name appears improperly, disseminated throughout the texture of his writing, *Souffles* explores the name as marker of an uncertain identity. Thus, for example, 'J'' blurs the distinction not only between proper names (in that it variously evokes both 'Jean' and 'Joyce') but between names and pronouns (in that it also presents as a remainder of 'je').[46] 'Je comprends que "J'" est son nom d'autre' ['I understand that "J'" is his other's name'] (18): in effect, for Cixous writing is haunted by the proper name *as other*. The manuscript contains a sequence reflecting on one's determination by one's proper name:[47]

> De Jean Genêt j'admire qu'abandonné un tel nom lui soit revenu à la place de père et mère. [. . .] Ce qu'un nom fait d'un homme, comment l'évaluer? De son nom d'une certaine manière Jean Genêt est le rejeton. En son nom son génie s'enracine. [. . .] Lui d'avance, son nom l'élève. Je ange net. Je ange. J'imagine qu'il s'angea. Ses gènes d'ange. (ts. 134–5; ms. 127–8)

> [About the abandoned Jean Genêt I admire that a name came to him in the place of father and mother. [. . .] How to evaluate what a name makes of a man? Of his name Jean Genêt is in a way the offspring. In his name his genius is rooted. [. . .] Already, his name raises him. Je ange net. Je ange. I imagine he angeled. His angel genes.]

On the one hand, this passage suggests a process of determination as robust as that of genetics: Genet's sublime writing is in part due to the resonances in his name of 'génie' (genie and genius), 'ange' (angel) and, as the following paragraph develops, 'généreux' (generous).[48] However, that the determination is far from a simple matter of cause and effect becomes obvious when the association between Genet and generosity leads into a consideration *a contrario* of the link between Cixous's own name and meanness:

> gosse, de mon nom les mauvaises langues faisant résonner quelques sous, cinq ou six, longtemps je me craignis une mesquinerie, je me sus complice des

mendiants, des avares, des troncs, des sébiles, des boîtes de fer-blanc, j'eus peur des petites monnaies, d'en être, d'en avoir, d'en manquer. (ts. 135; ms. 128)

[as a kid, nasty tongues made my name echo in some *sous*, five or six, for a long time I feared I was something mean, I knew myself to be complicit with beggars, misers, collection-boxes, begging-bowls, tin cans, I was afraid of small coins, of being them, having them, lacking them.]

Crucially, while at the level of the signified Cixous's relationship to her name would seem to be the opposite of Genet's, their troubling of the relationship between proper name and common noun – that is their very response to their name *as signifier* – is common – or proper? – to both. That commonality is further reflected in Cixous's use of 'troncs', a word whose homonymy links the collection-boxes she associates with her own name to trees, the plant-form with the strongest presence in *Souffles*. This compounds the link with herself: Helen was worshipped in Rhodes under the name Dendritis as the tree goddess. It also accentu-ates the similarity with Genet. By systematically spelling his name with a circumflex, Cixous highlights Genet's determination as plant rather than horse; furthermore, whereas Derrida and indeed Genet himself discussed 'genêt' as a flower, for Cixous Genet's name makes him a tree: 'd'être né rue d'Assas 22 de Gabrielle Genêt jamais vue (à jamais je join-drai l'infernal au lumineux, d'*être fleur et arborescent* je suis allié par la queue aux souterrains, aux morts par mon corps creux qu'il peut leur plaire d'emprunter pour remonter)' ['from being born 22 rue d'Assas of Gabrielle Genêt never seen (forever I will unite the infernal with the luminous, from *being flower and shrub* I am connected by the cock to those underground, to the dead by my hollow body that they may like to borrow to rise up again)'] (ms. 173; my emphasis).

In particular, Cixous sees her own name, like Genet's, as an indication of illegitimacy:

Dans cette ville où les noms étaient propres et riches, répertoriés, ordonnés, liés à des terroirs, provinces, nations, ou communs et tribaux, mon nom seul n'était d'aucun bord. C'était un batard de langues un enfant trouvé. [. . .] Jamais je ne m'y fis: mais ne pouvant sans me trahir le rejeter, je le voulus, je l'adoptai. [. . .] Inconsciemment, je le compris alors, mon nom m'avait fait écrire: il avait été si souvent cause en moi du plus bas, donc occasion du plus haut; par la blessure qu'il m'entretint les cortèges des langues s'étaient engouffrés jusqu'à mes poumons et mon cerveau. (ts. 135–6; ms. 128–9)

[In this city where names were proper and rich, listed, ordered, linked to lands, provinces, nations, or common and tribal, only my name was on no

side. It was a bastard of languages an abandoned child. [. . .] I never got used
to it: but not being able to reject it without betraying myself, I willed it, I
adopted it. [. . .] Unconsciously, I understood at that point, my name had
made me write: it had so often been the cause in me of the lowest, thus an
opportunity for the highest; by the wound it maintained in me streams of
languages had plunged right into my lungs and my brain.]

Here the name itself is in the place of illegitimate child or 'batard'
(another word spelt illegitimately, without its circumflex), the narrator in that of mother. While the rejected Genet became the 'rejeton' or
offspring, of his name, putting his name 'à la place de père et mère',
the narrator 'adopts' hers: in both cases an illegitimacy – that is an
improper or displaced filiation – generates a replacement genealogy.[49]
Rather than normalising the initial illegitimacy, however, this genealogy
seeks to extend and deepen it, *to create a line of illegitimacy*. 'My name
had made me write': Cixous's unclassifiable name appears to have been
a lesson in illegitimacy, an early apprenticeship that language could
be used to escape what, again borrowing Genet's voice, she calls the
'bizarre et universelle condamnation au filialisme':

D'aucuns pensent banalement: celle-là, parce que c'est ma mère, je dois
l'aimer. Moi, partout où je pousse – un peu de terre, et je me donne une
robuste naissance – je neutralise la mesquinerie de cette bizarre et universelle
condamnation au filialisme: de toutes les femmes je puis être le secret. Qu'en
mon corps conviennent des germes de toutes les races, c'est ma gloire. [. . .]
Qu'on ne m'envie pas ce destin: si j'ai jamais *gagné* (je ne veux pas dire mérité,
ni reçu en échange marchand, mais arraché à force de passion) quelque chose,
c'est cette âme détachée même de la montagne qu'elle couronna, d'où je puis
indifféremment, gratuitement, adorer celle qu'il me sied à tel moment de me
donner pour mère, sans distinction de classe, de culture, d'origine, de visage,
d'espèce: je me dois de n'être tenu par aucune restriction. (ms. 174)

[Some think banally: because she is my mother, I have to love her. For me,
wherever I grow – a little earth, and I can give myself a sturdy birth – I neu-
tralize the pettiness of the bizarre, universal condemnation to filialism: I can
be the secret of every woman. My glory is that seeds of all races are appropriate in my body. [. . .] That destiny should not be cause of envy: if ever I *won*
(I don't mean deserved, nor accepted in exchange, but snatched with the force
of my passion) something, it's my soul detached even from the mountain it
crowned, from where I can indifferently, freely, adore the one it suits me at
any moment to give myself for a mother, with no distinction of class, culture,
origin, face, species: I owe it to myself not to be bound by any restriction.]

At issue here is a generous, non-exclusive form of genealogy (from
genea, race/kind). His motherless status gives Genet the freedom to
'give' himself as many mothers as he wishes, irrespective of class, kind

or race. 'Qu'en mon corps conviennent des germes de toutes les races': the arcane use of the verb 'convenir' (which etymologically, from *convenire*, means to come together but in common parlance means to be appropriate, to suit) without an indirect object suggests that the filiation he invents is not a linear descent but a multiple hybridisation, a 'coming-together' of differences. The sudden shift from 'toutes les femmes' to 'toutes les races' is disconcerting; furthermore, the fact that the germs/seeds 'conviennent' in his body implies as much that his body harbours them (placing him in the position of mother rather than child) as that it derives from them. In Genet's genealogy, in other words, the *in*appropriate is appropriate, the unsuitable suits. 'Adorer celle *qu'il me sied* à tel moment de me donner pour mère': the appropriate mother is without any 'distinction of class, culture, origin, face, species', with whatever properties he desires. 'Ta mère: celle que tu aimes' ['Your mother: the one you love'] (208).

The very fact that the 'je' here is undecidably situated between Genet and Cixous, that Cixous's voice is never unambiguously her own, can itself be read as a reflection of Cixous's relationship with her own name. The effacement of her name accompanying the birth of the 'je' at the opening of *Souffles* can thus paradoxically be considered a signature gesture. Just as Genet's dissemination of his mother's proper name renders it ubiquitous, makes every word a signature, so her challenge to the very notion of the proper name as guarantor of a constant, fixed identity – a challenge reflected at every level of her writing in the perturbation of property that could be said to constitute the hallmark of her style – itself functions as a reminder, an echo, a resonance, of her own (im)proper name. She muses on the contradictory effects her name has had on her writing:

Aujourd'hui ce qui fut blessure d'amour-propre est au contraire prime de plaisir: non seulement j'ai à mon nom fait divers monuments, lui faisant ainsi un nom que nous n'avions pas prévu, mais encore indompté, traînant les langues à sa suite, il continue sa course à embûches, toujours s'adressant ses clins de lettres, ses ambages de sa place d'immigré. (ts. 136; ms. 129)

[Today what was a narcissistic wound is on the contrary a bonus pleasure: not only have I made several monuments to my name, making a name for it we hadn't foreseen, but yet untamed, dragging languages behind it, it continues on its path full of pitfalls, still addressing its winks of letters, its turns of phrase to itself from its immigrant place.]

On the one hand, Cixous's texts represent 'monuments' to her name, suggesting that they have served to consolidate and crystallise an identity, to soothe the wound to her 'amour-propre', self-esteem, that its early humiliations inflicted. Yet at the same time the name remains 'indompté', untamed, its movement unchecked, its contestatory force unrecuperated. Its continued disruptiveness is itself reflected in the displacement of two fixed expressions: 'ambages' is normally no longer used other than in the expression 'sans ambages', while 'clins de lettres' makes sense only in relation to 'clins d'œil'. The power of the proper name, in other words, is the insidious power of letters themselves, a power that lies not in a representational making visible but in letters' very indirectness, their subversive obliqueness. Giving voice to a 'place d'immigré', Cixous's name inscribes a marginality that resists appropriation. Her *practice* of her name, challenging rather consolidating identities, echoes the anonymous voice she associates with the mother.

Cixous's name, then, was one of her first 'mother-texts', providing her with a formative experience of the power of language, that is proof that the proper name can be used *improperly*. The message of *Souffles* is above all that anyone or anything can represent a mother. Cixous's name is also her creation: if 'Cixous' was the author's author, the author endlessly rewrote 'Cixous', finding it an infinite *sou*rce of *sou*rcils, *sou*rire, *sou*lèvement, *sou*lagement, *sou*plesse, *sou*liers *sou*ples, *sou*straction, *sou*hait, not to mention *sou*ffrance, or, of course, *sou*ffles . . . She breathes new life into her name by naming in a way that troubles the laws of property. In other words, she names *illegitimately*, in a way that bears a maternal mark, one not subordinated to the laws of property. Just as the mother is a metaphor, this book celebrates how a metaphor, the power of language to substitute one word for another, has the power to be a mother.

Notes

1. Hélène Cixous, 'Le Rire de la Méduse', *L'Arc*, 45 (1975), 39–54.
2. Hélène Cixous, 'Sorties', in Catherine Clément and Hélène Cixous, *La Jeune née* (Paris: 10/18, 1975), 115–246.
3. Hélène Cixous, *Le Rire de la Méduse et autres ironies*, preface Frédéric Regard (Paris: Galilée, 2010), 28.
4. Ibid.
5. Hélène Cixous, *Le Rire de la Méduse et autres ironies*, 58 ['Le Rire de la Méduse', 49].
6. 'The Laugh of the Medusa', *Signs*, 1:4 (Summer 1976), 875–93, at 887.
7. Ibid., 887n.
8. In their translation of Derrida's *H. C. pour la vie*, Herbrechter and Milesi translate 'art du vol' as 'art of lifting' to evoke both senses of the French *voler*; see HCE, 123.

9. Soon after they were made, the allegations of Cixous's biological essential-ism, made most influentially by Toril Moi in *Sexual/Textual Politics* (London: Routledge, 1988), were refuted in a number of publications; see especially Barbara Freeman's 'Plus corps donc plus écriture': Hélène Cixous and the Mind-Body Problem', *Paragraph*, 11:1 (1988), 58–70); Katherine Binhammer, 'Metaphor or Metonymy? The Question of Essentialism in Cixous', *Tessera*, 10 (1991), 65–79; and Peggy Kamuf, 'To Give Place: Semi-Approaches to Hélène Cixous'. I was therefore amazed to learn that as recently as 2005 Marie-Hélène Bourcier was still attributing essentialist positions to Cixous; see *Sexpolitiques: queer zones 2* (Paris: La Fabrique, 2005), 22. Such a determined non-reading that flies in the face of both Cixous's text and her academic commentators goes to show that the pieces are not 'dated', as has sometimes been proposed. The originality of Cixous's contribution has not yet fully been appreciated; the strong resist-ance it continues to encounter suggests that it still continues to carry a sig-nificant political charge.

10. *Le Rire et autres ironies*, 43n; 'The Laugh of the Medusa', 878–9.

11. *Le Rire et autres ironies*, 48, 49; 'The Laugh of the Medusa', 881, 882.

12. *Le Rire et autres ironies*, 48; 'The Laugh of the Medusa', 881.

13. Hélène Cixous, *Souffles* (Paris: Éditions des femmes, 1975). Unless other-wise indicated, page references in this chapter are to this text.

14. A number of critics have commented that Cixous never produced the read-ings she announced in 'Le Rire'; see, for example, Cynthia Running-Johnson, 'The Medusa's Tale: Feminine Writing and "La Genet"', *Romanic Review*, 80:3 (1989), 483–95, at 483. Cixous did, however, later publish on other aspects of Genet's writing in *Three Steps on the Ladder of Writing* (New York: Columbia University Press, 1993) and *Entretien de la blessure: Sur Jean Genet* (Paris: Galilée, 2011). For further discussions of the links between Cixous and Genet, see Cynthia Running-Johnson, 'Genet's "Excessive Double": Reading *Les Bonnes* through Irigaray and Cixous', *French Review*, 63:6 (May 1990), 959–66; and my 'Genet and Cixous: The InterSext', *French Review*, 72:4 (March 1999), 719–29.

15. It has often been signalled, for example by Running-Johnson, that *La Jeune née* sounds very close to 'La Genet'.

16. Documents concerning *Souffles* are contained in Box 9 of the Cixous archive. References to the manuscript will be preceded by ms., those to the typescript by ts.

17. For example, 'Jean' featured instead of 'il' and 'lui' in 'Il choisirait moins passivement que moi' (121; ts. 231bis) ['He would choose less passively than me'] and 'En lui liquider la mère devenue inutile. [. . .] Lui, ma mère, debout' (207; ts. 311bis) ['Liquidate in him the mother who has become useless. [. . .] Him, my mother, upright']. Similarly, the manuscript used the name where the published text reads 'Aussitôt J' intervient' (189; ms. 271bis) ['Immediately J' intervenes'] or 'La vue s'attarde, hésite, insiste sans se poser sur le buste de J' vu de loin' (205; ts. 310bis) ['Sight delays, hesi-tates, insists without resting on the bust of J' seen from afar'].

18. At a feminist level, in 'Sorties' Cixous deplores the fact that certain dis-courses function to recuperate the maternal by foreclosing the mother: 'Pas besoin de mère, pourvu qu'il y ait du maternel: et c'est le père alors qui fait

– est – la mère' ['No need for a mother, as long as there is some mother-liness: and it is the father, then, who acts the part, who is the mother'] (*Le Rire et autres ironies*, 73; *The Newly Born Woman*, 64). While the meta-phorical mother is not reducible to 'real' mothers, the converse also is true.

19. *Le Rire et autres ironies*, 60; 'The Laugh of the Medusa', 889.

20. The archives do not include drafts of the opening sequences, but compari-son of later passages with the documents which have survived shows that the published text is in general markedly more discontinuous than the earlier versions. The manuscript originally covered page after page in a continuous flow, with singularly few paragraph breaks; similarly, the broken syntax of the definitive text is in the main a late modification. For example, the passage 'En riant j'éloigne de nous la question inopportune. Après tout, qu'elle ait eu un fils . . . Ne me regarde pas. L'envie de . . . Me prend de lui passer la main dans le dos. Nu. De la toucher, – quelle ten-dresse. Non. Qu'on se . . . Oui. Si fort. Je pose mes doigts à la hauteur de sa nuque, comme ça. Pense "Je dois l'aimer pour un autre être mais qui?"' (141) ['Laughing I set the poorly-timed question at a distance. After all, whether she had a son . . . Does not concern me. The desire to . . . Takes me to run my hand over her back. Naked. To touch her, – what tenderness. No. If we . . . Yes. So strongly. I place my fingers high on the back of her neck, like that. Think "I must love her for another but who?"'] originally ran: 'En riant j'éloignai de nous la question qui m'était venue inopportuné-ment. Après tout, qu'elle ait eu un fils ne me regarde pas. L'envie me prit de lui passer la main dans le dos. A mes propres yeux ma tendresse pour la Primavère était inexcusable: Comme je posai mes doigts à la hauteur de sa nuque, je songeai que je devais l'aimer pour un autre être, mais lequel?' (ts. 260bis) ['Laughing I set the question that had occurred to me at a poor time at a distance. After all, whether she had a son does not concern me. The desire takes me to run my hand over her back. In my own eyes my tender-ness for the Primavère was inexcusable: As I placed my fingers high on the back of her neck, I thought that I must love her for another but which?"'].

21. This quotation in turn inscribes an uncertain identity: 'Selbst jetzo, welche denn ich sei, ich weiss es nicht' ['Which of them am I? Even now I do not know'], Johann Wolfgang Goethe, *Faust* 2, ed. Helmut Kobligk (Frankfurt: M. Diesterweg, 1973), l. 8875).

22. Søren Kierkegaard, *Fear and Trembling*, trans. Alastair Hannay (Harmondsworth: Penguin, 1985), 46.

23. As in *Les Commencements*, *Souffles* will exploit the homophony in French between *laid* (ugly) and *lait* (milk).

24. Examination of the manuscript version of this sequence reveals no trace yet of Rimbaud, or of the paragraph containing this quotation. The decision to space the text with the fragments of poem clearly came later, providing further confirmation that the text itself generated its sources as much as it derived from them.

25. Jacques Derrida, 'Fourmis', *Lectures de la Différence Sexuelle*, textes réunis et présentés par Mara Negrón (Paris: des femmes, 1994), 75; 'Fourmis', trans. Eric Prenowitz, *Rootprints*, 121.

26. Jean Genet, *Journal du voleur* (Paris: Gallimard, coll. Folio, 1949), 22.

27. Jacques Derrida, *Glas* (Paris: Galilée, 1974).

28. Jean-Paul Sartre, *Saint Genet: Comédien et martyr*, vol. I of Jean Genet, *Œuvres complètes* (Paris: Gallimard, 1952). While Derrida does not state directly that Sartre did not make the connection between 'sein' and 'saint', he points out that 'dans le *Saint Genet*, la question de la fleur, la question anthologique, entre autres, est infailliblement évitée. Avec celle de la "psychanalyse" et celle de la "littérature", par la plus agile et la plus intelligente des leçons d'ontologie phénoménologique de l'époque, à la française. Un développement pourtant la manque de peu. Notez qu'il commence ainsi: "Reste qu'on peut tout simplement *ne pas* le lire"' ['in *Saint Genet*, the question of the flower, the anthological question, among others, is infallibly avoided. Along with that of "psychoanalysis" and that of "literature", by the most agile and intelligent of the lessons in phenomenological ontology of the time, in the French mode. One development nevertheless narrowly misses it. Note that he begins thus: "The fact remains that one can simply *not* read him"'] (*Glas*, 18). Derrida thus suggests that Sartre did not in effect *read* Genet and that, blind to the work of the signifier, he missed the significance of the remarkable literary event that Genet's writing constituted.
29. *Glas*, 58.
30. 'La mère ne présenterait à l'analyse le terme d'une régression, un signifié de dernière instance, que si vous saviez ce que nomme ou veut dire la mère, ce dont elle est grosse. Or vous ne pourriez le savoir qu'après avoir épuisé tout le reste, tous les objets, tous les noms que le texte met à sa place (galère, galerie, bourreau, fleurs de toute espèce n'en sont que des exemples)' ['The mother would only present analysis with the end term of a regression, an ultimate signified, if you knew what the mother names or means, what she can produce. But you could only know that once you had exhausted all the rest, all the objects and names the text puts in her place (galley, gallery, executioner, flowers of all kinds are only examples)'], *Glas*, 163–4.
31. For a comparative study of Cixous and Teresa of Avila, see Elena Carrera, 'Teresa of Avila and Hélène Cixous: Corps-à-corps with the Mother', *Journal of the Institute of Romance Studies*, 2 (1993), 409–28. Understandably, given that she was presumably unaware of the saint's importance in the manuscript, the author does not take account of *Souffles*.
32. Teresa's quotation of the call in Psalm 55 for the wings of a dove ('Oh, my God, how clear is the meaning of that verse about asking for the wings of a dove and how right the author was – and how right we shall all be! – to ask for them! It is evident that he is referring to the flight taken by the spirit when it soars high above all created things, and above itself first of all; but it is a gentle and a joyful flight and also a silent one,' *Life*, ch. 20) is recalled in two of the mentions of doves in *Souffles*: 'Qui me donnera une aile comme à la colombe?' ['Who will give me a wing like the dove?'] (35), 'Une aile comme à la colombe?' ['A wing like the dove?'] (221).
33. In turn, the 'je' here is divided between Derrida and Genet. The columns in *Glas* echo those of Genet's 'Ce qui est resté d'un Rembrandt', where the writer seeks to come to terms with his discovery that all men share a 'même identité' ['same identity'] underlying their singular appearance. In particular, this identity, revealed to him by the 'si fragile regard' of a fellow-traveller, threatens to render powerless the entire symbolic order predicated

on the illusion of unique individuality, an order whose phallocentricity he loved to hate and whose erotic attraction for him, notwithstanding the violence of his attacks on it, is manifest at the end of the text in the nostalgia he acknowledges already for the future loss of power over him of a 'sexe érigé, congestionné et vibrant, dressé dans un fourré de poils noirs et bouclés' ('Ce qui est resté d'un Rembrandt déchiré en petits carrés bien réguliers, et foutu aux chiottes', *Œuvres complètes*, IV (Paris: Gallimard, 1968), 19–31, at 31) ['erect phallus, congested and vibrating, standing in a thicket of curly black hairs'] (Jean Genet, 'What Remains of a Rembrandt Torn into Little Squares All the Same Size and Shot Down the Toilet', *Fragments of the Artwork*, trans. Charlotte Mandell (Stanford: Stanford University Press, 2003), 91–102, at 101–2.)

34. See Jean Genet, *Miracle de la rose*, in *Œuvres complètes*, II (Paris: Gallimard, 1951), 454. These scenes are directly invoked at the beginning of *Souffles*: 'longeant des nuits-couloirs parvenir sans être arrêté par les matons, au ventre d'un condamné à mort et s'y nicher grâce aux mots de passe; à force de concentration faire comprendre aux barreaux d'une cellule la nécessité de s'écarter; les bras passés autour d'un pilier le réchauffer, lui faire perdre haleine' (33) ['pacing down night-corridors, without being stopped by the screws reach a condemned man's stomach and lodge there thanks to passwords; by dint of concentration make the bars of a cell understand the need to spread out; with arms passed around a pillar, warm it, make it lose breath'].

35. Notwithstanding the importance of the 'ineluctable modality of the audible' in *Souffles*, Joyce is not celebrated directly as one of its principal sources, although his presence can be deciphered behind the overdetermined J' in a passage announcing 'cette Irelande dont nul n'a encore dressé la carte' ['this Ire-land that nobody yet has mapped'] and focusing on the non-existence of a 'Prime Vérité' (188–92).

36. *Souffles* was originally to appear under the title *Vol/e*; see Christiane Makward and Hélène Cixous, 'Interview with Hélène Cixous', *SubStance*, 5:13 (1976), 19–37, at 34.

37. Frédéric Regard, 'AA', *Le Rire et autres ironies*, 13.

38. 'Nec ea re volebam frui quam furto appetebam, sed ipso furto et peccato' (Book 2, ch. 4).

39. Jean Genet, *Pompes funèbres* (Paris: Gallimard, collection 'Imaginaire', 1949), 297.

40. The last sentence is also reminiscent of Rilke's famous assertion in a letter to his Polish translator of the Duinô Elegies that 'we are the bees of the invisible'. As mentioned above, much of the typescript of *Souffles* was numbered 'Duinô'; Rilke maintains a strong presence in the published text in that many of its key leitmotivs such as angels, trees, birds/flight inscribe a relationship to his work that I unfortunately am unable here to examine in detail.

41. It was to be many years more before Cixous, in a series of texts beginning with *Les Rêveries de la femme sauvage*, would explore in depth the complexities of her identification with the colonised deriving from her colonial situation as an Algerian Jew, and as such belonging simply neither to the camp of the oppressor (because outside the circles of colonial power) nor to

that of the oppressed (because privileged relative to her Arab neighbours). I explore these questions in Chapter 6.

42. *Souffles* elaborates on this point, made earlier about 'Le Rire', in its own innovative way: 'Je n'ai jamais su, quand je volais en rêve ou en réalité, [. . .] si j'aspirais au vol pour le plaisir de voler (de détacher mon corps de ses terrestres obligations, de planer, de m'arracher à toute réquisition; de foutre en l'air l'ordre des poids et lois et des appartenances; de, m'évadant de l'espèce humaine, me dérober aux sommations du propre) ou pour le plaisir de voler (de prendre sans payer; de faire dérailler les valeurs, de mésuser de la cote; et aussi, en volant, non seulement de changer les choses de place, de nom, de cadre, de désorganiser le monde pour le recomposer à ma tête, mais en sus pour voler d'avoir à me changer moi-même entièrement; et jusqu'à me voler, me dérober)' ['I never knew, when I stole in dream or in reality, [. . .] if I aspired to theft for the pleasure of theft/flying (of detaching my body from its terrestrial obligations, of gliding, of wrenching myself free from all requisition; throwing in the air the order of weight and laws and belongings; of, escaping from humankind, evading the dictates of property) or for the pleasure of theft/flying (of taking without paying; of derailing values, misusing stock quotations; and also, in robbing/ flying, not only change the place, name and frame of things, disorganize the world to recompose it in my head, but in addition in flying/stealing to have to change myself entirely; to the point of stealing myself, escaping from myself)'] (163–4). The impossibility of distinguishing between the two meanings is exemplified not only in the repetition of the words 'pour le plaisir de voler' where logically one would expect something different, but further in the way the elaboration on each meaning has recourse to language equally appropriate to the other.

43. The absence of the circumflex in the context of a discussion of the 'reste' invites the reader to relate it to Derrida's discussion in *Glas* – whose subtitle is 'Que reste-t-il du savoir absolu?' ['What remains of absolute knowledge?'] and whose opening volley asks: 'quoi du reste aujourd'hui, pour nous, ici, maintenant, d'un Hegel?' ['moreover, what of the remainder today, for us, here, of Hegel?'] (*Glas*, 1) – of Genet's play on the circumflex: 'Le nom de la mère serait – communément – celui d'une plante ou d'une fleur, à la différence d'une lettre, l's tombé, ou d'un accent circonflexe, pour en cicatriser la chute. [. . .] Genêt nomme une plante à fleurs [. . .], genet une espèce de cheval. D'Espagne, pays qui importe beaucoup dans le texte. [. . .] Il est à cheval sur son nom propre. Il le tient par le mors. Comme un grand d'Espagne ou un accent circonflexe' ['The mother's name would – commonly – be that of a plant or flower, with a difference of one letter, the dropped s, or a circumflex accent, to cicatrize over the fall. [. . .] Genêt [*broom*] names a flowering plant [...], genet [*jennet*] a kind of horse. From Spain, a country that matters a lot in the text. [. . .] He is astride his proper name. He holds it by the bit. Like a Spanish noble or a circumflex accent'] (*Glas*, 48). In addition to highlighting the space of the lost letter and the difference between the two common nouns, the circumflex allows Genet to straddle both proper name and common noun and thus to trouble the difference between them.

44. Thus, for example, at one point Cixous reflects on the difference between

herself and Genet when faced with Solomon's dilemma: 'Il choisirait moins passivement que moi' ['He would choose less passively than me'] (121).

45. For other discussions of Cixous's name, see my 'Hélène Cixous's Improper Name,' *The Romanic Review*, 90:4 (1999), 481–97; Alison Rice, *Time Signatures: Contextualizing Contemporary Francophone Autobiographical Writing from the Maghreb* (Lanham, MD and Oxford: Lexington Books, 2006); and Elissa Marder, 'Birthmarks (Given Names)', *parallax* 44, 13:3 (2007), 49-61.

46. Elsewhere, the chain continues still further. Thus in 'My Algeriance', the 'J' stands for Jew: 'My mother, in the double grip of Nazi Germany and Vichy Algeria never said the word *Jew* in the street. Naïve, she said that's a *J*. Exorcism. Taboo. I knew well the subtle poisons of interdiction: interdictions interdict themselves. They self-mutilate themselves. All that was left of us was the letter J. J. became my first favorite letter: with great energy I said *je*' ('My Algeriance', 156). Proper nouns, common nouns, pronouns: Cixous's 'J' does not function to subsume all these under a common category but rather calls the irreducibly non-hierarchical relationship across different parts of speech to our attention.

47. Interestingly, Cixous's most developed meditation on this determination, many years later, again invokes Genet's name alongside her own: 'We must all deal with the unconscious effects of our proper name. We find this aspect of language's intervention in our destiny on the flesh of our imagination. We work on writers whose names are bearers of textual effects. This includes names that are seemingly insignificant, such as mine for example, an impossible name, but which has always produced signifying effects. Genet constantly puts his name to work in the French language' (*Three Steps on the Ladder of Writing*, 145).

48. In her early (semi-)theoretical and paratextual writings, Cixous associates generosity with Freud's genitality, as in her interview with Conley: 'The ideal harmony, reached by few, would be genital, assembling everything and being capable of generosity, of spending' (*Hélène Cixous: Writing the Feminine*, 131). Her development of Genet's 'generosity' in *Souffles* thus suggests that the structure manifest in the work of this homosexual writer who so forcefully celebrates the anus corresponds to a genital rather than anal stage of development.

49. In text after text Cixous emphasises the 'improper' aspect of her name. For example: 'My wild bristling sexual name unclean improper cutting like a Barbary fig, vulnerable, attacked, barbarian' ('My Algeriance', 157).

Chapter 5

Vital Tragedy? *Déluge*

'I live the tragic, I live myself tragically, I am totally occupied by the question of the tragic':[1] tragedy has always been at the root and heart of Hélène Cixous's work. As we saw with regard to *Dedans*, the loss of her father while she was only ten years old was a personal tragedy to which, for many years, she ascribed the motive force of her writing. Moreover, text after text suggests that her experience of political tragedy at an even earlier age was just as formative. Born in Algeria in 1937 to Jewish parents, her mother having read the signs of Nazi Germany early enough to leave it for Paris where she met Cixous's father, the author grew up in an environment profoundly marked by two of the tragedies that deeply scarred the twentieth century: the massacre of European Jewry and the violence and brutality of colonial Algeria. As Cixous comments in an interview: 'I was born political, in a sense, and it was even for political reasons that I began to write *poetry* as a response to the political tragedy.'[2]

What interests me particularly in this last statement is how Cixous inflects the discussion of tragedy towards a discussion of genre. Historically, the notion of tragedy is of course inseparable from the question of genre. The term emerged in Ancient Greece to describe a particular kind of drama, although in modern use the term is applied more frequently to 'real' events than to literary forms. Today, however, as Adrian Poole remarks, the word is ubiquitous in news coverage.[3] Cixous's theatre is undoubtedly tragic in this contemporary sense. The large-scale plays she wrote for Ariane Mnouchkine's Théâtre du Soleil remember for the most part political, historical calamities: the Cambodian genocide in *L'Histoire terrible mais inachevée de Norodom Sihanouk, Roi du Cambodge*; the combat from which arose the Partition of the Indian sub-continent in *L'Indiade ou l'Inde de leurs rêves*; the contaminated blood scandal in which hundreds of French hæmophiliacs lost their lives due to the venality of the doctors in charge of the blood transfusion service in *La Ville parjure*.[4] While not referring to a specific historical event in the same way, *Tambours sur la digue* offers an allegory of misgovernment and corruption with broad socio-political implications.[5] Cixous's less formalised collaborations with the theatre, too, foreground political questions; for example, in *Et soudain des nuits d'éveil* [*And Suddenly, Nights of Awakening*], created in 1997 'en harmonie' ['in harmony'] with Cixous, the Théâtre du Soleil opened its doors to the history of Tibet. These plays, which focus on the catastrophes of which contemporary humanity has shown itself capable, count among the most explicitly political, the most *conventionally* political, of all Cixous's writings. This is manifestly political theatre.

Nonetheless, it seems to me that Cixous's most powerful thinking about what 'tragedy' may mean is to be found in her fiction rather than these plays. While her theatre deals with tragic subjects, she has stated that the immediate, inescapable presence of the audience places a specific and particularly intense burden of responsibility on the author:

> Theater for me is tragedy, characters, combats against destinality, 'fate'. I think that only in a tradition with a profoundly political message does the theater have a reason for being. Particularly today, in quite an exceptional manner which distinguishes it from all other literary acts or practices, the theater structurally carries a responsibility in the instant. Therefore, when I write for the theater, I am in a state of incessant alert to responsibility, I verify at every moment of writing, to my right to my left in front around at a distance what I am in the process of writing, not because there is a superego, but because the theater is an activity that is turned toward the 'public', that is, the re-public, the audience, today: with the audience, for the audience; because the audience, that is to say, we ourselves, is the whole citizenry.[6]

We can see an example of the constraints arising from this consciousness of an ethical duty towards the audience in the ending of *La Ville parjure*. The 'action' proper of the play ends in a devastating flood let loose by the corrupt politicians, in which the city's *marginalisés*, including those who hunger for justice, are all swept to their deaths. But, feeling that this ending was 'exceedingly cruel for the audience',[7] Cixous felt herself obliged to add a final scene in which the dead congregate among the stars. This does not qualify as a 'happy ending', since nothing alleviates the characters' suffering. Nevertheless, the main effect of the final scene, which Cixous claims was the one time she 'consciously exerted the privilege of the writer to write according to his or her heart's desire',[8] is to mitigate the distressing impact on the audience. The dominant impulse in her theatre is that the tragic should not prevail.

It is perhaps telling in this respect that the only explicit quotation from Shakespeare in *Sihanouk* comes not from one of his tragedies but a 'history' play, *Richard II*.⁹ In an interview that ranges back over her work with the Soleil, the author lays a considerably greater emphasis on the 'epic' dimensions of her theatrical creations than on their 'tragic' side. For example, she recalls that she began to write what became *Sihanouk* 'd'une manière qui restait insufflée par ce qui me restait comme mémoire épique venant de Shakespeare' ['in a way that was instilled with my epic memory, from Shakespeare']. Or she explains that *L'Indiade* superseded an original plan to write a play about Indira Gandhi which she renounced when she realised, contrary to her expectations, 'qu'Indira Gandhi n'était pas un personnage intéressant. Que ce n'était pas un personnage de théâtre. Que c'était un personnage de journal, que ce n'était pas un personnage qu'on pouvait transformer pour en faire un personnage épique' ['Indira Gandhi was not an interesting character. She was not a theatrical character. She was a newspaper character, not one that could be transformed to make an epic character'].¹⁰ This is of course not to propose that epics and tragedies are distinct, opposable, categories; indeed, the starting point of Cixous's collaboration with the Soleil was the search for a people 'dont le sort tragique pouvait être l'image d'autres tragédies, d'autres histoires contemporaines' ['whose tragic destiny could be the image of other tragedies, of other contemporary stories'].¹¹ But it does suggest that her priority when seeking a subject for a play is that it have an epic dimension: that it be 'épopéeable' (epicable or 'saga-able').¹²

Fiction, on the other hand, appears to be Cixous's space of predilection for the exploration of tragedy. It is significant that her dramatic treatment developed in that direction; she herself signalled the evolution in her work for the Soleil 'vers de moins en moins de réalisme, ou de moins en moins de références à des données existantes, et de plus en plus d'inventions. De moins en moins d'actualité immédiatement lisible, jusqu'à atteindre la pure fiction avec *Tambours sur la digue*' ['towards less and less realism, or fewer and fewer references to existing facts, and more and more inventions. Less and less reliance on immediately readable current affairs, to the point of attaining pure fiction with *Drums on the Dam*'].¹³ Note also that she was talking about her fiction when she explained, in her interview with Kathleen O'Grady, that she wrote poetry as a response to a political tragedy greater than the individual: 'I could say that there is not a single one of my fictional texts that does not resonate with echoes of world history'. Even *Dedans* bears such a reading: 'my first narrative which was called *Dedans* reads in fact as an oblique ethico-political treatise on the conscious and unconscious situation in Algeria between the '40s and the '60s – one is not obliged to read it in that way, but that is what it is.'¹⁴ There is no opposition between one's suffering as a human being and one's suffering as a citizen.

For Cixous, then, fiction is best placed to explore tragedies of all scopes and origins. Not being subject to theatre's duty in the immediate present to its spectator, it allows her the space, and above all the *time*, to investigate scenes of appalling suffering as she desires. As we shall see, the time of tragedy is an intrinsically intermediate time, that is the time of narrative itself. This chapter will focus on *Déluge* [*Deluge*],[15] the narration of a calamitous time, a period of such extreme grief following the ending of a love-story that the narrator experiences the violent discontinuity between her previous and current selves as a death. In my view, this is the fictional text that offers Cixous's most developed reflection on tragedy. It is doubtless no accident that it is also one of the texts in which the 'echoes of world history' resonate the least; the same ethical impulse that led the writer to take the theatrical audience into account would have limited the freedom she allowed herself to take if the 'personal' tragedy it deals with was reflected on a broader scale in the suffering of others whose feelings she felt obliged to consider. However, far from wallowing in misery, the book obliges us to question what Cixous terms the 'attraction tragique' or tragic attraction (224), to rethink our assumptions about what tragedy means and why it appeals to us.[16]

In particular, Cixous explores in *Déluge* what we might understand by a tragic *life*. Most tragedies end in the afflicted character's death, a resolution which can be read as satisfying the longing for a state of quiescence theorised by Freud as the death instinct. Is a tragic life, where the character is grievously wounded yet does *not* die, more tragic than a tragic death, or does the very fact of survival – however painful it may be – preclude the finality associated with the tragic? To rephrase the question, in what way is it *more than tragic* if life continues? Is a work that is *more than* a tragedy a semi-tragedy?

We have returned indirectly here to the question of genre. Early in *Déluge*, the narrator asks: 'Comment s'appelle une pièce avec sangs et musique, avec deuil et jubilation? [. . .] Comment appeler ce genre sans le trahir' ['What to call a play with blood and music, mourning and jubilation? [. . .] What to call this genre without betraying it'], and claims to be able to think of no novel with an 'histoire semblable, à deux genres contraires' ['similar story, with two contrary genres'] (36–7). In the book's final pages, she wonders if she has written a 'comédie avec tragédie' ['comedy with tragedy'] (227) or a 'tragédie avec comédie' ['tragedy with comedy'] (229). Tragedy has of course been linked to comedy ever since its origins in Antiquity; as Adrian Poole explains, the purity of the genre has always been under threat from its 'inferiors'.[17]

Indeed, one probable motivation for the etymology of the term, derived from the Greek words for goat (*tragos*) and song (*ôdê*), was the chorus of satyrs from which Aristotle suggested the genre evolved, and whose presence remained manifest in the form of the satyr play that, along with three tragedies, each playwright entered in the Athenian Dionysia. Numerous theatrical precedents for a hybrid form exist, such as the parodic *hilarotragōdia* of which Bottom's play in Shakespeare's *A Midsummer Night's Dream* affords an example,[18] or, more pertinently, that playwright's tragedies, a constant reference for Cixous. *Déluge* includes an explicit mention of the porter in *Macbeth* (103), perhaps the most famous comic interlude in a tragedy.

What are the implications of the fact that *Déluge* both bears the hallmarks of exceptional tragedy, *is* a tragedy – yet is not *only* a tragedy? At issue again, especially, is the relation between tragedy and time: when is a tragedy not a tragedy? *When* is a tragedy defined as a tragedy? The narrator declares that she lives 'de vivre et mourir enchevêtrés en sonate' ['from living and dying entwined in a sonata'] (16): in this 'comedy with tragedy', or 'tragedy with comedy', life is the entwinement together of living and dying, of the fatal and the vital, of the tragic and the non-tragic. By definition, a tragic life is one where the tragedy, or the dying, continues, but also one where living continues. In a tragic life, the possibility always remains of wresting life from death.

Cixous's focus on the link between tragedy and life indicates to some extent a proximity with Nietzsche. Like Cixous, Nietzsche espouses a dualistic conception of tragedy, although for her tragedy is combined 'with' comedy whereas the dualism he elaborates is internal to the genre: the combination of the Apollonian and the Dionysian which he sees as tragedy's sublime characteristic. For Nietzsche, tragedy is ultimately affirmative since it allows us to intuit a terrible reality too unbearable to be directly confronted by mediating it æsthetically. Tragedy is the supreme example of art because it 'can turn these thoughts of repulsion at the horror and absurdity of existence into ideas compatible with life'.[19] Precisely because of its acceptance of the terrible as well as the harmonious, its engagement with the instinctive as well as the rational, because of its 'understanding of the unity of all things', tragedy is rooted in an 'affirmative instinct for life'.[20]

I want to suggest that the appeal of *Déluge*, the story of the end of a love-affair, paradoxically lies in its appeal to the libido, in the broad sense of life instinct. The existence of the book in itself bears witness to the drive to create in the very midst of death. Furthermore, the reflection it contains on the relation between tragedy and life and, especially, on the role that writing plays in ensuring that the story becomes 'more than' a tragedy, holds validity for Cixous's work in general. As she recently mused, 'Everything I write is tragic, but since I write, it's untragical-ised.'[21] This chapter will examine the (complicated) role Cixous's writing plays in helping to survive catastrophe, both in terms of enabling it to be accepted and in terms of mitigating one of its most disastrous aspects: the lack of a 'scene'. Telling the story, then, makes a vital differ-ence. That in turn is an insight whose validity may extend considerably beyond Cixous's work. *Déluge* invites us to consider that a tragedy told is always more than a tragedy that a tragedy, in other words, is always a semi-tragedy.

The Deluge

Déluge is the story of the 'agonie d'un Nous' ['agony of a We'] (68). The modern French *agonie* gives more equal weight to the two mean-ings of the term than its English equivalent: it means the suffering spe-cifically of one's dying moments as well as an extreme mental distress. In *Déluge*, it is not only the 'nous' that has come to an end. The book as a whole reliteralises the idea of a mortal anguish, an anguish so severe that the person suffering it ceases to exist. While the 'déluge' of the title does not appear until relatively late in the book, its paronym 'deuil' (mourning) features from the opening pages (13, 14): *Déluge* is the story of an 'I' in mourning, a *deuil-je*, in mourning specifically not only for her lost love and for the 'nous' they formed together but also for the self who died along with the relationship: 'En Deuil – c'est là que sont nos malades, au Pays Gris – où il n'y a pas de "moi", pas de je suis' ['In Mourning – that's where our invalids are, in the Grey Country – where there is no "me", no I am'] (69). This line calls to mind Louis XV's famous pronouncement: 'Après moi, le déluge' ['After me, the deluge']. *Déluge* is the book 'after me', a posthumous book, written after the self has ceased to be.

This cessation of the self is most insistently visible in the fact that, unusually in Cixous's corpus, a large proportion of *Déluge* is written in the third person. At the end of the first chapter, a complicated system with different diegetical layers is laid in place when the 'je' who initially assumed the narration withdraws, introducing a character to whom she hands over: 'Mon personnage s'appelle Clarice. Comme ce qui va lui arriver m'est inconnu et ne va pas m'arriver plus tard, je lui laisse la parole' ['My character's name is Clarice. As I don't know what is going to happen to her and it won't happen to me later, I will let her speak'] (18). The 'je' who speaks from the opening of the second chapter – '"Je cherche une porte, depuis des jours et des nuits, je cherche une porte ou une autre", disait-elle' ['"I have been looking for a door, for days and nights, I have been looking for one door or another", she said'] (21) – is thus presumably Clarice.[22] Occasionally, passages preceded by the italicised pronoun *Moi* [Me] return the narration to the opening 'je', as in the following example:

> Mais au fond je pense: Personne n'est innocent. Personne n'est coupable. Mais je ne sais pas l'expliquer. C'est seulement une vérité que je sens.
> (*Moi*: Clarice est innocente; et en même temps elle ne se laisse pas avoir; par rien.
> N.B.: L'expression: *ne pas se laisser avoir*. Et toutes les expressions avec *laisser*, voilà la signature (celle de Clarice). C'est une personne qui le plus souvent, *se laisse aller*. Et elle va.)

> *Clarice:*
> Mon espoir est de dire la vérité. Ses noms. (216)

> [But ultimately I think: Nobody is innocent. Nobody is guilty. But I cannot explain it. It's merely a truth I sense.
> (*Me*: Clarice is innocent; and at the same time she doesn't let herself be duped; by anything.
> N.B.: The expression: *not let oneself be duped*. And all expressions with *let*, that's her signature (Clarice's). She is someone who most often, *lets herself go*. And she goes.)

> *Clarice:*
> My hope is to tell the truth. Its names.]

However, while in this case the two narrative instances are clearly distinct, their separability is not always certain; for example it is impossible to decide when the 'je' returns the narration to Clarice after a similar interlude beginning on page 94. Their distinction is also made dubious by the earlier use, when 'je' introduced her character, of the same verb *laisser* – 'je lui laisse la parole' ['I will let her speak'] – which she here terms Clarice's 'signature' expression (indeed, the need for a parenthesis specifying that 'the' signature is that of Clarice is evidence of an uncertainty as to the distinction between them) and, especially, by the fact that, as in this quotation, Clarice too speaks/writes in the first person.

The diegetical organisation is further complicated when Clarice in turn gives way to Ascension, the principal character in the text. The passage where she decides to take on the name 'Ascension' makes clear that this name is a way of designating an *other* Clarice, a Clarice from the past:

– J'ai un problème: c'est le temps des verbes. Je ne peux pas dire 'je suis'. J'ai essayé 'j'étais'. Ce n'était pas plus vrai. La personne dont j'allais parler est un danger pour moi. J'étais elle pourtant, pas plus tard qu'hier, me semble-t-il, je notais tout à la première personne. Mais en ce moment, ici même où je veux entrer dans le livre, ce n'est pas ça, il y a rupture, surdité, il y a sécession, comme si plusieurs semaines avaient coulé cette nuit entre moi-même. [. . .] La difficulté exceptionnelle, c'est qu'il n'y a pas de présent pour le moment. [. . .]

– Et si vous disiez 'elle'? En attendant . . .

– Peut-être. Mais si c'est une elle, il faut trouver un nom qui ne m'éloigne pas. Presque tous les noms m'effarouchent. [. . .]

– Alors Ascension.

– Ascension!? Moi? Pourquoi pas 'Apparition'? (N.B.: Alors elle a ri. Le rire gai, voilé.)

– Vous avez bien appelé 'Virginia' un de vos personnages. Et malgré tout, elle m'est devenue familière, elle m'a touchée et moi aussi je l'ai touchée vivante. Je rêve d'une Ascension depuis trente ans.

– Soit. Cela ne l'empêchera pas de descendre. Mais jamais nom n'aura été si loin de mes possibilités. Mais les autres personnages, je garde leurs noms. David, Isaac, c'est eux. Maintenant je me tais. Je vais me retirer. (30–1)

[– I have a problem: the tense of verbs. I can't say 'I am'. I tried 'I was'. It wasn't any more true. The person I was going to speak of is a danger for me. Yet I was she, no later than yesterday, it seems, I noted everything in the first person. But at the moment, just here when I want to begin the book, it is no longer that, there is a break, deafness, there is a secession, as if several weeks had elapsed tonight between myself. [. . .] The enormous difficulty is that there is no present for the moment. [. . .]

– And if you said 'she'? While you are waiting . . .

– Maybe. But if it's a she, I will have to find a name that won't set me at a distance. Nearly all names scare me. [. . .]

– Then Ascension.

– Ascension!? Me? Why not 'Apparition'? (N.B.: Then she laughed. With a merry, veiled laugh.)

– You did call one of your characters 'Virginia'. And in spite of everything, she became close to me, she touched me and I in turn touched her alive. I have been dreaming of an Ascension for thirty years.

– So be it. It won't stop her from going down. But no name will ever have been so far from my possibilities. But I'm keeping the names of the other characters. David, Isaac, it is them. Now I will be quiet. I am going to withdraw.]

Clarice's declaration of silence following the introduction of Ascension and her use of the verb *se retirer* (withdraw), the same verb the first 'je' employed to describe her own eclipse (18), invite us to read her relationship to her character as a figure of the relationship of 'je' to Clarice. In other words, just as the use of the third person and a different name is a device enabling Clarice to continue her story about a self she no longer

is, so the introduction of Clarice can be considered a means of representing the self the 'je' she herself was, 'no later than yesterday'.[23]

The successive diegetical layers thus inscribe and repeat a chasm at the
level of the subject – a chasm which constitutes the subject – to which
the break-up has given rise, encapsulated in the unusual locution 'entre
moi-même' ['between myself'] and thematised sporadically elsewhere in
elements such as the coining of the word 'postvivre' ['postliving'] (35).
Furthermore, as the following quotation illustrates, this process of division does not stop with the split between Clarice and Ascension:

> *Ascension:*
> Je ne suis pas je. La rupture m'arrive à chaque page.
> *Ascension:*
> Alors, écris // rompu // me dis // je.
> En pièces. En rêves. En deux. En deuil. En dehors.
> *Ascension:*
> Côté jour en deuil. Mais côté nuit ailleurs.
> Où? Sous la nappe. En secret.
> Alors, écris en secret, me dis-je.
>
> Deuil et joie je ne coïncide pas. (41)

> [*Ascension:*
> I am not I. Breaking happens me on each page.
> *Ascension:*
> So, write // broken // I tell // myself.
> In pieces. In dreams. In two. In mourning. Outside.
> *Ascension:*
> Day side in mourning. But night side elsewhere.
> Where? Under the cloth. In secret.
> So, write in secret, I tell myself.
>
> Mourning and joy I do not coincide with myself.]

The 'rupture' Ascension asserts discursively is mirrored formally in the
syntax disjointed by the slashes and in the serial notation of the same
name where one would expect different characters. Ascension is clearly
not only mourning her beloved, appositely named David; she is in 'en
deuil' because she herself is 'en deux'.

Déluge, then, is a book of mourning for a dead self, in fact a murdered
self: it tells 'l'histoire d'un assassinat' ['the story of an assassination']
(32). This assassination is all the more terrible at one level in that 'la
femme, si assassinée qu'elle soit, ne meurt pas' ['the woman, however
assassinated she may be, does not die'] (33). The narrator[24] wonders if
the story is perhaps the ultimate tragedy, the 'tragédie des tragédies'
['tragedy of tragedies'], precisely because 'c'est une tragédie qui n'y

arrive pas. Qui n'arrive pas à son point de perfection. Finalement, il n'y a pas de scène. Je veux dire: elle n'a pas de théâtre' ['it's a tragedy that never gets there. That doesn't attain its point of perfection. Finally, there is no stage. I mean: no theatre'] (35–6). Death of the soul is in some sense *more* tragic than death of the body because it is not visible: 'De nos jours, quant à l'âme, rien n'est reconnu: ni maladie ni homicide. Comme si l'âme n'était pas le corps même du corps. Des millions et des millions d'assassinés n'ont jamais pu obtenir d'être reconnus comme tels, même par leurs mères, même par leurs enfants' ['In our days, when it's a matter of the soul, nothing is recognized: neither sickness nor homicide. As if the soul were not the very body of the body. Millions and millions of assassinated people never succeeded in being recognized as such, even by their mothers, even by their children'] (36). The tragedy thus appears compounded by its failure to achieve representation.

In a number of paratexts, Cixous similarly situates the tragic primarily in the lack of a witness to one's suffering. Tragedy is the absence of a 'we':

> Là où il n'y a pas de témoin. Nous-mêmes nous ne sommes pas nos propres témoins. Nous sommes sans nous. Sans Dieu. Dieu ne nous ayant pas suivi. Nous, étant dans l'abandon de Dieu. Le signe de ces scènes: même Dieu n'y arrive pas, même moi. C'est la tragédie selon Celan, selon Eschyle, la tragédie de personne, la tragédie selon Akhmatova.

> [There where there is no witness at all. We ourselves are not our own witnesses. We are without us. Without God. God not having followed us. We, being in the abandonment of God. The sign of these scenes: even God doesn't make it there, even I. This is tragedy according to Celan, according to Æschylus, the tragedy of no one, tragedy according to Akhmatova.][25]

Or, as Cixous will assert fifteen years later: 'The most incontestable example of the tragic, in my view, is *solitude*.'[26] The effect of the solitude is double, as she explains in another piece dating from the same period of *Déluge*. On the one hand, it means that one has nobody to weep with: 'Il y a un bonheur affreux dans les pleurs, dans certains pleurs, qui est lié au spectacle, à la représentation, au fait qu'il y a des témoins. On pleure devant témoins, en compagnie. On ne s'en rend pas compte puisqu'on souffre. Mais c'est quand même un bonheur. Le malheur, c'est personne avec qui pleurer' ['There is a frightful happiness in tears, in certain tears, which is connected to the theatre, to representation, to the fact that there are witnesses. One weeps in front of witnesses, in company. In a certain way, one is happy. One doesn't realize it because of the suffering. But it brings happiness just the same. Unhappiness is having no one to weep with'].[27] In addition, the absence of a witness makes suffering ridiculous: 'Une chose que j'ai troujours trouvée belle et terrible et intransposable: c'est à quel point les personnages de tragédie sont *à rire* – c'est-à-dire nous – quand ils sont sans public' ['Something that I've always found beautiful and terrible and untransposable: the degree to which the characters of tragedy are *laughable* – that is, to us – when they are without an audience'].[28] Adrian Poole notes the importance tragedies give to witnessing the other's pain: 'To us, the readers, spectators, and viewers, they are third persons, as we are to them, separated by the frame of fiction. Tragedies abound with bystanders, advisors, and counsellors.'[29] The fictional witnesses cannot remedy the characters' suffering, but at the level of the diegesis they can provide the stage whose absence aggravates Cixous's narrator's pain; within a play, they also offer a figure *en abyme* of the play's audience. No such witness soothes the character's pain in *Déluge*. Yet Cixous's theatrical metaphor serves to highlight the gap between the diegesis and the narrative: the very fact of telling a tragic story, even an unremittingly catastrophic one, supplies an audience at another level, outside the imaginary universe.

Within *Déluge*, then, the tragedy is that the tragedy does not end in representation, that the tragedy *does not end*: 'La douleur d'aujourd'hui, c'est de ne pas mourir quand mourir est la solution. Une tragédie qui ne finit pas, imaginez!' ['Pain today is not dying when dying is the solution. Imagine a tragedy that never ends!'] (35). Within the book's imaginary universe, the tragedy is unparalleled. From the beginning, the narrator announces that the break-up constitutes an apocalypse of unrivalled proportions: 'Dans mon histoire jamais femme n'aura connu pire douleur à cause de l'homme qu'elle aimait. Les larmes mouilleront ses vêtements jusqu'aux genoux et ses papiers tous les jours pendant bien des mois' ['In my story no woman will ever have known worse pain because of the man she loved. Tears will wet her clothes down to the knees and her papers every day for many a month'] (16). The book's title thus first bears reading in relation to the narrator's response to the disaster which befell her, as the flood of tears wept over the loss of the man she loved. But not only is a deluge itself a form of disaster, for Cixous it appears to figure the tragic disaster par excellence, in that calamity strikes in this form in two of her plays (*La Ville parjure* and *Tambours sur la digue*): 'There is something awful about floods because it is human beings that create them, and human beings are carried off by what they themselves have unleashed.'[30]

The idea that the tears the narrator weeps represent an event of the same order as the calamity that annihilated her chimes with the attempt, throughout the book, to understand the other's point of view. Unlike in

Cixous's plays, this tragedy is not a matter of injustice since, as the writer hypothesises elsewhere, in matters of love we are all both innocent and guilty:

> Comment, dans la scène privée, le bourreau – toi ou moi – se sent victime de la victime. Comment la victime est bourreau du bourreau. Ce qui rend très difficiles nos relations de persécutions amoureuses. Je pensais à la faute de la victime. Je pensais à la véritable tragédie qui est que la victime est coupable d'être victime. [. . .] Nous sommes tous des innocents coupables. Nous sommes coupables d'être innocents.

> [How, in private, the executioner – you or I – feels the victim of the victim. How the victim is the executioner of the executioner. Which makes our relations of persecution in love very difficult. I was thinking about the fault of the victim. I was thinking about the tragic truth that the victim is guilty of being victim. [. . .] We are all guilty innocents. We are guilty of being innocent.][31]

While tragedy typically 'presents situations in which there is a desperate urgency to assign blame',[32] the attempt to attribute responsibility unilaterally to one party when what is at issue is as obscure and complicated as one's affective attachments is more likely to create a scapegoat (the goat again) than to administer justice. In *Déluge*, the narrator displays an exceptional, rather saintly, willingness to comprehend that, from his point of view, David is as innocent as herself: 'finalement je ne sais jamais qui n'est pas victime, qui n'est pas meurtrier. [. . .] Le meurtre tue, mais cela n'empêche personne d'être innocent' ['in the end I never know who is not a victim, who not a murderer. [. . .] Murder kills, but that doesn't prevent anyone from being innocent'] (118). And to accept that, by causing him the 'mécontentement aigu du bourreau que la victimitude de la victime offense gravement' ['sharp unhappiness of the executioner gravely offended by the victim's victimhood'] (91), her own hurt is guilty of hurting him. She is at fault as well as him.

I shall come back later to the part the narrator may have played in causing the tragedy. Let us first note another image which invites us to consider the disaster more as a fatal accident than as an event timely action could perhaps have avoided. While the word 'désastre' (disaster) never appears in *Déluge*, the story is explicitly related to disaster in the literal sense of the word, evil star (*astre*), when the narrator compares it to the destruction of the dinosaurs following the impact of an asteroid:

> Mais du point de vue impersonnel ce que je suis en train d'écrire est l'histoire de la disparition des dinosaures. [. . .] La disparition a été instantanée: en deux ou trois milliers d'années, ils ont été effacés comme s'ils n'avaient jamais vécu, trois cents millions d'années ont été annulées et oubliées. Est-ce un

cataclysme ou est-ce une catastrophe? Selon moi ce fut un cataclysme: un jour d'automne une météorite colossale est tombée sur nous. [. . .]

La vie était difficile, mais il y avait des solutions. Jusqu'au jour où un astéroïde est tombé sur notre terre. Les dinosaures sont tombés avec l'astre. Eux si lents soudain frappés de précipitation. (159–61)

[But from an impersonal point of view what I am in the process of writing is the story of the disappearance of the dinosaurs. [. . .] The disappearance was instantaneous: in two or three thousand years, they were obliterated as if they had never lived, three hundred million years were nullified and forgotten. Is it a cataclysm or is it a catastrophe? According to me it was a cataclysm: one Autumn day a colossal meteorite fell down on us. [. . .]

Life was difficult, but there were solutions. Until the day when an asteroid fell on our earth. The dinosaurs fell with the star. Those who were so slow suddenly precipitated into haste.]

From an 'impersonal point of view', the tragedy was an act of God, just as in the grand scheme of things the two or three thousand years it took for the dinosaurs to die out completely represents a mere instant. 'Cataclysme' and 'catastrophe' are generally considered close synonyms for disaster in French as in English; both words are overdetermined with relevant connotations: the etymology of 'cataclysme', from the Greek *klusmos*, 'flood', links it to the eponymous deluge, while 'catastrophe' has the specifically theatrical meaning of the denouement of a tragedy, an ending prepared in advance by the plot. The distinction between the two words seems here to concern less the mode in which disaster struck than the time it took. This quotation echoes an earlier passage, where the difference of point of view between David and Ascension concerning the end of their relationship above all involves a temporal difference:

Mais selon David la fin est arrivée brutalement. Dix minutes avant, la vie continuait. Tout d'un coup dans la régularité, il y a eu un accident. Une pure singularité. [. . .] Un cataclysme.

D'un coup des dizaines d'années effacées.

Mais d'un autre point de vue on peut se demander si c'était vraiment un cataclysme; – si ce n'était pas plutôt une catastrophe. La fin avait peut-être commencé depuis quelque temps. (156–7)

[But according to David the end happened abruptly. Ten minutes previously, life was continuing. Suddenly in that regularity, there was an accident. A pure singularity. [. . .] Un cataclysme.

At one blow tens of years wiped out.

But from another point of view one can ask if it was really a cataclysm; – if it wasn't rather a catastrophe. The end had perhaps already begun for some time.]

For David, the disaster was a fortuitous act of God, a sudden accident, pure chance, whereas for the narrator, in retrospect it could have been foreseen. The difference constructed here between a 'cataclysme' and a 'catastrophe' is that in the latter case the ending is ongoing: it *takes time*.

From the beginning, the writing points to a cessation, an ending which is not final. 'C'était l'entredeux' ['It was the intervening period']: the first chapter title – repeated as the text's opening sentence/paragraph (11) – immediately signals that something is over, while at the same time situating *Déluge* in an intermediate rather than final time-space. Asserted *in medias res* with no indication of what the gap interrupted, it first calls to mind the 'entre-deux-guerres' or interwar period, a suggestion that finds corroboration later in the text when the narrator asserts: 'Ceci est un après. Mais après la bataille s'élève la bataille d'après la bataille, un cantique tremble dans le vent noir. [. . .] Et rien ne s'éloigne plus vite de la mémoire de notre chair que la peine de guerre' ['This is an afterwards. But after the battle rises the battle after the battle, a song trembles in the black wind. [. . .] And nothing recedes quicker from the memory of our flesh than the pain of war'] (32). The 'entredeux' thus evokes a gap between battles, a pause after death before the dying recommences. The repetition of 'deux' in the following sentence further assimilates the gap to a breakage, a violent end: 'le monde se divise sans cesse en deux camps, entre le Rhin et le Danube, s'il y a de l'amitié, elle se divise en deux, s'il y a une pierre, l'épée la brise en deux, sommes nous d'une nature, elle se tourne en deux' ['the world is endlessly divided into two camps, between the Rhine and the Danube, if there is friendship, it is divided in two, if there is a stone, the sword breaks it in two, if we are of one nature, it turns into two'] (11). Textual time is that of a disintegration which especially entails, as we have seen, the spiritual dissolution of the subject: 'Je en tronçons, entre deux l'âme se tord' ['I in sections, between the two the soul twists itself'] (25).

Yet insofar as the term 'entredeux' means an interval, it necessarily inscribes some sort of future.[33] The key question is whether this future is merely going to repeat the past, continue the dying, or whether it will bring about some form of rebirth. The claim that the story is one of unparalleled grief is followed by a concession: 'Dans mon histoire jamais femme n'aura connu pire douleur à cause de l'homme qu'elle aimait. Les larmes mouilleront ses vêtements jusqu'aux genoux et ses papiers tous les jours pendant bien des mois. *Mais il y aura la surprise*' ['In my story no woman will even have known worse pain because of the man she loved. Tears will wet her clothes down to the knees and her papers every day for many a month. *But there will be a surprise*'] (16). This warning – or rather the opposite of a warning, the notification of something positive to come – makes the story the inverse of the *Nibelungen* which, after Montaigne's *Essais*, are the first intertext explicitly mentioned,[34] and whose terrible beauty the narrator later attributes to the fact that from the beginning we are told that the 'grande joie' ['great joy'] the characters look forward to experiencing 'va être changée, malgré nous malgré nous en la grande douleur' ['is going to be changed, in spite of us in spite of us into a great suffering'] (95). From the beginning of *Déluge*, we know that however tragic the narrator's story is, it has another aspect. It is *more than tragic* both in that it is tragic in the extreme and in that it is non-tragic: 'Oui, mais ce livre ne va pas être une simple tragédie. Parce que, d'un autre côté, – il y a la joie. Oui. Je sais déjà des choses que le Récit m'a laissé entendre' ['Yes, but this book is not going to be a simple tragedy. Because, on the one hand, – there is joy. Yes. I already know things that the Narrative let me understand'] (32). Furthermore, it is specifically because of this 'joie' that the protagonist, 'however assassinated she may be', does not die (33). Let us recall here that the series of 'Ascensions' reflected a discontinuity within the narrative instance both diachronically and synchronically: 'Deuil et joie je ne coïncide pas' (41). Ascension is torn not only between the self she was and the self she is, but between grief and joy at the one time. *Déluge* is the story of a *deuil-joie* as well as of a *deuil-je*.

Intervening Joy

Bearing this in mind, the text's opening 'entredeux' appears considerably more complex than a respite between two phases of a disaster. At issue is not that the disaster has not yet ended in tragedy, but rather that it *has already* done so, already brought about the annihilation or 'assassination' of the principal character. The 'entredeux' in which Clarice finds herself confronted with the dilemma concerning the tense of the verbs is a posthumous time, after death but before rebirth: 'La difficulté exceptionnelle, c'est qu'il n'y a pas de présent pour le moment. Je piétine du rien. C'est une fissure dans ma vie, entre fin et résurrection, moment tordu, inhabitable, où brutalement l'air n'arrive pas. [. . .] Six mois, un an, deux ans, inexister' ['The exceptional difficulty is that there is no present for the moment. I am trudging along on nothing. It's a gap in my life, between end and resurrection, an uninhabitable, twisted moment, where brutally no air gets through. [. . .] Six months, a year, two years, inexisting'] (30). Whereas in conventional tragedy the focus of the audience's suspense is on whether the end will come, *Déluge* leaves its reader wondering whether a new beginning will come, that is whether this intermediate time of non-existence will give way to a time when a future will again be possible. Paradoxically, this 'in-between time' is pure time, time as duration. It is the antithesis of the miraculous 'instant' Cixous eulogised, for example, at the end of *Jours de l'an*; it is time unrelieved by the timelessness experienced at moments of joy:

> Le temps de ces années d'entre-temps, je le connais, il est lent lourd épais goutte à goutte, entre chaque goutte un arrêt, tout le contraire de cet air gai, frais, sans durée que nous respirons quand nous ne sommes pas blessés. Dans la tragédie il n'y a que du temps. [. . .] Dans la joie, nous sommes délivrés des nombres, des dates, deux font un, un est tout, pas de calcul, pas de numéro nulle part, tout est légèreté sans division
> Il n'y a pas le Temps. [. . .]
> Dans la tragédie les années passent, le temps reste, toujours aussi pesant. (94)

> [I know the time of these between-time years, it is slow heavy thick drop by drop, between each drop a stop, the very contrary of the bright, fresh air without duration we breathe when we are not wounded. In tragedy there is only time. [. . .] In joy, we are freed from numbers, dates, two make one, one is all, no calculation, no number anywhere, all is lightness with no division
> There is no Time. [. . .]
> In tragedy years pass, time remains, always as heavy.]

At a structural level, the 'entredeux', the textual time of *Déluge*, is thus the time of all tragedy, the intermediate time between an initial misfortune and the final outcome, a time during which time itself weighs heavily.[35] However, it is markedly different from the teleological time of classical tragedy in which the timeline is unified by a clear causality, in accordance with Aristotle's rule that 'well-constructed plots must neither begin nor end in a haphazard way'.[36] 'Goutte à goutte, entre chaque goutte un arrêt': just as the 'entredeux' is cut off from the time before and after it, so its constituent moments are unrelated. Hence the impossibility of voluntarily determining how long this time of duration must be endured: 'personne ne peut passer de l'entredeux au temps suivant consciemment. Il faut s'échapper' ['nobody can pass consciously from the intervening period to the following time. Escaping is the only way'] (53).

This is not to suggest that there is no agency involved in this 'escaping' from time spent merely marking time. On the contrary, *Déluge* can be read as a sustained effort to 'laisser la mort derrière soi' ['leave death behind one'] (171). The death in question involves the hurt the victim continues to cause herself in the wake of her desertion as much as that inflicted by her forsaker; Cixous focuses attention above all on the need for the narrator to stop being her own 'executioner', as metaphorised for example in her inability to eat the fish she loved. As the paronymy in French between 'poisson' (fish; 51) and 'poison' (68) further suggests, the narrator has difficulty nurturing herself following the blow of the separation; after the other's 'assassinat' comes

> l'auto-assassinat, pas le suicide, l'assassinat obligatoire de soi-même, comment cela s'appelle ce qui vient après l'amour, cet innommable qui est de l'amour coupé avec les propres dents, amour déchet, amour pourri asphyxié, étranglement d'amour, langue énorme et durcie, douleur durcie farcie, et qui n'est pas la haine, qui n'arrive pas à cette santé-là, qui est le cadavre d'amour pas enterré jamais enterré (169)

> [the auto-assassination, not suicide, the obligatory assassination of oneself, what to call what comes after love, the unnameable which is love cut with its own teeth, love waste, rotten asphyxiated love, the strangling of love, an enormous hardened language, a hardened stuffed pain, that isn't hatred, that doesn't attain that particular health, that is the unburied never buried corpse of love]

The 'entredeux' is thus also the time during which the narrator is trapped without the ability to give life to herself, 'entre fin et résurrection'.

The time of *Déluge*, then, hovers less between two deaths than between fatality and vitality. The crucial difference between the narrator and the dinosaurs is precisely that the outcome of the 'entredeux' – extinction, in the case of the latter – is not yet decided in her case. *Déluge* is a story of dying embers: 'Des années des dizaines d'années après la fin, l'amour mort demeure dans l'entredeux et fait des braises. Tout à coup, d'un jour à l'autre c'est une cendre, un vieux vent l'envoie se mêler à l'anonyme cendre universelle. Ici finit le mien' ['Years tens of years after the end, the dead love remains in the interval and makes embers. Suddenly, from one day to another it's ashes, an old wind sends it off to mingle with the anonymous universal ash. Here ends mine'] (27). Embers, as distinct from ashes, can be reignited. Similarly, the mere fact of not yet being dead *and buried* means necessarily that the drive to live subsists:

> Mais Freud a dit que la libido veut vivre malgré tout malgré tout malgré tout malgré rien malgré nous.
> Ce qui était démontré pour l'instant par le fait qu'elle n'était pas morte, et malgré tout elle se mourait, mais tout en mourant seulement n'était pas morte, c'était à cause de la libido. (81)

> [But Freud said that the libido wants to live in spite of everything in spite of everything in spite of everything in spite of nothing in spite of us.

Which was shown for the moment by the fact that she was not died, and in spite of everything she was dying, but while only dying was not dead, it was because of libido.]

Or, to adapt Cicero's maxim: while there is dying, there is life. In the 'entredeux', this time of pure time, time devoid of all eternity, there is still time for life to begin again, for her libido to reassert itself: *there is still time*.

This is true of all tragedy, whose action concerns the intermediate time we have seen to be that of narrative itself, the time before the final ending. The difference in *Déluge* is that the catastrophe comes at the beginning rather than the end. If Cixous's text helps us to explore the nature of tragedy, it is precisely because it opens up a difference between a story that may initially progress tragically but where a turn of events leads to a happy ending (a story which wouldn't be a tragedy, a 'non-tragedy'), and one where the tragic and the 'comic' are entwined from the beginning. Rather than tragedy marking the end of life, for Cixous tragedy is an integral part of life: as the narrator says, 'le déluge est notre condition, mais il n'est pas notre fin' ['the deluge is our condition, but it is not our end'] (177). This idea of tragedy as an integral part of life rather than something opposed to it is at the heart of a generous, non-judgmental conception of the human condition as a situation where not only 'vivre et mourir' ['living and dying'] are 'enchevêtrés', entwined, but where 'la *même* personne est un enchevêtrement, l'enchevêtrement règne, tous nous sommes enchevêtrés, nous-mêmes avec nous-mêmes, les uns avec les autres' ['the *same* person is an entwining, entwining reigns, we are all entwined, ourselves with ourselves, each with each other'] (40), each of us at once betrayer and betrayed, perpetrator as well as victim of violence.

At the end of Cixous's text, life unequivocally prevails over death; the last sections are punctuated by a series of statements indicative of a new beginning: 'Elle approchait de la douce impersonnalité. Fin de la tragédie' ['She was approaching sweet impersonality. End of the tragedy'] (174), 'Elle avait cessé de mourir' ['She had ceased dying'] (221), 'Aujourd'hui, c'est le futur?' ['Today is the future?'] (227).[37] As well as Ascension's victimhood, the closing pages thus bring the 'entredeux' to a close. However, it would be a mistake to read the 'entredeux', the time of Ascension's efforts to stop being 'cette propre ennemie de soi-même qu'une personne atteinte de trahison devient' ['the enemy of oneself that someone affected by betrayal becomes'] (58), simply as a time before rebirth, that is *before* joy: 'Une joie c'est ça: notre besoin de faire-part de notre naissance au monde' ['A joy is that: our need to announce our birth to the world'] (86).

For, relatively early in the book, the narrator asserts: 'Non, non ceci n'est pas un livre sur la trahison. C'est un livre sur la joie. Qui se sauve' ['No, no, this is not a book about betrayal. It is a book about joy. That escapes'] (59). The detachment of the final clause in a separate sentence creates an amphibology, making both 'livre' and 'joie' possible subjects of the verb *se sauver* (a verb which itself associates salvation with the flight or escape necessary to leave the 'entredeux' behind: 'Il faut s'échapper'). But most important of all is the use of the present tense. In effect, the book (the 'entredeux') is *already* punctuated by joyful moments: Ascension's pleasure of momentarily forgetting her grief while noticing three swallows (whose association with the spring in itself thematises a rebirth) (58), the 'cadeau' or 'grâce' or 'chance' represented by a dream (85), the 'chance' again which befalls her 'dans les collines aux trois rocs' ['in the hills with three rocks'] when, in a landscape reminiscent of the Three-Rock Mountain of the Wicklow hills, a lamb's suckling its mother in an 'orgie de lait' ['orgy of milk'] transports her to a time 'd'avant nos haines et nos trahisons' ['before our hatreds and our betrayals'], a space where 'il n'y avait pas [. . .] d'autre ennemi que la mort' ['there was [. . .] no other enemy than death'] (179–80). If *Déluge* is 'un livre sur la joie', it is because the 'entredeux' is *already* a time of (intermittent) joy. The difference between it and the *Nibelungen* is not so much that in the latter joy gives way to tragedy whereas in the other tragedy gives way to joy; it is rather that in *Déluge* 'deuil' and 'joie' are intertwined to such an extent that which of them will prevail hangs in the balance:

> Le ciel est lourd sur le pays des Nibelungen. Mais dans ce livre-ci, on ne sait pas qui va être sauvé qui ne va pas être sauvé, à quelle heure. On souffre d'impatience, mais il y a une chance, il y a de l'air et des chants; il y a des taxis et du Secret.
> [. . .] Deuil et joie vont comme deux amis ne se séparant jamais, hormis dans un seul combat à la fin. On ne sait pas qui alors l'emportera. (94–5)

> [The sky is heavy over the country of the Nibelungen. But in this book, one doesn't know who will be saved, who will not be saved, at what time. One suffers impatiently, but there is a chance, there is some air and some songs; there are taxis and a Secret.
> [. . .] Mourning and joy go like two friends never separating, other than in a single combat at the end. One doesn't know who will then prevail.]

Notwithstanding the relatively small proportion of the text for which it accounts in *quantitative* terms, the central focus in *Déluge* is the interruption of the interruption, the intermittent joy which, by dint of the narrator's painful struggle, punctuates what she is determined will be only an interstitial 'entredeux' in her existence.

Writing the End of Tragedy

'Il y a une chance, il y a de l'air et des chants': *chance* (which in French, in addition to its paronymy with 'chants' (songs), means luck as well as hazard), is a key signifier in *Déluge*. Joy is a matter of chance,[38] something explicitly ruled out of Aristotle's notion of a well-constructed tragic plot. In particular, the narrator, striving to accept the cataclysmic upheaval in her life without recrimination, attributes to chance the abrupt change of identity in David in which (from his point of view) the cataclysm originated: 'C'est l'histoire d'un homme appelé David, toute sa vie David, et tout d'un coup l'homme va dire: nous nous sommes tous trompés. J'étais Hans. Si incroyable que cela soit, c'est Hans' ['It is the story of a man named David, all his life David, and suddenly the man will say: we were all mistaken. I was Hans. However incredible it may be, it was Hans'] (33). The anacoluthic shift in both pronoun and tense draws attention to the last clause. 'C'est Hans', 'C-Hans', 'C-hance': the aleatory (and therefore ultimately non-condemnable) nature of David's metamorphosis into Hans is subsequently corroborated by the narrator's wondering if David 'aura été un accident de Hans' ['will have been an accident of Hans'] (39). 'Chance' thus links in to a textual chain inscribing the narrator's efforts to see the break up which had such tragic consequences for her from David's point of view, that is as due to 'chance' rather than 'méchanceté' (unkindness or nastiness).[39] But as the association between joy and chance in the above examples reveals (and as the paronomasia between 'chance' and 'chants' in the previous quotation further accentuates), 'chance' is above all associated with the joyful interludes in the narrator's grief. Indeed, in a key passage, the name 'Chance' is explicitly given to the unexpected manifestation of a joyful 'éternité', in an astonishing prosopopœia whose own animation of the inanimate heralds its revitalising, restorative function:

> (*On entend la joyeuse petite trompe de l'éternité. Et elle entre.*)
> La voici, le personnage insaisissable de cette histoire. La Chance d'Ascension.
> C'est bien elle,
> Voici qu'elle arrive, le personnage-surprise de cette histoire, l'héroïne est en soie bleu sombre, les cheveux tendres, les vêtements, la voix qui rappelle au jour, tout en soie. (72)

> [(*The joyful little trumpet of eternity is heard. And she enters.*)
> There she is, the elusive character of this story. Ascension's Chance.
> It is indeed she,
> Here she comes, the surprise-character of this story, the heroine is in dark blue silk, her hair soft, her clothes, the voice recalling the day, all in silk.]

As 'heroine' of the story, Ascension's 'Chance' is necessarily of central importance; however, as a 'personnage insaisissable', a 'personnage-surprise', it is elusive, difficult to bring into focus. In effect, the pros-opopœia serves to focus attention on the difficulty of bringing such a 'personnage' into focus. This character remains 'insaisissable': is it a metaphor for Ascension herself, as the terms 'personnage' and 'héroïne' might suggest, or a quality or property associated with Ascension in a more metonymical relation of contiguity? Is it feminine, as the repeated use of feminine pronouns and nouns ('elle entre', 'la voici', 'c'est bien elle', 'elle arrive', 'héroïne') to describe an otherwise masculine 'person-nage' highlights, or is the marked discrepancy between masculine and feminine a reflection of an uncertainty in its gender? In particular, is it the heroine *although* or rather *because* it is elusive and unpredictable? Is the 'Chance' which can save Ascension precisely that of having a secret existence which manifests itself only indirectly, unexpectedly, as for example in dreams – or in writing?

These same questions arise in relation to the other dramatic personi-fication in *Déluge*, the astonishing characterisation of writing itself as 'Isaac': 'J'aime. "Isaac": c'est le nom que j'ai donné à mon amour, pour qu'il ait un nom. Parce que si je dis simplement j'aime "écrire", ce n'est pas ça. C'est un tel mystère' ['I love. "Isaac": it's the name I gave my love, so that it would have a name. Because if I simply say I love "writing", it's not that. It's such a mystery'] (134). Mireille Calle-Gruber has highlighted what an extraordinary gesture this constitutes: 'Je ne connais pas de coup d'écriture de cet ordre-là: qui concrétise en relation amoureuse, passionnelle, ce qui nous dépasse et qui est désir, pulsion d'écriture' ['I do not know a stroke of writing of that order: that takes what goes beyond us and which is a desire, a drive to write, and makes it concrete in a relationship of love, of passion'].[40] Cixous explains that the personification is motivated by the question of 'la présence de l'écriture vécue comme tiers: du fait que quelqu'un écrit et de ce que cette présence entraîne comme conséquences dans les rela-tions interpersonnelles' ['the presence of writing experienced as a third party: of the fact that someone writes and of the consequences that presence leads to in interpersonal relations'].[41] While any pursuit not shared by both people in a couple can give rise to jealously or a feeling of exclusion, the fact that the 'elsewhere' of artistic creation is a space of intense pleasure can strain a relationship to the utmost. In *Déluge*, the narrator comes to wonder if, in fact, the treasured resource that writing represents, the sense of an inviolable inner core it endowed her with, was not also to blame for the break up. David's departure was such a cataclysmic bolt from the blue because she had never 'été effleurée par l'idée d'être abandonnée, occupée qu'elle était par l'idée inverse' ['the thought of being abandoned had never even crossed her mind, she was so taken up with the opposite idea'] (122). She realises that while she had no doubt he would be devastated if she left him, she may never have granted him the reassurance that she could not live without him. In contrast, she had expressed how absolutely necessary Isaac was to her existence: 'Une fois, il y a longtemps, elle s'était dit tout d'un coup qu'elle ne pourrait plus jamais vivre sans Isaac' ['Once, long ago, she had suddenly thought that she could no longer live without Isaac'] (130). What seemed to her a 'cataclysme' might, in effect, be rather a 'catastrophe', its seeds sown in advance, insofar as the existence of Isaac prevented anybody else from feeling able to fill the world for her. Her 'fault' was that she did not make David feel he was indispensable: 'Mais parfois, tristement, baissant la tête, elle craignait: "s'il n'y avait pas toujours eu Isaac pour me tirer du feu à la dernière minute, me serais-je laissée anéantir par un David? [. . .] Ai-je privé David de mon néant?"' ['But sometimes, sadly, lowering her head, she feared: "if there had not always been Isaac to rescue me from the fire at the last minute, might I have allowed a David to annihilate me? [. . .] Did I deprive David of my destruction?"'] (141).

However, if writing cost her David, it was also the chance that enabled her to survive him: 'J'ai besoin d'isaac pour supporter david' ['I need isaac to be able to bear david'] (141). Numerous indications in the text invite us to make a connection between Isaac and 'la Chance d'Ascension'. The lead-up to his introduction in the chapter 'Sous la nappe' is presented as a return to Ascension's 'secret': 'Comme je l'ai dit il y a des dizaines et des dizaines de pages, Ascension a un – secret' ['As I said tens and tens of pages ago, Ascension has a – secret'] (130). More importantly, he too is an extraneous source of joy: 'Je cherchais à: joie. Et j'ai entendu: Isaac. Pour me sentir vivre, pour me vivre vivant, j'ai besoin de parler à Isaac, et de m'entendre parler' ['I looked under: joy. And I heard: Isaac. To feel myself live, to live myself as living, I need to talk to Isaac, and to hear myself talk'] (134). The description of his appearance in response to the narrator's prayers furthermore echoes that of Ascension's 'Chance' in a number of important respects. Isaac is directly compared to 'chance' in that his arrival cannot be voluntarily decided, can only be gratefully accepted:

> Ce jour-là cet Isaac, celui qui arrive, s'est manifesté comme la chance même. C'était la chance. C'est d'une telle simplicité qu'on ne peut pas le raconter. On voit ce qu'on a peut-être rêvé, mais rêvé comme rêve, pour vivre en rêve et jouer en rêve. Et soudain, c'est la réalité. En plein milieu du rêve, une île dans un océan de rêves, et c'est la terre. C'est elle. C'est lui. C'est la réalité. Mais la

réalité aux traits parfaits, comme dans le rêve. La chance c'est ça. La chance arrive. Nous regarde. On se voit. (148)

[That day this Isaac, the one who arrives, appeared like chance itself. It was chance. It's so simple one can't recount it. One sees what one has perhaps dreamed of, but dreamed like a dream, to live in a dream and play in a dream. And suddenly, it's reality. In the very middle of the dream, an island in an ocean of dreams, there is land. It's she. It's he. It's reality. But reality with perfect features, as in a dream. That is chance. Chance happens. Concerns us. One sees oneself.]

Furthermore, not only is 'his' gender uncertain – as is audible here in 'une île', in addition to the juxtaposition 'C'est elle. C'est lui' – but also his status as a character:[42]

Mais voilà: Isaac n'est personne. Il est le nom propre de sa moitié mystérieuse; ou le nom de son existence; ou bien le nom de son pays personnel ou
   Isaac est Ascension?
   Plus loin.
   Homme ou Femme? Alors là vraiment, qui peut répondre? Isaac est toute la différence intérieure d'Ascension. Mais la propre différence d'Ascension varie au contact de la différence intérieure des gens. (136)

[But there it is: Isaac is nobody. He is the proper name of her mysterious half; or the name of her existence; or the name of her personal country or
   Isaac is Ascension?
   Further.
   Man or Woman? Now there truly, who can respond? Isaac is all Ascension's inner difference. But Ascension's own difference varies with the contact of people's inner difference.]

Isaac 'n'est personne', is nobody/not a person, yet the possibility of confusing him with Ascension suggests some degree of anthropomorphic comparability. And, just as Ascension's 'Chance' was elusive, Isaac names some-(one? thing? time? place?) indefinable, impossible to pin down, her *shifting* 'inner difference'. Both 'la Chance d'Ascension' and 'Isaac' can thus be read as provisional names for a secret force, a joyful source, which forms a hidden dimension to Ascension's existence and whose elusive nature is further conveyed by the shift from the (predominantly feminine) one to the (predominantly masculine) other.[43]

Writing, then, appears to function as a privileged example of the joyful intervention – literally, coming *between* – necessary for the narrator to 'passer de l'entredeux au temps suivant'. Writing is a mode of accessing, or being transported to – we may note that the 'taxi' which was another source of joy contains all the sounds of 'Isaac' – a secret 'source', a word which in French has the additional meaning of a spring of fresh water, the image par excellence of a life-enhancing rather than a catastrophic flow of water:

> il suffisait pour cela qu'Ascension se rende dans l'autre galaxie, l'éternelle et nouvelle, dans le Secret. Comment nous passons du brasier à la source: l'âme décide entièrement des blessures et des guérisons. Quand la fin est proche, il y a toujours la force cachée, le modeste logis à la frontière du néant. Là sont gardés le gâteau, le papier, le secours du Récit, le secret de l'ange, la lumière qui ne s'éteint pas, le temps qui ne rouille pas. Là jaillit la parole qui dit toujours: oui. (82)

> [for that, it was enough for Ascension to go to the other galaxy, the eternal and new one, in the Secret. How we pass from the fire to the spring: the soul decides entirely on wounds and healings. When the end is near, there is always the hidden force, the modest lodging at the border of nothingness. There are kept the cake, paper and succour of the Narrative, the angel's secret, the light that doesn't go out, time that doesn't rust. There springs forth the word that always says: yes.]

'La parole qui dit toujours: oui': writing is inherently affirmative. In particular, *narrative* ('le Récit') has a secret power, the power of the secret. Narrative creates a time in which time can be preserved, an unending resource with which to withstand the tragedy of life. At the beginning of the book, we saw that the tragedy seemed all the worse in that it lacked a 'scene', a 'theatre'. This hymn to the hidden yet inexhaustible resources of the 'Récit' already invites us to interpret the more positive ending of *Déluge* as due, at least in part, to the telling of the story. The book's final pages corroborate the idea that the representation of the 'entredeux' helps to bring it to an end, that writing a tragedy helps to perform the end of the tragedy, and thereby to perform the beginning of something else. At the end, Cixous returns to the analogy between the dinosaurs and Ascension:

> Un jour l'astre tombe sur la terre. Tout de suite après la chute, le présent est terriblement long. Mais plus tard trois cent millions d'années entreront dans quelques pages. Pendant que je l'écris cette histoire est en train de passer. [. . .]
>   Pendant que je l'écris, ce livre, déjà, ce n'est plus lui? C'est peut-être déjà 'plus tard'?
>   N.B.: En vitesse: Hier – chaleur étouffante – une gare – imminence, accélération. A travers les vitres je vois D. d'un côté, A. de l'autre. Dehors il pleut. Je voyais double. [. . .] Il entrait. Le même. Il s'asseyait en face d'Ascension. Comme si c'était lui. Comme si c'était elle. C'était lui. C'était elle. Je voyais. Ce n'était pas lui. Ce n'était pas elle. Je voyais les deux en même temps. Les vitres étaient à l'intérieur. Il pleuvait. Ascension ne pleurait pas. C'était le déluge. A l'intérieur. Entre nous le déluge. L'eau tombait avec un fracas

assourdissant. On n'entendait que le déluge, musique dure, faite seulement pour remplir l'énormité du silence avec des flots de pierre et de rochers. (225)

[One day the star falls to earth. Immediately after the fall, the present is terribly long. But later three hundred million years will go in a few pages. While I am writing it, this story is passing. [. . .]

While I am writing it, the book already is no longer it? It is perhaps already 'later'?

N.B.: Quickly: Yesterday – stifling heat – a station – imminence, acceleration. Through the windows I see D. on one side, A. on the other. Outside it is raining. I was seeing double. [. . .] He was going in. The same. He was sitting down opposite Ascension. As if it was him. As if it was her. It was him. It was her. I could see. It wasn't him. It wasn't her. I could see both at the same time. The windows were inside. It was raining. Ascension was not crying. It was the deluge. Inside. Between us the deluge. The water fell with a deafening din. All that could be heard was the deluge, a hard music, made only to fill the enormousness of the silence with floods of stone and rocks.]

'Pendant que je l'écris cette histoire est en train de passer': the time of writing is the time it takes to *tell a story*, to move the story on to a new present where, happily, both David and Ascension are still alive, although no longer the same people they were before. 'Après moi le déluge' has given place to 'entre nous le déluge': the deluge which originally destroyed the 'nous' now paradoxically enables a link between them, converting the 'entredeux' into an 'entre nous'.[44] And, crucially, accepting that 'nous' marks the separation of 'tu' and 'je' rather than their union, that 'nous' exists only disjointedly, visible only with 'double' vision, allows a future finally to begin again for the 'je': 'Aujourd'hui c'est le futur? Déjà?' ['Today is the future? Already?'] (227). The end of the book reclimbs the diegetical layers of the beginning: Clarice, specified as the narrator of this passage, finally gives way to 'Moi' for the text's concluding paragraphs.

Telling the tragedy has therefore played a vital role in *Déluge*: vital both in the sense of necessary, essential, and in the sense of revitalising, bringing the victim back to life. As such, tragedy appears to have an effect on the narrator analogous in many respects to the cathartic effect Aristotle famously defined tragedy as having on the spectator. But what of Cixous's *reader*? To consider the question most often associated with tragedy: what kind of pleasure does the reader derive from this book which is not only a tragedy, which is more than a tragedy? Ascension's rebirth at the end of the text is described as that of a 'femme ayant échappé physiquement à l'attraction tragique' ['woman having physically escaped from the attraction of tragedy'] (226): what does this tragic attraction consist of, and does the fact that tragedy does not finally prevail take away from its enjoyment?

With respect to the reader's pleasure, Cixous appears comparatively close to Nietzsche's idea that the audience finds in tragedy a way to embrace the depths of human suffering without being overwhelmed. For Cixous, the tragic story has a similarly mediating function; the narrative helps the reader to take cognisance of, and indeed *enjoy*, the painful underside of life:

> Pourquoi nous avertir, si nous n'y pouvons rien? nous plaignons-nous. C'est pour que vous pleuriez plus et mieux et plus longtemps, dit le Récit, afin que sous les pluies de larmes poussent les bancs de fleurs qui fêteront l'éclat du sang. De quoi vous plaignez-vous? Je ne vous trompe pas. Je vous donne à pleurer. C'est une riche joie. [. . .]
>
> Moi, le Récit, je vous donne le temps, je ne vous l'ôte pas, j'ouvre par mes paroles le livre de la mort; et à la Mort aussi je donne le temps vivant, ce temps qu'elle n'a jamais; je vous donne la mort à goûter à mourir [. . .] c'est une chance unique, celle de pouvoir s'adonner en entier, en toute certitude, de toutes nos forces, à la fête du regret. (96)

> [Why warn us, if we can't do anything about it? we complain. It's so that you will cry more and better and longer, says the Narrative, so that under the showers of tears will grow banks of flowers celebrating the glory of blood. What are you complaining of? I am not deceiving you. I am giving you something to cry about. It is a rich joy. [. . .]
>
> I, the Narrative, give you time, I don't take it away from you, by my words I open the book of death; and I also give Death living time, the time it never has; I give you death to taste to die for [. . .] it is a unique chance, to be able to give oneself wholly, in all certainty, with all our strengths, to the feast of regret.]

Narrative is the *space of time*; it gives us: time. Telling a tragic story means that the deluge of tears can make flowers grow, that bloody death produces joy. 'Je vous *donne* à pleurer', 'je vous *donne* le temps', 'je *donne* le temps vivant', 'je vous *donne* la mort à goûter à mourir': time and death itself – the very stuff of tragedy – are gifts to be savoured as well as suffered. The *amor fati* the narrator aspires to achieve – 'vienne un Amor Fati, oui à la violence sonne l'Amor Fati' ['let an Amor Fati come, yes let the Amor Fati sound out to violence'] (42) – will not enable the narrator to escape from tragedy; on the contrary, it finds its supreme home in tragedy. Tragedy affirms life in all its dimensions, including its darkest underside.

The tragic attraction of *Déluge* is therefore the attraction of tragedy in general. Embracing tragedy as part of life, the book gives its reader the pleasure of tasting the abyss, of vicariously experiencing disaster, of affirming profound suffering as an inalienable part of life. It can be argued to be *more* than a tragedy in this respect, in that it is motivated by a vital principle. Note, however, that Cixous's text invites us pre-cisely to envisage that the same is true more generally: to the extent that the impulse to tell a tragic story originates in 'an affirmative instinct for life', to quote Nietzsche's phrase again, all tragedy is more than a tragedy.

But there is another, more distinctive, sense in which *Déluge* is more than a tragedy. As we have seen, it is not merely at the end of the book that the narrator escapes the 'attraction tragique'. *From the outset*, the narrator's focus is on arduously carving out, and therefore creating, space for moments of joy. This book sets itself apart from most tragedies in that it succeeds in opening the telling of a tragic story to the possibility that the worst will be interrupted. In other words, even at the level of the diegesis in which suffering is given its full due, death is not allowed to divorce itself from life. The writing of *Déluge* is marked by a profound resolution that the vital instinct should prevail. It exemplarily illustrates how, even in the darkest throes of agony, Cixous's writing is rooted in the attempt to foster life.

Notes

1. 'Enter the Theatre', 26.
2. Kathleen O'Grady, 'Guardian of Language: An Interview with Hélène Cixous', *Women's education des femmes*, 12:4 (Winter 1996–7), 6–10; available online at http://bailiwick.lib.uiowa.edu/wstudies/cixous/, con-sulted 17 September 2013.
3. Adrian Poole, *Tragedy: A Very Short Introduction* (Oxford: Oxford University Press, 2005), 3. For other recent accounts of tragedy and the tragic, see A.D. Nuttall, *Why Does Tragedy Give Pleasure?* (Oxford: Oxford University Press, 1996); Peter Szondi, *An Essay on the Tragic*, trans. Paul Fleming (Stanford: Stanford University Press, 2002); Terry Eagleton, *Sweet Violence: The Idea of the Tragic* (Oxford: Blackwell, 2003); and Jennifer Wallace, *The Cambridge Introduction to Tragedy* (Cambridge: Cambridge University Press, 2007). George Steiner reconsid-ers his classic *The Death of Tragedy* (Oxford: Oxford University Press, 1961) forty years later in '"Tragedy", Reconsidered,' *New Literary History*, 35:1 (2004), 1–15.
4. Hélène Cixous, *L'Histoire terrible mais inachevée de Norodom Sihanouk, Roi du Cambodge*, Nouvelle édition revue et corrigée (Paris: Théâtre du Soleil, 1987) [*The Terrible But Unfinished Story of Norodom Sihanouk, King of Cambodia*, trans. Juliet Flower MacCannell, Judith Pike and Lollie Groth (Lincoln, NE: University of Nebraska Press, 1994)]; *L'Indiade ou l'Inde de leurs rêves et quelques écrits sur le théâtre* (Paris: Théâtre du Soleil, 1987) [*The Indiad, or The India of Their Dreams*]; *La Ville parjure ou le réveil des Erinyes*, Nouvelle édition revue et augmentée (Paris: Théâtre du Soleil, 2010) [*The Perjured City, Or the Awakening of the Furies*, trans.

Bernadette Fort, *Selected Plays of Hélène Cixous*, ed. Eric Prenowitz (London and New York: Routledge, 2004)].

5. Hélène Cixous, *Tambours sur la digue* [*Drums on the Dyke*] (Paris: Théâtre du Soleil, 1999).

6. Hélène Cixous and Bernadette Fort, 'Theater, History, Ethics: An Interview with Hélène Cixous on "The Perjured City, or the Awakening of the Furies"', *New Literary History*, 28:3 (Summer 1997), 425–56, at 428.

7. Ibid., 450.

8. Ibid., 449.

9. Sihanouk's description of Cambodia as 'this other Eden, this demi-paradise, c'est nous, this happy breed of men, this little world, this blessed plot, cette forteresse que s'est bâtie la Nature contre la contagion du monde et le bras de la guerre, cet ANGKOR, c'est nous!' (57) is a direct borrowing from John of Gaunt's lamentation on the state of England ('ANGleterre', in French) under Richard (*Richard II*, 2.i.724–32). For Cixous's borrowing from Shakespeare, see also Catherine Franke and Roger Chazal, 'Interview with Hélène Cixous', *Qui parle*, 3:1 (1989), 152–79.

10. 'Auteur au Théâtre du Soleil: Entretien avec Hélène Cixous', http://www. theatre-du-soleil.fr/thsol/IMG/pdf/Auteur_au_Theatre_du_soleil.pdf; 'On Theatre: An Interview with Hélène Cixous', in *Selected Plays of Hélène Cixous*, ed. Eric Prenowitz (London: Routledge, 2004), 25–34 (13 and 14).

11. 'Auteur au Théâtre du Soleil: Entretien avec Hélène Cixous'; 'On Theatre: An Interview with Hélène Cixous', 13.

12. 'Auteur au Théâtre du Soleil: Entretien avec Hélène Cixous'; 'On Theatre: An Interview with Hélène Cixous', 14.

13. 'Auteur au Théâtre du Soleil: Entretien avec Hélène Cixous'; 'On Theatre: An Interview with Hélène Cixous', 12.

14. 'Guardian of Language: An Interview with Hélène Cixous'.

15. Hélène Cixous, *Déluge* (Paris: Éditions des femmes, 1992). Unless otherwise indicated, page references in this chapter are to this text.

16. For a first discussion of Cixous's reworking of the tragic, see Eberhard Gruber's 'Réécriture du tragique', in *Hélène Cixous: Croisées d'une œuvre*, Actes du Colloque de Cerisy-la-Salle, ed. Mireille Calle-Gruber (Paris: Galilée, 2000), 163–87, where he elaborates the notion of a 'para-tragic' writing in relation to *L'Histoire (qu'on ne connaîtra jamais)* and *La Ville parjure*.

17. *Tragedy: A Very Short Introduction*, 5.

18. Ibid., 70.

19. Friedrich Nietzsche, *The Birth of Tragedy*, trans. Shaun Whiteside, ed. Michael Tanner (London: Penguin, 1993), 40.

20. Ibid., 52 and 9.

21. Hélène Cixous in conversation with Adrian Heathfield, *Writing Not Yet Thought* (London: Performance Matters, 2011).

22. In *Hélène Cixous, Photos de racines*, Cixous states that the 'Clarice' in *Déluge* is not meant to represent the 'real' Clarice Lispector whose importance for Cixous is well known: 'C'est une fiction . . . C'est un nom. Clarice est un synonyme' (100) ['It's a fiction . . . It's a name. Clarice is a synonym'] (*Rootprints*, 91). She goes on to explain that she feels at liberty to fictionalise people who 'ne craignent rien car ils sont morts – et parce qu'ils sont

forts' ['cannot be hurt because they are dead – and because they are strong']. The choice of the name thus appears motivated by the fact that it is a name which will to some extent *resist* a simply referential reading. See also Gill Rye, *Reading for Change: Interactions between Text and Identity in Contemporary French Women's Writing (Baroche, Cixous, Constant)* (Bern: Peter Lang, 2001), 119–20.

23. Gill Rye reads Cixous's use of the third person as a widening of the narrator's personal loss to a 'meditation on loss in more universal terms' (*Reading for Change*, 141).

24. For simplicity, unless otherwise indicated, 'the narrator' shall refer to the narrative instance operative at the relevant textual moment.

25. 'Quelle heure est-il, ou La porte (celle qu'on ne passe pas)', 93; 'What Is It O'clock?', 74.

26. 'Enter the Theatre', 26.

27. Hélène Cixous, 'En octobre 1991 . . .', *Du Féminin*, ed. Mireille Calle-Gruber (Sainte-Foy and Grenoble: Le Griffon d'argile and Presses Universitaires de Grenoble, 1992), 115–37, at 134; 'In October 1991 . . .', trans. Keith Cohen, *Stigmata: Escaping Texts*, 35–49, at 47.

28. Ibid., 126–7 and 42.

29. *Tragedy: A Very Short Introduction*, 66.

30. 'Enter the Theatre', 21.

31. 'En octobre 1991 . . .', 120; 'In October 1991 . . .', 38.

32. *Tragedy: A Very Short Introduction*, 45.

33. For Elizabeth Berglund Hall, the 'entredeux' is an eternal present; see 'Mundane Interruptions: The Insignificance of Hélene Cixous's *Le Jour où je n'étais pas là*', *Romanic Review*, 100:3 (May 2009), 329–44, at 330).

34. At the same time that Cixous was writing *Déluge*, she was also writing *L'Histoire (qu'on ne connaîtra jamais)* [*The Story (We Will Never Know)*], a rewriting of the *Nibelungen* that was directed by Daniel Mesguich in Paris at the Théâtre de la Ville in Spring 1994, appearing in book form the same year (Paris: Éditions des femmes, 1994). An analysis of the *Nibelungen* is also to be found in 'En octobre 1991 . . .'.

35. For Lacan, too, tragedy is an 'entredeux', in his case specifically an 'entre-deux-morts' ['between-two-deaths']. In his interpretation of *Antigone*, the appeal of tragedy lies in the fact that '[c]'est bien d'une illustration de l'instinct de mort qu'il s'agit' ['it's a matter of illustrating the death instinct'] ('L'Essence de la Tragédie: Un commentaire de l'*Antigone* de Sophocle', *Le Séminaire Livre VII: L'éthique de la psychanalyse* (Paris: Seuil, 1986), 327). For a discussion of Lacan's treatment of tragedy, see Alenka Zupančič, 'Ethics and Tragedy in Lacan', *The Cambridge Companion to Lacan*, ed. Jean-Michel Rabaté (Cambridge: Cambridge University Press, 2003), 173–90.

36. *On the Art of Poetry*, 41.

37. In other passages, the narrator's renewed gusto for life, if scarcely 'life-giving' in the sense that it augurs the view of relationships as intrinsically savage that Cixous develops so cogently in *L'Amour du loup et autres remords* (Paris: Galilée, 2003), suggests that she has successfully left the place of victim behind: 'L'envie de tuer renaissait' ['The desire to kill was being born again'] (188), 'Enfin le goût de tuer plutôt que d'être tuée

revenait' ['At last the pleasure of killing rather than being killed was return-ing'] (201).

38. 'Chants', 'taxis' and 'Secret' are other significant signifiers which will reap-pear.

39. The chain of signification is of course overdetermined; it can also be read, for example, in connection with the escape from victimhood signalled by her renascent capacity for hatred (*haine*) as well as for killing, as in the fol-lowing example where I have highlighted words with a paronomastic rela-tion to 'chance' in bold: 'Mon Dieu le mot **haine** est venue m'aider, [. . .] **haleine** de feu, mais ce ne fut jamais un sentiment, seulement le **han!** que vomit l'âme qui se rend [. . .] "Il faut qu'elle meure!" trouvai-je **Han!** cette paix de feu qui vient tuer la guerre!' ['My God the word hatred came to help me, [. . .] breath of fire, but it was never a feeling, only the han! vomited by the soul as it surrenders [. . .] "She must die!" I found Han! This peace of fire that comes to kill war!'] (212).

40. *Photos de racines*, 102; *Rootprints*, 93.

41. Ibid.

42. Isaac further inscribes uncertainty in a variety of other ways. He names not only the process ('écrire') and the addressee of writing ('j'ai besoin de parler *à* Isaac' ['I need to talk *to* Isaac']), but also the source in which writing originates: 'Quand j'attends l'appel d'Isaac, il m'est impossible de résister' ['When I am waiting for Isaac's call, I cannot resist'] (135); a space: 'Ascension s'élance en Isaac' ['Ascension launches herself into Isaac'] (138); and a time: 'Pendant Isaac personne ne meurt' ['During Isaac nobody dies'] (138).

43. The importance of the provisionality of this naming can also be seen in the shift between what the names Clarice and Isaac represent in *Jours de l'an* (whose final chapter imagines a very different – and signally more utopian – story about a relationship between two characters with these names) and how Cixous uses them in *Déluge*. While the repetition is doubtless signifi-cant, what Isaac 'means' in each is specific to the particular text and context.

44. The narrator's final acceptance of the separation between herself and David makes it possible for a new friendship on different, more remote, terms to begin: 'Déjà tu m'es proche, a-t-elle essayé de se dire, comme l'ami pas encore aimé, le bon étranger' ['Already you are close to me, she tried to tell herself, like a friend who has not yet been loved, a good stranger'] (223).

Chapter 6

The Time of Hospitality:
Les Rêveries de la femme sauvage

Over the last ten years or so, the idea has gained currency of a periodisation of Cixous's *œuvre*. For example, Elissa Marder precedes her analysis of Cixous's transformative play on her family's 'given names' with the postulation that during the decade following 1991, 'Cixous's writing takes a marked and distinctive turn. A different turn inwards and outwards from what comes before. The texts that she writes during these years take the form of an "auto-analysis" or even an "auto-odyssey".'[1] Claire Boyle sees a 'new autobiographical cycle' begin in 2000 with a more explicit investigation of Cixous's past.[2] More recently, a call for proposals for a volume to be edited by Elizabeth Berglund Hall, Eilene Hoft-March and Maribel Peñalver Vicea on 'Cixous since 2000' aims 'to reveal some of the dominant themes of her contemporary work, and to discern the ways in which Cixous's most recent writings differ – or not – from her earlier texts'.[3] As the parenthetical 'or not' here patently reveals, the notion of a secure periodisation of Cixous's work proves problematical even as the idea emerges. These various periodisations are predicated on significantly differing identifications of a turning point in Cixous's work: 1991 in one case, 2000 in the others. *Les Rêveries de la femme sauvage* [*Reveries of the Wild Woman*], the book that will be the focus of reading in this chapter,[4] is the only text that belongs to both these attempts to outline a temporal shift in Cixous's output; published in 2000, it is situated at the beginning of a distinct time period in one case, and towards the end of one in the other. Marder's choice of 1991 as a decisive moment of change in Cixous's work is all the more intriguing given that *Or: Les letters de mon père* [*Or: My Father's Letters*] and *Osnabrück*, the other two texts which she places, along with *Les Rêveries*, 'at the heart of this auto-odyssey', were similarly written towards the end of the 1990s,[5] whereas other fictions Cixous published between 1991 and 1996 do not figure in her argument.[6] The difficulties of categorising the writer's work in terms of time with any certainty or robustness are blatantly obvious, as Marder herself acknowledges, recognising that 'virtually everything – even down to every last event and detail – that "happens" in the texts dating from this specific period was always already present in the texts that came before it'.[7]

The alinearity Marder touches on here constitutes an obstacle in the way of any endeavour to elaborate a classification of Cixous's output over time. All systems of periodisation are arbitrary to some extent, in that they seek to divide a history into distinct blocks with precise beginnings and endings. Some periodisations, however, prove more productive than others. When the history in question itself constitutes a constant process of rebeginning, as the analyses of the previous chapters have shown is the case with Cixous's texts, the question arises as to whether the usefulness of the periodisation is limited merely by the approximateness or lack or granularity that typically accounts for its convenience in the first place. In other words, the problem with a periodisation of Cixous's work is not only the standard criticism that it is a heuristic solution that doesn't take sufficient account of the complexity of the phenomenon it seeks to explain. It is that the very existence of the kind of temporal shift the purpose of a periodisation is to highlight is highly questionable in relation to Cixous's *œuvre*. This comes across clearly in *Rencontre terrestre* [*Encounters: Conversations on Life and Writing*], the series of interviews between the author and Frédéric-Yves Jeannet which discuss her books in roughly the (linear) order in which they appeared. The dominant gesture in the conversation is that of teasing out the differences from text to text, eschewing the temptation to impose a grouping on texts from the same period retrospectively.[8] Cixous remarks that while each book can be situated in a linear chronology,

> j'ai tendance à considérer maintenant mes textes comme gravitant en une 'œuvre', dans le cercle indéfini d'un tout autrement-éloigné de moi: les livres sont tous des lettres expédiées dans le futur, et lues en mon absence, après moi (moi vivante ou moi morte). Dans ce futur qui est celui de la lecture, le temps est annulé, le *Portrait du soleil* n'est pas plus éloigné en perspective que *Déluge*. [. . .]
>
> Quel âge a un livre? Qu'est-ce qu'un âge? Qu'est-ce que l'âge? Quel âge ai-je? Je ne se sais plus. Les livres se passent au large de l'âge. [. . .]
>
> Mes livres s'éloignent très vite de moi, pour rejoindre ce temps sans date où ils séjournent, échappés totalement à l'époque. Ainsi lis-je Stendhal ou Dostoïevski contemporainement, l'un à l'autre à moi à vous.

> [I have a tendency now to consider my texts as gravitating toward a 'work', in the vague circle of a whole otherwise-distant from me: the books are all letters mailed to the future, and read in my absence, after me (me alive or me

dead). In this future which is that of reading, time is annulled and *Portrait* is no further away in perspective than *Déluge* (1992). [. . .]

What age is a book? What is an age? What is age? What age am I? I no longer know. Books happen off age's shore. [. . .]

Very quickly books distance themselves from me, to find that time-with-out-date in which they remain, utterly eluding period. Hence I read Stendhal or Dostoevsky as contemporaries, with one another, with me, with you.][9]

For Cixous, once they are written and launched into the world, all her books are the same age, belong to the same time of reading. This idea that all texts, once 'born', are contemporaries of each other, echoes the connection she explored in *Manne* between the Russian poet Osip Mandelstam and the statesman Nelson Mandela who, although separated by time and space, are linked by a common 'greatness of soul'.[10] However, this agelessness characterises not only her own texts, but those of Stendhal, Dostoevsky, Mandelstam, etc. What interests me particularly is the intimation of a contemporaneity specific (though not necessarily exclusive) to Cixous's texts. As the conversation with Jeannet continues, she suddenly moves away from the question of the agelessness produced by a common time of reading to note a different kind of contemporaneity at the level of writing, one that, precisely, is not a question of 'period':

Une immémorialité enveloppe les livres, pour la plupart, et même s'ils font référence à des événements historiques datés. *Portrait du soleil* j'aurai(s) pu l'écrire demain. Et qui sait si je ne vais pas y être amenée . . .

N.B. Je ne dirais pas cela également de tous mes textes. Certains, je ne les réécrirais plus, ils étaient des moments. D'autres sont des racines de temps, ils repousseront en rejetons.

[Books, most of them, are enveloped in a kind of immemorial-ness, even if they refer to dated historical events. *Portrait du soleil* I could (have) write (written) tomorrow. And who knows whether I won't be brought to that . . .

N.B. I wouldn't say this in the same way of all my texts. Some of them, I would no longer write, they were moments. Others are time's roots, they will send up shoots.][11]

The fascinating thing about this quotation is the distinction it makes between books that are 'moments' and those that are 'time's roots', rooted in time. In contrast with usual models of periodisation which group books of the same 'moment' together, here the ones that are 'moments' and which could only have been written at one particular time appear to exist in isolation, outside any temporal relation. Those which are rooted in time are related to others in time, but to others of a *different* time, 'rejetons', shoots or offspring, a different generation of books.

The question of generation is in fact key. 'Des racines de temps' might better be translated as 'roots of time' to convey the ambiguity of the genitive, both objective and subjective, of the French. Books root in time, give rise to other books at a later date. From a comment later in the interview, for example, it seems that it took thirty years for *Neutre* to 'repousser', grow again, produce an offshoot, in *Le Jour où je n'étais pas là*:[12]

> Vous y trouverez le premier portrait avorté de l'enfant manqué, celui qui a/ est une lettre ratée (vous noterez l'étrangeté de la notation chromosomique: nous sommes des lettres plus ou moins bien rédigées, parfois il y a faute d'orthographe). *Neutre* était l'effort suprême pour déterrer le secret. Je n'ai fait que changer de fosse. Et c'est seulement l'an dernier que les mots ont fini par creuser une galerie jusqu'à l'air libre pour témoigner du Jour où je n'étais pas là. Cela n'a pu se faire – mon fils est mort en 1961 – que parce que mon fils avait enfin fini sa mort, ou fini de mourir, c'est long à mourir, de mourir un mort, il faut, quarante ans, se taire.

> [You'll find there the first aborted portrait of the botched child, the one who has/is a wrong letter (note the strangeness of chromosomal notation: we are letters written more or less well, sometimes there's a spelling mistake). *Neutre* was the supreme effort to dig up the secret. All I did was shift it to another grave. Only last year did the words finally tunnel out into the open to bear witness to the Day I wasn't there. This could only happen – my son died in 1961 – because my son was finally done with his death, or done dying, it takes a long time to die, to die a death, you need to be silent for forty years.][13]

Alternatively, we could say that it took forty years for the son's death to find expression in a book. *Le Jour où je n'étais pas là* is also a root *of* time, the product of a temporal process that cannot be accelerated.

It seems that the stories which take a long time to tell are especially those relating to the different generations of the narrator's family, those concerning her 'scènes primitives' or primal scenes, to be understood not in the strict psychoanalytical sense of the child's witnessing parental sex but in the broader sense of any originary childhood scenes.[14] As early as *Jours de l'an*, Cixous's work is characterised by a reflection on the impossibility of accessing such scenes directly. Commenting in this book (the first in which she broaches the idea of the 'book-she-does-not-write', although this is not the reason Jeannet considers it a turning-point in her work[15]) on the fact that Thomas Bernhardt deals with his childhood only in the fifth volume of his autobiography, she declares: 'l'enfance, nous y arrivons à la fin' ['childhood, we get there in the end'].[16] According to Cixous, Dante too could only tell his story in reverse, by taking a path that led him first in the opposite direction away from the story he wanted to tell:

Pour raconter une certaine histoire, il faut parfois raconter une autre histoire; et aller jusqu'à la brûler. On ne fait pas exprès. On veut aller à la Rose. Sur le chemin on rencontre la lonza. Pour faire l'ascension, on commence par descendre. On croise Virgile. Comment ne pas se laisser mener? Et ainsi de chant en chant on s'éloigne, de fascination en oubli, c'est ainsi que l'on va à la Rose, inversement.

[In order to tell a certain story, sometimes we must tell another story, and go so far as to burn it. We don't do this on purpose. We want to go to the Rose. On the way we meet the lonza. In order to ascend, we begin by descending. We cross paths with Virgil. How not to let ourselves be led? And thus from canto to canto we ramble, from fascination to forgetting, this is how we get to the Rose, inversely.][17]

Certain stories can only be approached backwards, by telling a different story first.

In Cixous's own case, the most obvious 'about-turn' involves her mother. She explicitly declared in 1991: 'Écrire de ma mère, je l'ai fait de manière extrêmement succincte. Ce n'est rien, en fait, ce que j'ai fait. Il me semble que nous ne pouvons pas écrire de notre mère. J'en suis sûre. C'est une des limites de l'écriture' ['As for writing about my mother, I've done it with extreme succinctness. What I've done, in fact, amounts to nothing. It seems to me that we can't write about our mother. I'm sure about it. It's one of the limits of writing'].[18] Leaving aside the question of whether the reason for the mother's relative absence until then within Cixous's work was structural rather than personal (whether it was *the* mother in general or *her* mother in particular who resists writing), the date of this declaration is interesting. Although it was uttered the year following the publication of *Jours de l'an*, and although Marder cites it as one of the justifications for her choosing 1991 as a cut-off point in Cixous's *œuvre*,[19] it indicates that Cixous did not at that point antici-pate that the situation it described would change, and did not have her mother in mind as a figure it would take a particularly long time to explore in writing. In the texts published since 1999, however, Cixous's mother has emerged as the most prominent character of her texts, domi-nating many of them thematically,[20] and offering an accompanying voice to the narrator even in texts focused on other figures (for example, *Le Jour où je n'étais pas là*), other questions (for example, *Si près*[21]). Cixous has herself reflected on the contradiction, first in her contribu-tion to the conference held in 2003 to mark the acquisition by the Bibliothèque Nationale de France of her archive, and subsequently to observe that already in 1991 the process of writing about her mother had 'sans doute' ['doubtless'], if unknowingly, already begun:

Pourtant, en octobre 91, j'avais écrit et déclaré publiquement à Kingston au Canada devant mon amie Mireille que je n'écrirai jamais de livre sur ma mère, [. . .] et tout de suite après j'ai fait le contraire, un modèle de parjure innocent, ou plutôt de parjure. [. . .] En octobre 91 c'était trop tard, le livre avait sans doute déjà commence, les guerres aussi commencent bien avant la guerre et les crimes sont à se commettre longtemps avant le couteau, sinon rien n'aurait jamais lieu.

[Nevertheless, in October 91, I had written and publicly declared in Kingston Ontario before my friend Mireille that I will never write a book about my mother, [. . .] and immediately afterwards I did the opposite, a model of innocent perjury, or rather of perjury. [. . .] In October 91 it was too late, the book had doubtless already begun, wars too begin well before war and crimes are being committed long before the knife, otherwise nothing would take place.][22]

Recognising that something is not happening may be the first sign that it is happening, or more precisely the first sign by which it is seen retrospectively to have been happening. That pre-happening is needed for the event in question to 'take place'. *Time* is necessary, in certain cases, for a *place* to be taken.

The mother is just one figure in and of the book Cixous 'does-not-write'. Others involve her 'enfant manqué', the son whose death she did-not-write in *Neutre*, and Algeria, the place of her childhood.[23] Just as Cixous declared she would never write about her mother, so she explained in 1988 that she had no desire to return to her birthplace:

Oran est pour moi la ville de mémoire: je garde un trésor étrange. Je sens que j'ai envie de ne pas retourner à Oran. J'ai envie de garder Oran dans une virginité de mémoire. Parce que si j'y retourne, cela provoquera une grande joie, mais cela provoquera aussi ce que provoquent tous les retours, l'effacement du souvenir, et le remplacement d'un souvenir ancien par un souvenir récent. Je n'ai pas envie. Oran, je l'ai vécue dans la magie absolue.

[Oran is for me the city of memory: I keep a strange treasure. I feel that I want not to return to Oran. I want to keep Oran in a virginity of memory. Because if I return there, it will cause a great joy, but it will also cause what all returns cause, the erasure of memory, and the replacement of an old memory by a recent memory. I don't want that. Oran was for me an experience of absolute magic.][24]

Similarly, too, Cixous changed her mind in this respect. On the same model as her Kingston declaration, this announcement of an intention never to return to her birthplace may have been the first step of that return. 'Mon Algériance', first published in 1997, was the first indication that an urge to explore, that is, to recreate, her country of origin was building inside her. However, it was not until *Osnabrück* had freed a 'galerie jusqu'à l'air libre' enabling her mother to (begin to) take a place in her work that Cixous could create a further passage 'out into the open', which ultimately divided into two separate books, *Les Rêveries de la femme sauvage* (about returning to Algeria) and *Le Jour où je n'étais pas là* (about the loss of her son). *Les Rêveries de la femme sauvage*, which was in turn to be followed by a number of other texts dealing with Algeria, generating a large supplement of critical interest in her as a Francophone postcolonial author,[25] therefore comes into being always already separated, not merely from its author but from other narratives of loss.

As we shall see, separation is originary in Cixous's relationship with Algeria. The subtitle of *Les Rêveries de la femme sauvage* is 'Scènes primitives' ['primal scenes']; Cixous's Algerian primal scene is dominated above all by the fact that, right from the beginning, she was not at home in her homeland. The extent to which one is made to feel at home is a key criterion of hospitality; the Algeria Cixous remembers is notably *in*hospitable in every respect. *Les Rêveries de la femme sauvage* probes with singular acuity how the colonial situation made hospitable relations impossible when the narrator was a child, either with the Arab population or the French colonisers – or indeed between the narrator's family and the broader Algerian Jewish community. At one level, there is a tragic dimension insofar as the text shows very clearly why Cixous never felt welcome in Algeria.[26] Yet, as we saw in Chapter 5, Cixous has no interest in writing unremitting tragedy. What interests me in this text is the hospitality she finds herself eventually able to extend to Algeria. Especially, my focus here is to investigate the *time* of hospitality, the time it took for Algeria to take (its) place in her work.

An Originary Separation

Forty-five years separate the publication of *Les Rêveries de la femme sauvage* from 1955, the year Cixous left Algeria to live in France; for most of that time, ever since 1962 when her mother was told to leave the country in the aftermath of the War of Independence, she had no contact with it. The book's opening line introduces the idea of a return there, but it is immediately evident that at issue here is a return to the origin in no way structured by the metaphysics of presence which have been the focus of so much deconstructive attention over the last forty years:

> *Tout le temps où je vivais en Algérie je rêvais d'arriver un jour en Algérie, j'aurais fait n'importe quoi pour y arriver,* avais-je écrit, *je ne me suis jamais*

trouvée en Algérie, il faut maintenant précisément que je m'en explique, comment je voulais que la porte s'ouvre, maintenant et pas plus tard, avais-je noté très vite, *dans la fièvre de la nuit de juillet, car c'est maintenant, et probablement pour des dizaines ou des centaines de raisons, qu'une porte vient de s'entrebâiller dans la galerie Oubli de ma mémoire, et pour la première fois, voici que j'ai la possibilité de retourner en Algérie, donc l'obligation . . .*

['*The whole time I was living in Algeria I would dream of one day arriving in Algeria, I would have done anything to get there,* I had written, *I never made it to Algeria, it is right now that I must explain what I mean by this, how I longed for the door to open, now not later,* I had scribbled, *in the fever of the July night, for it is now, and probably for dozens or hundreds of reasons that a door has cracked open in the Oblivion Wing of my memory, and now for the first time I may be able to return to Algeria, therefore I must . . .*][27]

There is no fantasy whatsoever of an original presence. Since the narrator dreamed of arriving in Algeria during the entire period she lived there, she was already apart from Algeria even then: her lost country of origin was never present in the first place. This separation at the very heart and origin of the narrator's relationship with her native country dominates *Les Rêveries de la femme sauvage* thematically; the majority of its scenes deal with events which were experienced as exclusions – at the level of the family as much as at the wider level of Algerian society – and which made her violently aware of her sexual, social and religious difference. As the passage quoted above emphasises, this relation of separation still continues to produce effects decades later, in that the writing of the return to the divided or unreachable origin is in turn divided, split from itself. The text begins not with reported speech but with a reported *writing* that is clearly distinguished graphically by the italics (and the quotation marks) not only from the subsequent narrative but also from the comment clauses – 'avais-je écrit', 'avais-je noté très vite' ['I had written', 'I had scribbled'] – that thus stand out from the whole of the paragraph of which they form a part.[28] Likewise, the tense used underscores that the time of writing is split, the pluperfect signalling a temporal difference between the earlier writing and the present narration. The present is divided; indeed, the repeated 'now' clearly refers not to the implicit present of narration, but to the (past) moment when, according to the following paragraph, the book emerged 'en pleine nuit de juillet' ['in the middle of the July night'] for the first time. The return to the past-which-was-never-present thus takes place via a writing highlighting that 'now' belongs to the past.

In addition, it becomes clear that the above quotation is all that is left of three pages that were written that night, the others having mysteriously disappeared. At the chapter's end, the narrator explicitly compares the grief this loss causes her to 'cette sorte de *maladie algérie* que je faisais en Algérie ou qu'elle me faisait, cette sensation d'être possédée par une sensation de dépossession et la réponse que je produisais, ce combat pour conquérir l'introuvable qui peut me conduire à l'autodestruction, tout comme autrefois, ici, dans mon bureau, après si longtemps' (16–17) ['that sort of *Algerian disorder* I used to get in Algeria or that Algeria got to me, that feeling of being possessed by a feeling of dispossession and the response I produced to this, that struggle to vanquish the unfindable that can lead to self-destruction, just like old times, here, in my study, after so many years' (7)]. The book which begins by noting a separation at the very core of the narrator's relationship to her country of origin has analogously suffered a loss or separation at its own origin.

The question thus arises of knowing if or to what extent *Les Rêveries de la femme sauvage* as a whole repeats or reproduces the narrator's early relationship with Algeria. The first chapter's final paragraph leads us to believe that, at the time of writing, the narrator herself is of the opinion that she has succeeded in breaking away from her previous pattern:

> Alors par un effort déchirant je rompis avec moi-même je me tranchai je ne sais comment, comme si je m'étais saisie à bras-le-corps, et je m'enlevai à cette scène d'engouffrement. Ensuite, toujours sans savoir comment, je me doublai moi-même. Et je mis ma propre folie à ma propre œuvre. Par un tour je me renversai, je retournai moi-même en sens contraire. J'avais perdu un trésor irremplaçable. Et c'est cette perte irremplaçable elle-même qui allait remplacer les pages dont je n'admettais pas encore la mort, même si, le temps passant, je m'approchais d'un abandon des recherches c'est-à-dire d'un abandon d'un membre de mon âme. (17)

> [Then with an excruciating effort I broke with myself I severed myself I don't know how, it's as if I took hold of myself, and I dragged myself away from this scene of being sucked up. Next, still not knowing how, I made myself in two. And I put my own madness into my own work. By some kind of magic, I faced myself in the other direction. I had lost a treasure I couldn't replace. And this irreparable loss was going to take the place of the pages whose demise I could not yet admit, even if, as time went by, I was getting closer to giving up the search that is to giving up a limb of my soul. (7)]

She stops herself from being engulfed by 'slicing' herself in two (*trancher*, a verb which can also mean to decide between alternatives, favour one side over another), 'doubling' herself, thus perpetuating within herself the division which had caused her such suffering during her childhood but which will now provide her with a means of replacing the irreplaceable, accommodating what cannot be accommodated. In effect, Cixous already suggests here that once separation is achieved and accepted, it can function 'en sens contraire', in the other direction, so that for the first time a return becomes possible. Separation literally *turns into* return: '*Par un tour* je me renversai, je retournai moi-même en sens contraire.' 'Tour' in French means turn as well as trick (I shall come back to the magic involved later). A return is thus a double turn, one which repeats rather than negates the original turning away, measuring rather than seeking to abolish the distance travelled. Or, put differently, return is only possible when the break is final.

We shall see that the text as a whole confirms this reading. But first I want to highlight the significance in the book's first paragraph of the fact that the divided present of this 'now' opens a door in the 'Oblivion Wing' of the narrator's memory, revealing for her 'la possibilité de retourner en Algérie, donc l'obligation . . .', the requirement to return to Algeria once it has become possible to do so. The door has figured regularly in Cixous's writing since her earliest texts as an image of openness.[29] Opening the door is a standard gesture of hospitality. I want to suggest that this door does not so much belong within a hospitable sphere as open up the very possibility of a space of hospitality. For the first time, Cixous's narrator will display a hospitable attitude towards her native country, notwithstanding the fact that Algeria figures within the text above all as *in*hospitable, a place of brutal exclusions, violent rejections and wars. Furthermore, *Les Rêveries* heralds a time of hospitality in that what is at stake is precisely the time that *will have* proven necessary for the narrator to be able to welcome Algeria as part of herself. The extent to which this time of hospitality is a phenomenon of writing is of especial interest.

At this point, let me briefly recall the distinction Derrida made between a 'hospitality of right' and an 'absolute hospitality'.[30] The former is conditional insofar as it is extended only to the guest who has satisfactorily obeyed the request 'de décliner et de garantir son identité, comme à un témoin devant un tribunal' ['to state and to guarantee his identity, as you would a witness before a court'],[31] a request which in effect obliges the guest to prove he or she shares a code belonging to the host, or to which the host belongs. In contrast, the latter makes it incumbent upon me to open my home 'à l'autre absolu, inconnu, anonyme et que je lui *donne lieu*, que je le laisse venir, que je le laisse arriver, et avoir lieu dans le lieu que je lui offre, sans lui demander ni réciprocité (l'entrée dans un pacte) ni même son nom' ['to the absolute, unknown, anonymous other, and that I *give place* to them, that I let them come, that I let them arrive, and take place in the place I offer them, without asking of them either reciprocity (entering into a pact) or even their names'].[32] The thinking about hospitality that is at work in Cixous's book recalls Derrida's distinction insofar as it posits a difference between two different types of hospitality. '– Invitée? demandai-je. – Invitée? Non!' (97): the lack of hospitality consistently encountered by the narrator's mother in Algeria turns out to be the reverse side of a limited, circumscribed hospitality. Even in Germany, prior to her life in Algeria, the mother did not go to others' homes:

> jamais je ne vais chez les Juifs dit ma mère j'étais encore très allemande ensuite les gens commençaient à être sionistes ce que je n'ai jamais été, chaque fois qu'il y a un nationalisme je ne vais pas, j'ai toujours été internationale. Quand nous avons quitté l'Allemagne, j'ai toujours dit 'chez nous' 'chez eux' [. . .] Ce 'chez nous', ça m'a passé dès que je suis arrivée à Oran. (107)

> [I never went to Jewish homes says my mother I was still very German next people began to be Zionist which I never was, every time there is some kind of nationalism I don't go, I have always been international. When we left Germany, I always said 'back home' 'over here' [. . .] 'Back home' is a thing I got over when I arrived in Oran. (62)]

Going 'chez les Juifs' would mean accepting hospitality offered her *as a Jew*, agreeing to confine herself within a particular (national) identity. She refuses this 'conditional' hospitality, one dependent on the guest's identity and extended at some level in order to consolidate the host's identity or ipseity. As Derrida explains, the host places himself at the mercy of his guest, risks becoming his guest's *hostage*, another word linked etymologically to host and hospitality. But such a conditional hospitality is equally emprisoning for the guest: each becomes hostage of the other.[33] The mother's refusal of any hospitality based on a prior identification with the other (and thus an exclusion of those not sharing that identity), a refusal which eventually leads her to relinquish use of the pronoun 'nous', explains for the narrator why she was never invited anywhere in Algeria:

> Une personne qu'on ne peut pas haïr franchement comme il est normal quotidien et juste pour les clients de haïr les Français, on ne peut pas l'aimer non plus. Elle est étrangère. Brève étendue étrangère. [. . .] Avec elle, sentent les clients, pensai-je, et je prenais le mot *sentent* plutôt que le mot *pensent* car cette chose, qui a toujours fait d'elle une invitée-évitée, et de nous des ininvités par contiguïté, échappe à la pensée: c'est un manque de sens des hostilités qui s'accompagne de son contraire. (108)

> [Somebody you cannot simply hate as it is normal everyday and just for patients to hate the French, you cannot love either. She is foreign. A brief expanse of foreignness. [. . .] With her, the patients feel, I thought, and I took the word *feel* rather than the word *think* because this thing that has

always made her the uninvited guest, and us uninvited by association, eludes thought: it is a lack of the sense of hostility cheek by jowl with its opposite. (63)]

Paradoxically, her lack of a 'sens des hostilités' ['sense of hostility'] is the reason she is never invited. Being impossible to situate unambiguously as friend or enemy, an undecidable *hostis*, it is in fact less because she is 'étrangère', foreign, than because she is sensed to be 'international', that is: *foreign to any national allegiance*, that she is not welcome as a guest.

Nonetheless, the prevalence of this limited or conditional hospitality is leavened by the gleam of the possibility of an 'absolute' hospitality. Oran, Cixous's birthplace, figures as a city that 'ne transforme pas les arrivants en étrangers' (138) ['doesn't turn newcomers into foreigners' (78)], a city where the heterogeneity of the population does not generate the same violent reactions as in Algiers, such that in deciding to move his family to Clos-Salembier in the capital, the narrator's father 'a fait l'erreur d'échanger le paradis pour l'Enfer en croyant faire tout le contraire' (142) ['made the mistake of trading paradise for Hell all the while believing he was doing the contrary' (80)]. The narrator remembers her father's mother feeding Mohamed, a beggar who lived in the entrance to their apartment building: 'Mémé remplit la gamelle à ras bord. Elle nourrit son. Son qui, son quoi, son hôte son autre, il est venu, elle ne sait pas qui est venu, elle remplit la boîte en fer-blanc' (140) ['Grandma fills the tin right to the brim. She looks after hers. Her who, her what, her host, her guest, her other, he has come, she doesn't know who has come, she fills the tin can' (79)]. She is hospitable to any comer regardless of their social, national or religious identity, with no precondition, allowing any 'autre' [other] in need to become her 'hôte' [guest]. 'Elle nourrit son': in an untranslatable pun, the grandmother's readiness to feed the hungry whoever they may be equates her with a *nourrisson*, the newborn baby who, according to her 'international' daughter-in-law midwife, is always a 'nouveau-né international' (107) ['international newborn' (62)], not yet having developed a national allegiance. Her son, the narrator's father, displays a similar internationalism when he gives a lift to two Arab hitch-hikers who are all the more astounded by the 'hospitalité inattendue' ['unexpected hospitality'] that they believe him to be French. According to the narrator, it is rather 'en tant que déchet craché destitué des Français d'une part et d'autre part en tant qu'idéal du moi médecin' ['on the one hand as a piece of detritus spit out rejected by the French and on the other hand as my ideal of a doctor'] that he stopped to offer them a lift:

c'est donc il faut se le dire, en tant que genre particulier d'Arabe que mon père un arabizarre s'est arrêté [. . .] mais il ne faut pas le dire à nos deux passagers

– que mon père est un véritable arabe sous les fausses apparences d'un jeune et beau médecin français, étant d'ailleurs juif, ce qui pouvait peser sur un plateau ou l'autre de la balance – car ce serait ôter aux deux hôtes enchantés le sentiment merveilleux que dans ce pays malade et maudit de haine et totalement impossible, malgré tout, tout était possible. (46–7)

[it is therefore, I repeat, as a peculiar kind of Arab that my father an ara-bizarre stopped [. . .] but this we mustn't tell our two passengers – that my father is really an Arab beneath the façade of young and dashing French doctor, being Jewish what's more which could tip the scales either way – for this would deprive our two enchanted guests of the marvellous feeling that in this sick and cursed with hatred and totally impossible country, in spite of everything, anything could happen. (25)]

The marvel is both that the father's complex of identifications should make the hospitable gesture possible *and* that the two delighted 'hôtes' be unaware that this was the case, enabling them to believe that when the 'auto' – another word in the chain reinforcing the idea of the self as harbour to the *hôte/autre* – stopped, it was the most other other possible (a Catholic Frenchman) who opened the door to let them in.

'Ce serait *ôter* aux deux *hôtes*': time after time the homophony in French highlights the link between the question of hospitality and that of separation. To quote Derrida again: 'Aujourd'hui une réflexion sur l'hospitalité suppose, entre autres choses, la possibilité d'une délimitation rigoureuse des seuils ou des frontières: entre le familial et le non familial, entre l'étranger et le non étranger, le citoyen et le non-citoyen, mais d'abord entre le privé et le public, le droit privé et le droit public, etc.' ['Nowadays, a reflection on hospitality presupposes, among other things, the possibility of a rigorous delimitation of thresholds or frontiers: between the familial and the non-familial, between the foreign and the non-foreign, the citizen and the non-citizen, but first of all between the private and the public, private and public law, etc.'].[34] But what if this threshold cannot be 'rigorously delimited'? Can one offer hospitality to the other that one represents for oneself? To return to the narrative instance, was the problem where Algeria was concerned, for Cixous, one of needing to separate *enough* from her origins to be able to welcome it again as other, respecting its alterity?

Endless Separations

The narrator's memories of her Algerian childhood are dominated by scenes of separation. Thus, for example, the arrival of the bicycle jointly longed for by herself and her brother for more than four years has the effect not of uniting them but of bringing about a separation between them. The brother experiences their mother's choice of a girl's bicycle as a present for his thirteenth birthday as a castration all the more painful that she didn't mean to hurt him: 'Toute ma vie je soulignerai le pire; maman n'a *même pas voulu me castrer.* Toute sa vie elle n'a même pas perçu l'homme, ni le fils, ni la femme, ni la mère' (37) ['My whole life I shall emphasize the worst; Mummy *did not even want to castrate me.* Her whole life she took no notice of the man, nor the son, nor the woman, nor the mother' (18)]. For the brother, the mother's refusal or inability to recognise his (sexual) difference paradoxically differentiates him violently from his sister by defining him, at the decisive age of puberty, as castrated. For his sister, too, the bicycle divides them, although for her the difference it installs is not primarily sexual; it lies rather in the distance at which henceforth each holds Algeria. Notwithstanding the humiliation of its missing bar, her brother sets off on the bicycle day after day to discover the country, whereas she gives up borrowing it after some children in the street bring home to her the difference between their poverty and her relative wealth by throwing a case against the wheel the first time she uses it: 'Ce vélo nous a vraiment séparés, pensai-je, jusque-là nous ne faisions qu'un frère avec sœur intérieure et inversement maintenant je n'étais plus que sœur sans frère intérieur' (53) ['That bike really drove a wedge between us, I thought, up to then we were just one brother with an internal sister and vice versa now I was nothing but a sister with no internal brother' (30)].

The bicycle thus confronts the narrator with the abyss separating her from her Arab neighbours as much as with the new gap which has opened up between herself and her brother. Able and ready to defend herself on foot, in a relationship 'd'égale à égal', a relationship between sexual equals, she renounces the bicycle in order to avoid the hostile relations her using it would oblige her to deal with.[35] The separation from her brother and the separation from her neighbours thus intersect, as can be seen most powerfully in the scene where the narrator and her brother speak through the bars of the entrance to their house on his return home after running away in resentment at being given the bicycle:

> Nous nous regardons. Entre nous le portail, impossible. Je suis malheureuse. Je suis malheureux. Je suis mon frère de l'autre coté. Ensemble nous poussons lentement le portail. La grappe de gosses se détache. Le portail impossible passe entre nous, à nouveau, entre nous les enfants à deux pains et nous les enfants sans pain. (36)

[We looked at one another. Between us the gate, impossible. I am miserable. I am miserable. I am my brother on the other side. Together we push slowly on the gate. The bunch of kids comes unstuck. The impossible gate comes between us, again, between us the children with two loaves and us the children without loaves. (18)]

In a complex new version of the figure of the door, the gate constrains us to consider the *difficulty* of passing from one side to the other. The gate opens here only to close again, forming another barrier; no sooner is a separation negotiated than another presents itself. The bar missing from the bicycle has led to a proliferation of bars: the gate is the site of not one but two different separations (first between brother and sister, then between them and the children hungry for bread), two different configurations of the line between inside and outside, as the sliding reference of the pronoun 'nous' (we) reveals. 'Nous nous regardons': at issue in this scene are in effect two 'nous' placed 'en regard', as is said in French, facing or opposite each other, two different, intersecting pluralities: the whole the narrator forms with her brother although at the same time cut off from him, and the whole that, once he has come inside, she and her brother form with the children who remain outside. 'Entre nous': here the homonymy in French between the preposition and the verbal form 'entre' Cixous has much exploited suggests not only that the gate cuts them off from each other but also that the pronoun 'nous' *enters*, as a character in the theatre,[36] a new entity whose novelty and importance are stressed by its eight inscriptions in the space of the short quotation (if we include '*nou*veau'). This is a key turning-point where – contrary to her mother who initially feels she belongs to a 'nous' from which she subsequently takes her distance – the narrator realises she is part of a whole that cuts her off from herself, from the unhappy other she (also) *is*: 'Je *suis* mon frère de l'autre côté.' Hence the unforgettable play on words: 'Moi, pensais-je je suis *inséparabe*' (45) ['Me, I thought, I am *inseparab*' (24)]. She is *one* with the Arabs from whom she must unavoidably remain apart.[37]

The difference for the narrator between her relationships (especially with her brother) within the family[38] and her relationship to those outside is that in the latter hostility never flips over into its opposite, into hospitality. Her relationship with her Arab neighbours is structured dissymmetrically: 'je voulais être de leur côté mais c'était un désir de mon côté de leur côté le désir était sans côté' (45) ['I wanted to be on their side but it was a desire on my side on their side the desire had no side' (24)].[39] An analogous dissymmetry characterises her later friendships, first as a Jewish girl with a Catholic friend, aptly named Françoise: 'Je ne peux pas entrer dans la maison de Françoise [. . .] il est strictement interdit aux Juifs d'entrer dans cette maison mais il n'est pas totalement ni strictement impossible qu'elle apparaisse dans la maison des Juifs' (126) ['I cannot enter Françoise's house [. . .] it is strictly forbidden for a Jew to enter this house but it is not totally nor strictly impossible that she make an appearance in the house of the Jew' (72)], and later as a pupil seeking to make friends with the only three Muslim girls to attend her predominantly Catholic secondary school: 'J'étais avec elles et elles n'étaient pas avec moi [. . .] j'étais avec elles sans elles moi qui à moins d'elles ne pouvais être moi' (151–2) ['I was with them and they were not with me [. . .] I was with them without them me who except for them could not be me' (85)].[40] Likewise, the narrator's mother, although very different in character from her daughter, faces a similar rejection from her Arab employees when she wishes to remain in Algeria after Independence: 'Ils voulaient être sans moi et j'étais toujours là, ils étaient avec moi dans l'immeuble sans que je fusse avec eux' (163) ['They wanted me gone and I was still around, they were with me in the building without me being with them' (93)].

'*Tout le temps où je vivais en Algérie je rêvais d'arriver un jour en Algérie*': if the narrator never had the feeling she belonged in the country she was nevertheless part of, it was thus principally because she felt herself constantly excluded by her cohabitants. There was *no end to the exclusion*. 'L'expulsion pour nous mon frère et moi [. . .] était la forme même de notre existence et de notre relation au monde depuis la maison du Clos-Salembier' (61) ['Expulsion for my brother and me [. . .] was the very form of our existence and relationship to the world from the Clos-Salembier house' (35)]: the expulsion did not succeed in expelling. Living in Algiers for the narrator was tantamount to experiencing an ongoing expulsion, a state metaphorised by the *placenta previa* evoked by the mother which precipitates premature labour but where the placenta obstructs the cervix and prevents the baby's head from emerging. Leaving Algeria in 1955 thus constituted an attempt to bring about an expulsion paradoxically in order to bring the *process* of expulsion to an end. The attempt was not destined to know success quickly; when back in Algeria in 1971 to see her mother, the 'obstruction' (166/94) she feels on her head tells her that she has not yet managed to achieve separation. As always with Cixous, inside and outside change places: it is while she is *inside*, before her symbolic birth, that she feels most excluded.

The narrator is different in this respect from her mother who, in contrast, has no difficulty in taking her distance, in leaving or at least transforming the hostile scenes she finds herself bound up with:

Et alors même qu'elle s'était retrouvée rejetée, mise en quarantaine définitive à l'âge de trente-six ans, toutes les portes d'hospitalité et d'amitié verrouillées de l'intérieur, [. . .] ma mère [. . .] a tout de suite trouvé le chemin de l'Hôpital, celui-là où, sans trembler sans penser même une minute qu'elle y pourrait trembler, celui-là où mon père son mari était décédé, elle va s'inscrire pour des études de sage-femme. Avec son aptitude remarquable au rétablissement. On lui ôte son arbre, elle passe d'un bond au faîte de l'arbre à côté. Et de là, de l'Hôpital devenu le sien, elle crée en quatre années le nouveau monde (55)

[And even when she found herself cast out, quarantined for good at the age of thirty-six, all the doors of hospitality and friendship bolted from within, [. . .] my mother [. . .] without losing a second made her way to the Hospital, the very one where, without trembling without it even crossing her mind that she could tremble in that place, the very place where my father her husband had died, and signs up to become a midwife. With her astounding aptitude for recovery. Remove her tree and she bounds to the top of the next one. And from there, from the Hospital she can now call hers, before four years have passed, she creates the new world (31)]

Where there is inhospitality, the mother 'tout de suite', immediately, finds the *hospital*, a space of healing rather than war, birth rather than murder. She has a special talent for 'rétablissement', a word meaning recovery but also suggesting putting down roots in a place. In fact, she has no need for roots, accommodating impermanence as a monkey swings from tree to tree: 'On lui ôte son arbre, elle passe d'un bond au faîte de l'arbre à côté.' As Lacan famously showed in 'L'Instance de la lettre dans l'inconscient', *arbre* is an anagram of *barre*.[41] Here, the mother manages to turn the very figure of the exclusion afflicting her daughter (and son) into something living. Moreover, as a midwife she spends her life bringing about a life-giving separation in others: 'Un lien pense-t-elle est fait pour être coupé, un désir sevré. Je me demande, se demande mon frère, si elle n'est pas devenue sage-femme par penchant inné ou acquis pour les coupements de cordon' (58) ['A tie she thinks is made to be broken, a desire to be cut off. I wonder, my brother wonders, if she didn't become a midwife out of an innate or acquired tendency to cut cords' (33)].

Breaking Bread

A measure of the distance travelled by the narrator since her time in Algeria is seen in the penultimate paragraph of the text when she says:

Mais maintenant plus j'en parle et plus j'y reviens surtout avec mon frère plus je me sens chez moi au Clos-Salembier maintenant et rétrospectivement, autant j'étais jetée dehors assaillie repoussée clouée au portail autant j'y suis chez moi maintenant que je n'y suis plus enchaînée [. . .] autant maintenant le Clos-Salembier est en moi et je tiens à chacun des endroits que j'ai fuis et chaque instant détesté détestable est pour moi une transfigure vitale que je n'échangerai pour aucun instant doux et modéré au monde. (167)

[But now the more I talk about it and the more I go back there especially with my brother the more I feel at home in the Clos-Salembier now and retrospectively, to the degree I was thrown out assailed expulsed nailed to the gate so I am at home there now I am no longer chained up [. . .] the Clos-Salembier has become part of me and I am attached to each of the places I fled and each hated hateful moment is for me a vital transfigure that I wouldn't exchange for any kinder gentler moment in the world. (95)]

If, 'maintenant' ['now'], the narrator is at home ('chez moi') in Clos-Salembier, something has changed radically. Whereas *in* Algeria she was always outside, 'now' she is far enough away from Clos-Salembier to be able to return to it, to feel at home ['chez moi'] there. But Clos-Salembier is also 'in' her: she welcomes it, offers it a shelter without wanting to change it any longer, able now to value the unique specificity that she previously detested. The fact that *Les Rêveries de la femme sauvage* depicts Algeria with all its faults, in all its inhospitality, can thus be read not as the sign of the narrator's old hostility towards it but on the contrary as the sign of a new hospitality on her part, a new readiness to accept it as it is. What was previously detestable is now a 'transfigure vitale': if Algeria is now transfigured, it is not that the narrator has transformed it by attributing to it or recognising in it qualities it did not have but rather that she is now able to draw something positive from the same qualities which previously repulsed her.

What, then, is the link between this final 'now' and those we saw at the beginning of the book? As a shifter (in the linguistic sense of the term), 'now' refers to the time of enunciation. How significant is it that it should be at the end of the book that the narrator admits to harbouring Clos-Salembier within herself? Has telling the story played a part in bringing about this new hospitality? Significant in this respect is the fact that the book is in the shape of a Möbius strip, its end repeating its beginning: 'Je me suis redressée dans mon lit en pleine nuit et avec le crayon gras qui est toujours couché à côté de ma main j'ai écrit à grands traits dans le noir: *Tout le temps où je vivais en Algérie je rêvais d'arriver un jour en Algérie*' (168) ['I sat up in my bed in the middle of the night and with the soft lead of the pencil always within reach I scrawled in the dark: *The whole time I was living in Algeria I would dream of one day arriving in Algeria*' (96)]. On the one hand, this circular structure enclosing the narrative signifies that the change making the book possible had in some sense already taken place before it begins (i.e. between the narrator's leaving Algeria and her writing the book), that its writing must needs be related to an extra-narrative time. On the other hand, it emphasises that the narrative is the space of a difference: the time in which the return takes place is an irremediably *narrative* time.

The most significant shift in *Les Rêveries de la femme sauvage* is the narrator's recognition that separation has not separated her from Algeria, but rather (already) turned into a return. Hence the first explanation for the fact that the narrator has 'la possibilité [...] donc l'obligation' ['the possibility [...] thus the obligation'] to return to Algeria: to be able to do so is already to do so. A key textual moment emphasises that the break with her native country represented a change in, rather than the end of, the relationship. The narrator becomes aware of a similarity she had never noticed over the course of forty years between 'la maison qui a succédé à la maison du Clos-Salembier' ['the house which has taken the place of the Clos-Salembier house'] and 'la maison du Clos-Salembier' ['the Clos-Salembier house'] (71/41). When her brother claims that nothing in it is reminiscent of Algeria, she comments: 'Tout rappelle à mon frère que rien ici ne lui rappelle en rien l'Algérie. C'est ainsi que nous communions assis dans les fauteuils qui ne sont pas les fauteuils du Clos-Salembier, qui ne-sont-pas-les-fauteuils c'est-à-dire que ce sont les non-fauteuils du Clos-Salembier' (87) ['Everything reminds my brother that nothing here reminds him in the least of Algeria. This is how we commune sitting in the chairs that are not the Clos-Salembier chairs, that are-not-the-chairs that is to say that they are the non-chairs of the Clos-Salembier' (50)]. Stating the lack of a relation is itself evidence of a relation; a non-relation is one among a number of possible modes of relation. Similarly, some pages later the narrator's mother is perplexed at her own abrupt change of topic, finding herself having passed inexplicably from the Clinic to the Commissariat de Police, sensing vaguely (according to her daughter) that 'les lieux qui n'ont aucun rapport ont communiqué d'une façon invraisemblable' (98) ['places which have nothing to do with one another have become communicable in the most improbable fashion' (58)]. What does not communicate nevertheless communicates. Furthermore, the reader cannot help but observe that in French the verb 'communiquer' in turn communicates with 'communier'.[42] 'C'est ainsi que nous *communions*' ['This is how we *commune*']: although seated apart, each in their own armchair, brother and sister are brought together by the *lack* of relation between the narrator's armchairs and those of their childhood home. Whereas the bicycle which they were to share and which was to enable them to discover their environment came between them, 'now' the lack of a relation proves a bond.

But in French 'communier' also means to receive the Christian Eucharist. Surprisingly, at the beginning of the text, the italicised lines – scribbled down in darkness for fear that putting on the light would put to flight the nocturnal 'Venant' ['Comer'] who 'dictated' (10/3) them to her – are at once metaphorised as a *host*:

> Puis une fois reçu le viatique absolu je m'aventurai à allumer, et comme si j'avais à la bouche, à la bouche de l'âme et de la main, et sur ma langue de nuit l'hostie qui répand chair et sang du Venant dans mon corps, tout en suçant et absorbant, j'avais écrit à la suite de la première semence quatre grandes pages de lignes serrées en caractères épais hâtifs [. . .] quatre immenses pages avec toutes les qualités du viable, ce qui pour moi signifie que je n'ai plus qu'à pousser plus loin, ce commencement une fois donné, il n'y a plus qu'à poursuivre dans la direction (10)

> [Once the absolute viaticum had been received I ventured to switch on the light, and as though I held the Host to disperse the Comer's flesh and blood through my body in my mouth, in my soul's mouth and my hand's, and on my night tongue, as I let it dissolve, in the trace of that initial seeding, I had scrawled four big, single-spaced pages [. . .] four immense pages with every sign of being viable, which for me means I have only to forge ahead, once I've been given the beginning, I have only to push on, you just have to carry on the same way (4)]

Writing is a viaticum, the Eucharist given *in extremis* as food for the journey into death, the body and blood of Christ given to save the other's (eternal) life. Here, however, the viaticum has the effect of preparing the narrator not for death, but for giving birth. Whereas the 'je' is initially in the place of the dying person *receiving* the host, the effect of the host is to transform her into the one *giving* life, the 'semence' of the viaticum leading immediately to a text that to all appearances is 'viable', that is one capable of living a separate existence. 'Je n'ai plus qu'à pousser plus loin' ['I only have to push on']: writing figures from the outset as a process of pushing; however, unlike the expulsions of Algeria, it describes a birth that successfully brings a pregnancy to term, one that not only gives life to the child being born but also enables the person giving birth to 'pousser' further, continue to grow. By virtue of this association with birth and life ('vie' is disseminated forcefully throughout the French passage in *v*iatique, a*v*enturai, a*v*ais, *v*iable, poursui*v*re and most conspicuously in Venant), writing is unmistakably linked at the beginning of the book to a specifically creative, nourishing separation.

The hospitable dimension of writing is reinforced by the fact that communion recalls the scene of hospitality at its simplest, the breaking of bread together (in contrast, the unlikelihood of the hostile relations separating the narrator and her brother from their Arab neighbours ever becoming hospitable is adumbrated in the description of the children on the other side of the gate as 'sans pain', lacking in bread). But, as already stated, here the one who *receives* the bread is the one who *gives* life. The guest becomes the nourisher, the corollary of which is that being hospitable nourishes the host. Writing thus appears to install a circle of hospitality, although not in the sense in which Derrida's 'conditional' hospitality is circumscribed, extended in order to consolidate a sense of community. Rather, the hospitality of writing seems circular in that the very positions of host and guest are placed in question. Cixous's text generalises the ambiguity created by the fact that in French the word 'hôte' means both host *and* guest; it becomes effectively impossible to determine if the narrator 'receives' the host as a gift or as a guest. In this context, the choice of a Eucharistic metaphor, the ultimate Christian image, by a writer whose Judeity is so central to her sense of identity invites reading as the sign of an exceptional and unconditional openness. Cixous deploys the metaphor of communion not in order to consolidate a missing or regretted community but rather in a way which inscribes a desire for communion *outside* one's community, a communion that would transcend the limits of any specific community.[43] The readiness to open the door of her text to an image from a community of which she is not part, of which she displays no desire to be part, betokens a readiness to make room for an otherness with whom she has little or no relation that tallies closely with Derrida's notion of an 'absolute' hospitality. The narrator displays a hospitality analogous to her grandmother's by welcoming within her very body the 'Venant', the visitor satisfying no prior condition other than being the one who comes.

It is not without importance that the 'Venant' whom the narrator welcomes into her writing, welcomes by writing, itself comes within the sphere of writing. Furthermore, insofar as 'le langage *est* hospitalité' ['language *is* hospitality'],[44] what comes is already hospitable. The capital letter which both announces and emphasises its links throughout the book with *Vélo*, *Ville*, etc. calls our attention to the fact that, well in advance of the theatrical image of the bicycle, letters are the first thing to circulate speedily in *Les Rêveries de la femme sauvage*.[45] The hospitable nature of their circulation finds confirmation most obviously in the conversation between the narrator and her mother concerning invitations. After asking her mother if she had ever been invited to people's homes in Algeria, the narrator's italicisation of the word *invitée* when recounting her reply offers a clue as to the reason for the abrupt shift from the Clinic to the Commissariat which had left her mother perplexed: 'Chaque fois que je suis *invitée* à passer au Commissariat ...'

(98) ['Each time that I am *invited* to go down to the station . . .' (58)]. It
was the *word* 'invitée' – the narrator later stresses that she had deliberately chosen this 'mot incongru' ['incongruous word'] – that apparently
transported her suddenly from one place to the other: the only 'invitation' she had received in Algeria had been to present herself at the police
station. At the same time as it evokes the lack of hospitality the mother
encountered in Algeria, then, the text signals how hospitable *language*
can be, not only in that words communicate by evoking other similar yet
different words – *communiquer/communier, inviter/inciter*, etc. – but
especially in that different meanings coexist without excluding each
other. A few pages later, the hospitality of the word 'invité' is explicitly
reflected upon:

> – Invitée, dis-je, pensant aux innombrables invitations qu'envoie à rêver le
> mot invité invitation, *invitus invitam*, à ses ressources fabuleuses, *dimisit*,
> maudites, subtiles, contraires à ses irisations latines, ses retors, ses secrets,
> ses jalousies, ses cœurs, les uns bons et sucrés, les autres mielleux, les autres
> amers et mensongers, (103)

> [– Invited, I say, thinking of the countless invitations the word invited con-
> jures up, invitation, *invitus invitam*, its fabulous resources, *dimisit*, accursed,
> subtle, contrary to its Latinate shimmers, its twists, its secrets, its jealousies,
> its hearts, some good and sugary, others honeyed, others bitter and lying,
> (60)]

The word 'invité' clearly *invites*. This quotation details how it opens
up or 'gives place' to other words, making room not only for obviously
related words such as 'invitation' but also for others whose connection
to 'invité' may not be what it seems. For example, 'envoie' is considerably closer than one might think in that it comes from the low Latin
inviare, a paronym of *invitare*, the word in which 'invitation' originates.
Likewise, the choice of the word 'jalousies' is overdetermined, firstly
because it translates the latin *invidiæ*, another paronym of *invitatio*,
but also because its synonym 'envies', in turn paronomastically close to
'envoie', does in fact derive from *invitare* . . . But perhaps the most fla-
grant example is that, notwithstanding the evident paronymy, the words
invitus invitam are related not to the family of *invitare* but to the adjective *vitus*, from *vis* (you want). They mean 'against his wishes, against
her wishes', and act as a reminder that a word can signify in ways
'contraires à ses irisations latines', its various meanings contradicting
each other, its 'ressources' (whose etymological root is *resors*) fabulous
also *because* it has 'retors' (a word which, used as a noun instead of as
the more usual adjective, adds yet another twist), secret associations
proliferating in all directions and thoroughly defying the possibility of

privileging one line of filiation over another. Furthermore, beyond the network of relations at the level of material form, the word's resources here include intertextual echoes. In light of the *invitus invitam*, the italicised *dimisit*, 'sent away' (a word which in turn echoes the verb 'envoie'), recalls the line from Suetonius foregrounded by Racine in his Preface to *Bérénice*: 'Titus reginam Berenicen [. . .] dimisit invitus invitam'. Indeed, as a tragedy culminating not in death but in separation, when Titus's declaration of love finally convinces Berenice to agree to leave, *Bérénice* bears a structural resemblance to the narrator's encounter with a Berber boy which she suggests might have blossomed into a positive relationship had she not shortly afterwards left Algeria, an encounter which she specifically recalls as a 'rencontre dont l'autre nom est adieu' (156) ['the meeting whose other name is adieu' (88)]. Conversely, *Les Rêveries de la femme sauvage* as a whole can be deemed a farewell whose other name is return.

The list of words harbouring each other, giving place to each other, could go on: invitation/irisation, the various meanings of 'mielleux' (sugary/false/hypocritical), etc. The way Cixous's writing exploits the 'fabulous resources' of words, their 'secrets' (from *secretus*, meaning separate, set apart) invites us to consider it in its own way as a form of 'retors', defined by the *Robert* as a 'tissu fabriqué avec du fil retors' ['textile made with twisted yarn']: her text is made up of rebellious, refractory elements, welcoming rather than rejecting chance encounters between words. Above all, the return to the origin as reflected in this last quotation – that is, the return to the origin of the *word* – serves not to confirm an identity or cement an allegiance based on a common descent but rather to savour a mysterious strangeness, to discover a network of differences where words are enriched by contact with other, unexpected words and become iridescent.

This essentially inappropriable otherness of a linguistic origin returns us to the question of the specific role language, and especially *writing*, plays in the emergence of the narrator's newfound hospitality towards her own country of origin. Again according to Derrida, language is characterised by being *both* what constitutes me as myself, and as such is inseparable from my innermost identity, *and* an otherness in constant renewal. As he states: 'ce qui ne me quitte pas ainsi, la langue, c'est aussi, *en réalité, en nécessité*, au-delà du phantasme, ce qui ne cesse de se départir de moi. La langue ne va qu'*à partir* de moi. Elle est aussi ce dont je pars, me pare et me sépare. Ce qui se sépare de moi en partant de moi' ['that which doesn't leave me in this way, language, is also, *in reality, in necessity*, beyond the fantasy, that which never ceases to depart from me. Language only works *from* me. It is also what I part from, parry, and separate myself from'].[46] This circularity inherent in language ('ce dont je pars [. . .] ce qui se sépare de moi en partant de moi') bears a close resemblance to the circularity of the narrator's relationship with Algeria as reflected in the structure of *Les Rêveries de la femme sauvage*. That circularity – the fact that the narrator had to break the link completely before she could return to her native country, that only by leaving it could she welcome being part of it – appears independent of the text's existence; a certain time had to elapse before she could bear Algeria, in any sense of the English verb. As such, the hospitality I have argued she displays towards it was not merely generated by writing the book. Nevertheless, Cixous's exploration of the hospitality of language insists that writing also plays a performative, irreducible role in its emergence. It is because narrative *makes*, that is, *gives* time that writing is incomparably propitious to the kind of hospitality *Les Rêveries de la femme sauvage* displays, one which seeks not to mend a broken relation but rather to cherish it as it is. Cixous reminds us that 'tout ce qui encore est indicible est déjà lisible' (156) ['everything that is still unsayable is already readable' (88)]. Telling her 'inséparabité' allows her to separate from it without violence, that is to express or expel in a new, 'viable' form her complicated, convoluted relationship with her Algerian origins in a way that neither simplifies nor embellishes it but rather, in accordance with the laws of hospitality, admits it such as it is and lets it be.

Notes

1. Elissa Marder, 'Birthmarks (Given Names)', *parallax*, 13:3 (2007), 49–61, at 52.
2. Claire Boyle, 'Writing Self-Estrangement: Possessive Knowledge and Loss in Cixous's Recent Autobiographical Work', *Dalhousie French Studies*, 68 (Fall 2004), 69–77, at 70.
3. See http://www.fabula.org/actualites/cixous-depuis-2000-cixous-since-200 0_56545.php, consulted on 16 June 2013.
4. Hélène Cixous, *Les Rêveries de la femme sauvage: Scènes primitives* (Paris: Galilée, 2000) [*Reveries of the Wild Woman: Primal Scenes*, trans. Beverley Bie Brahic (Evanston: Northwestern University Press, 2000)]. Unless otherwise indicated, page references in this chapter are to these texts.
5. Hélène Cixous, *Or: Les letters de mon père* [*Or: My Father's Letters*] (Paris: Éditions des femmes, 1997); *Osnabrück* (Paris: Éditions des femmes, 1999).
6. Marder explains that 1991 was the year in which Cixous published *L'Ange au secret* [*The Angel with a Secret*] (Paris: Éditions des femmes, 1991), but does not discuss its significance for her argument. Over the following years, Cixous also produced *Déluge* [*Deluge*] (1992); *Beethoven à jamais, ou l'existence de Dieu* [*Beethoven Forever, or the Existence of God*] (Paris: Éditions des femmes, 1993); *La Fiancée juive: de la tentation* [*The Jewish*

Fiancée: Of Temptation] (Paris: Éditions des femmes, 1995); and *Messie* [*Messiah*] (Paris: Éditions des femmes, 1996).

7. 'Birthmarks (Given Names)', 52.

8. That said, Jeannet in turn will finally posit a 'césure' ['cæsura'] in Cixous's work, which he identifies as taking place with *Jours de l'an* (Paris: Éditions des femmes, 1990); see *Rencontre terrestre*, 124; *Encounters*, 131.

9. *Rencontre terrestre*, 43–4; *Encounters*, 40–1.

10. See Hélène Cixous, *Manne: aux Mandelstams aux Mandelas* (Paris: Éditions des femmes, 1988).

11. *Rencontre terrestre*, 44–5; *Encounters*, 41.

12. Hélène Cixous, *Neutre* [*Neutral*] (Paris: Grasset, 1972); *Le Jour où je n'étais pas là* (Paris: Galilée, 2000) [*The Day I Wasn't There*, trans. Beverley Bie Brahic (Evanston: Northwestern University Press, 2006)].

13. *Rencontre terrestre*, 53; *Encounters*, 51.

14. For Ned Lukacher, the primal scene signifies 'an ontologically undecidable intertextual event that is situated in the differential space between historical memory and imaginative construction, between archival verification and interpretative free play' (*Primal Scenes: Literature, Philosophy and Psychoanalysis* (New York: Cornell University Press, 1986), 24).

15. For a discussion of the 'book-she-did-not-write', see especially Hélène Cixous, 'Le livre que je n'écris pas', in *Genèses Généalogies Genres: Autour de l'œuvre d'Hélène Cixous*, sous la direction de Mireille Calle-Gruber et Marie-Odile Germain (Paris: Galilée/Bibliothèque nationale de France, 2006); and *Tours promises* (Paris: Galilée, 2004). I have discussed *Jours de l'an* in the light of the 'book-she-did-not-write' in 'Where Thinking Is Not What We Think', *New Literary History*, 37:1 (2006), 179–95.

16. Hélène Cixous, *Jours de l'an* (Paris: des femmes, 1990), 85; *FirstDays of the Year*, trans. and preface Catherine MacGillivray (Minneapolis and London: University of Minnesota Press, 1998), 56.

17. *Jours de l'an*, 185–6; *FirstDays of the Year*, 124. Cixous furthermore inter-prets the Romanian Germanophone poet Paul Celan's inversion of his original name, Ancel, in similar terms, as a necessary contrary or counter-movement through which alone advance is possible: 'Celan, le poète au nom renversé, le poète qui avait commencé par être appelé Ancel, puis avait cessé d'être appelé Ancel, puis s'était appelé lui-même: Celan, et c'est ainsi qu'il était sorti de l'oubli dans lequel on l'avait glissé, *en s'appelant contrai-rement* [. . .] C'est seulement ainsi que l'on peut s'avancer, en commençant par la fin, la mort la première, la vie ensuite, ensuite la vie chancelante, si chancelante, si chance, si celante' (*Jours de l'an*, 14) ['Celan, the poet with the name in reverse, the poet who started out being called Ancel, then stopped being called Ancel, then called himself Celan, and thus had emerged from the forgetting into which we had slipped him, *by calling himself contrarily* [. . .] Only thus are we able to advance, by beginning at the end, death first, life next, chancy, secret life, so celative, so elative, so celantive, so *celante*' (*FirstDays of the Year*, 9)].

18. Hélène Cixous, 'En octobre 1991 . . .', 133–4 ; 'In October 1991 . . .', 47.

19. 'Birthmarks (Given Names)', 52.

20. See especially Hélène Cixous, *Osnabrück*, *Benjamin à Montaigne: Il ne faut pas le dire* (Paris: Galilée, 2001), *Hyperrêve* (Paris: Galilée, 2006), *Ciguë:*

Vieille femmes en fleurs (Paris: Galilée, 2008), *Ève s'évade* (Paris: Galilée, 2009), *Revirements dans l'antarctique du cœur* (Paris: Galilée, 2011). For a reading of *Osnabruck* in the light of this change, see my 'The Place of the Mother: Hélène Cixous's *Osnabrück*,' *Paragraph*, 27:1 (2004), 6–20.

21. Hélène Cixous, *Si près* (Paris: Galilée, 2007).

22. *Tours promises*, 95–6.

23. The list is, in fact, endless. We can note, for example, that one of Cixous's most recent texts, *Abstracts et brèves Chroniques du temps: I Chapitre Los* (Paris: Galilée, 2013), is presented in the first sentence of the *Prière d'insérer* or review slip as 'un chapitre du *Livre-que-je-n'écris-pas*' ['a chapter of the *Book-I-do-not-write*']. An interesting question might be to ask which, if any, of Cixous's texts are *not* instalments of the 'book-she-does-not-write'.

24. Hélène Cixous, 'Une Virginité de mémoire', in *Mon Algérie: 62 personnalités témoignent*, ed. Monique Ayoun and Jean-Pierre Stora (Paris: Acropole, 1988), 88–90.

25. One instance of this was the somewhat controversial decision by the editorial board of the newly founded journal *Expressions maghrébines* to devote one of its first numbers to Cixous's work. A section of this chapter originally appeared in French in that number under the title '*Les Rêveries de la femme sauvage* ou le temps de l'hospitalité' (*Expressions maghrébines*, 2:2 (2003), 55–69).

26. This tragic dimension is the focus of Mireille Rosello's reading of the text in 'Frapper aux portes invisibles avec des mots-valises: la *malgériance* d'Hélène Cixous', in *Le Dire de l'hospitalité*, ed. Lise Gauvin, Pierre L'Hérault and Alain Montandon (Clermont-Ferrand: Presses Universitaires Blaise Pascal, 2004), 61–74. In this essay, which unfortunately appeared too late for me to cite it in the first version of this chapter, Rosello admires Cixous for recognising the unavoidable violence of any request for hospitality on the part of anyone placed, as Rosello assumes Cixous was placed, as an 'Européenne en Algérie', that is a potential guest rather than a host (70).

27. Hélène Cixous, *Les Rêveries de la femme sauvage*, 9; *Reveries of the Wild Woman*, 3. Henceforward, page references in this chapter are to this text and its translation unless otherwise indicated.

28. In the English version, the comment clauses are given in italics which obscures this difference. I have reinstituted them in the translation given above.

29. See, for example, Stevens's *L'Écriture solaire d'Hélène Cixous*, 166–73.

30. For a comprehensive discussion of Derrida on hospitality, see Judith Still, *Derrida and Hospitality: Theory and Practice* (Edinburgh: Edinburgh University Press, 2010). For the tension Derrida sees between an ethics and a politics of hospitality, see Mireille Rosello, *Postcolonial Hospitality: The Immigrant as Guest* (Stanford: Stanford University Press, 2001), 11–13. For a comprehensive discussion of the relationship between deconstruction and postcolonial theory, see Michael Syrotinski, *Deconstruction and the Postcolonial: At the Limits of Theory* (Liverpool: Liverpool University Press, 2007).

31. Jacques Derrida, *De l'Hospitalité: Anne Dufourmantelle invite Jacques Derrida à répondre* (Paris: Calmann-Lévy, 1997), 31; *Of Hospitality: Anne*

Dufourmantelle invites Jacques Derrida to respond, trans. Rachel Bowlby (Stanford: Stanford University Press, 2000), 27.

32. *De l'Hospitalité*, 29; *Of Hospitality*, 25.

33. *De l'Hospitalité*, 53 and 111; *Of Hospitality*, 53–4 and 125. Cixous twice uses the metaphor of the hostage (68 and 76), a figure of a (sudden, hostile) transformation of an inside into an outside which corresponds thematically to the reversals that her writing practises systematically.

34. *De l'hospitalité*, 47; *Of Hospitality*, 49.

35. For a theoretical problematisation of how sexual difference complicates models of hospitality, see Still's *Derrida and Hospitality*, ch. 3 (93–142).

36. Cixous exploits this uncertainty in a range of texts, and in particular in the privileged position of the title: *Entre l'écriture* [*Enter Writing*], 'Entre le théâtre' ['Enter the Theatre'], etc.

37. My reading diverges from Rosello's in relation to her interpretation of this passage in terms of an 'idéal d'inséparabité' ['ideal of inseparabity'] ('Frapper aux portes', 73). As I understand the text, the narrator's 'inseparabity' was not an impossible ideal of a borderless union but rather the source of her suffering, the condition which bound her to the Arab neighbours with whom at the same time she could not exist.

38. There is also a fault line within the family between the two children, on the one hand, and the mother and grandmother, on the other. These intrafamilial fault lines are, however, constantly shifting: 'Je parlerai [. . .] de ce fossé vertigineux qui se creusait entre nous et elles. Tout ceci se passait à l'intérieur de la maison. / Mais à l'extérieur nous reformions la famille pour résister aux diverses attaques venant des camps ennemis' (30) ['I shall speak [. . .] of the dizzying abyss which opened between them and us. All this was inside the house. / But outside we became a family again, to fend off a variety of attacks from the enemy camps' (14)].

39. Given that *Les Rêveries de la femme sauvage* was written after Derrida's study of Cixous's work in 'H. C. pour la vie, c'est à dire . . .', where he identified a unilaterality meaning that, for her, 'il n'y a pas d'autre côté que [. . .] le côté de la vie' (HC, 43) ['there is only one side [. . .] and this side is that of life' (HCE, 36)], this passage is particularly interesting in that it suggests that the dissymmetry of Cixous's world-vision has its origin in the dissymmetrical structure of her first relationships in Algeria.

40. Cixous's asymmetrical relationship with one of these girls, Zohra Drif, imprisoned for her activities during the Algerian War of Independence and in later years a prominent member of the Algerian Senate, became the central focus of two later texts, 'Lettre à Zohra Drif', *Lectora: revista de dones i textualitati*, 7 (2001), 183–8, available online at http://www. ub.edu/cdona/Lectora_07/CREACI%D3N/H%C9L%C8NE%20 CIXOUS_Lettre%20%E0%20Zohra%20Drif.pdf and *Si près*. For a consideration of the specificity of the return to Algeria in the latter (which followed Cixous's first journey to the country after many years), see Marta Segarra, 'Allégorie du voyage en Algérie', in *Rêver croire penser*, 155–60.

41. Jacques Lacan, 'L'Instance de la lettre dans l'inconscient, ou la raison depuis Freud', *Écrits* (Paris: Seuil, 1966), 493–528, at 503; 'The Instance of the Letter in the Unconscious, or Reason since Freud', in *Ecrits: A Selection*, trans. Bruce Fink (New York: Norton, 2002), 138–68, at 146.

42. In fact, the published translation translates 'communions' as 'communicate' rather than 'commune'.
43. Similarly, and in line with her renouncing the plural pronoun 'nous', the narrator's mother does not have 'le sentiment d'appartenir à une communauté' (101) ['the feeling of belonging to a community' (59)].
44. *De l'hospitalité*, 119; *Of Hospitality*, 135. Cixous articulates a similar idea when she contrasts the 'stormy, intermittent hospitality of the [French] State and of the Nation' with the 'infinite hospitality' of its language ('My Algeriance', 55).
45. Jennifer Yee pays welcome attention to Cixous's 'linguistic play and invention' in 'The Colonial Outsider: "malgérie" in Hélène Cixous's *Les Rêveries de la femme sauvage*', *Tulsa Studies in Women's Literature*, 20:2 (2001), 189–200.
46. *De l'hospitalité*, 85; *Of Hospitality*, 91.

Works Cited

Works by Hélène Cixous

This is a list only of those of Cixous's texts referred to in the book, not an exhaustive record of her publications to date.

L'Exil de James Joyce ou l'art du remplacement (Paris: Grasset, 1968).
Dedans (Paris: Éditions des femmes, 1986 [1969]).
Les Commencements (Paris: Éditions des femmes, 1999 [1970]).
Neutre (Paris: Grasset, 1972).
Portrait du soleil (Paris: Denoël, 1973).
Souffles (Paris: Éditions des femmes, 1975).
'Le Rire de la Méduse', *L'Arc*, 45 (1975), 39–54.
Partie (Paris: Éditions des femmes, 1976).
Anankè (Paris: Éditions des femmes, 1979).
Le Livre de Promethea (Paris: Gallimard, 1983).
La Venue à l'écriture, in *Entre l'écriture* (Paris: Éditions des femmes, 1986 [1976]).
L'Histoire terrible mais inachevée de Norodom Sihanouk, Roi du Cambodge, nouvelle édition revue et corrigée (Paris: Théâtre du Soleil, 1987 [1984]).
L'Indiade ou l'Inde de leurs rêves et quelques écrits sur le théâtre (Paris: Théâtre du Soleil, 1987).
Manne: aux Mandelstams aux Mandelas (Paris: Éditions des femmes, 1988).
'Une Virginité de mémoire' in *Mon Algérie: 62 personnalités témoignent*, ed. Monique Ayoun and Jean-Pierre Stora (Paris: Acropole, 1988), 88–90.
'De la scène de l'Inconscient à la scène de l'Histoire', in *Hélène Cixous, chemins d'une écriture*, ed. Françoise van Rossum-Guyon and Myriam Diaz-Diocaretz (Paris and Amsterdam: Rodopi/Presses Universitaires de Vincennes, 1990).
Jours de l'an (Paris: Éditions des femmes, 1990).
L'Ange au secret (Paris: Éditions des femmes, 1991).
Déluge (Paris: Éditions des femmes, 1992).
'En octobre 1991 . . .', in *Du Féminin*, ed. Mireille Calle-Gruber (Sainte-Foy and Grenoble: Le Griffon d'argile and Presses Universitaires de Grenoble, 1992), 115–37.
Beethoven à jamais, ou l'existence de Dieu (Paris: Éditions des femmes, 1993).

'Contes de la différence sexuelle', in *Lectures de la différence sexuelle*, textes réunis et présentés par Mara Negrón (Paris: Éditions des femmes, 1994), 31–68.

'Quelle heure est-il, ou La porte (celle qu'on ne passe pas)', in *Le Passage des frontières: Autour du travail de Jacques Derrida*, ed. Marie-Louise Mallet (Paris: Galilée, 1994), 83–98.

L'Histoire (qu'on ne connaîtra jamais) (Paris: Éditions des femmes, 1994).

La Fiancée juive: de la tentation (Paris: Éditions des femmes, 1995).

Messie (Paris: Éditions des femmes, 1996).

Or: Les letters de mon père (Paris: Éditions des femmes, 1997).

Osnabrück (Paris: Éditions des femmes, 1999).

Tambours sur la digue (Paris: Théâtre du Soleil, 1999).

Les Rêveries de la femme sauvage: Scènes primitives (Paris: Galilée, 2000).

Le Jour où je n'étais pas là (Paris: Galilée, 2000).

'Lettre à Zohra Drif', *Lectora: revista de dones i textualitat*, 7 (2001), 183–8.

Portrait de Jacques Derrida en Jeune Saint Juif (Paris: Galilée, 2001).

Benjamin à Montaigne: Il ne faut pas le dire (Paris: Galilée, 2001).

'Ce corps étranjuif', in *Judéités: Questions pour Jacques Derrida*, ed. Joseph Cohen and Raphael Zagury-Orly (Paris: Galilée, 2003), 59–83.

Rêve je te dis (Paris: Galilée, 2003).

L'Amour du loup et autres remords (Paris: Galilée, 2003).

'De la démoncratie en littérature ou Le Diable sans Confession', in *La Démocratie à venir: Autour de Jacques Derrida*, ed. Marie-Louise Mallet (Paris: Galilée, 2004), 189–223.

'Fichus et caleçons', in *Derrida: Cahier Derrida, Cahiers de l'Herne*, 83, ed. Marie-Louise Mallet and Ginette Michaud (Paris: Éditions de l'Herne, 2004), 56–61.

Tours promises (Paris: Galilée, 2004).

Insister: A Jacques Derrida (Paris: Galilée, 2006).

'Le livre que je n'écris pas', in *Genèses Généalogies Genre: Autour de l'œuvre d'Hélène Cixous*, sous la direction de Mireille Calle-Gruber et Marie-Odile Germain (Paris: Galilée/Bibliothèque nationale de France, 2006).

Hyperrêve (Paris: Galilée, 2006).

'Ce qui a l'air de quoi', in *L'Événement comme écriture: Cixous et Derrida se lisant*, ed. Marta Segarra (Paris: Campagne Première, 2007), 11–71.

Si près (Paris: Galilée, 2007).

Ciguë: Vieille femmes en fleurs (Paris: Galilée, 2008).

Ève s'évade (Paris: Galilée, 2009).

La Ville parjure ou le réveil des Erinyes, nouvelle édition revue et augmentée (Paris: Théâtre du Soleil, 2010 [1994]).

Hélène Cixous, *Le Rire de la Méduse et autres ironies*, preface Frédéric Regard (Paris: Galilée, 2010).

Revirements dans l'antarctique du cœur (Paris: Galilée, 2011).

Entretien de la blessure: Sur Jean Genet (Paris: Galilée, 2011).

Abstracts et brèves Chroniques du temps: I Chapitre Los (Paris: Galilée, 2013).

Co-authored works

(with Catherine Clément) *La Jeune née* (Paris: 10/18, 1975).
(with Mireille Calle-Gruber) *Hélène Cixous, Photos de racines* (Paris: Éditions des femmes, 1994).
(with Jacques Derrida) *Voiles* (Paris: Galilée, 1998).
(with Frédéric-Yves Jeannet) *Rencontre terrestre* (Paris: Galilée, 2005).

Works by Hélène Cixous in translation

The Exile of James Joyce, trans. Sally Purcell (New York: David Lewis, 1972).
'The Laugh of the Medusa', *Signs*, 1:4 (Summer 1976), 875–93.
Inside, trans. Carol Barko (New York: Schocken Books, 1986).
'Coming to Writing' and Other Essays, intro. essay Susan Rubin Suleiman, ed. Deborah Jenson and trans. Sarah Cornell, Deborah Jenson, Ann Liddle and Susan Sellers (Cambridge, MA: Harvard University Press, 1991).
Three Steps on the Ladder of Writing, trans. Sarah Cornell and Susan Sellers (New York: Columbia University Press, 1993).
The Terrible But Unfinished Story of Norodom Sihanouk, King of Cambodia, trans. Juliet Flower MacCannell, Judith Pike and Lollie Groth (Lincoln, NE: University of Nebraska Press, 1994).
FirstDays of the Year, trans. and ed. with a preface by Catherine MacGillivray (Minneapolis and London: University of Minnesota Press, 1998).
Stigmata: Escaping Texts (London: Routledge, 1998).
'In October 1991 . . .', trans. Keith Cohen, in *Stigmata: Escaping Texts* (London and New York: Routledge, 1998), 35–49.
'What Is It O'clock? or The Door (We Never Enter)', trans. Catherine A. F. MacGillivray, in *Stigmata: Escaping Texts* (London: Routledge, 1998), 57–83.
'My Algeriance, in other words: to depart not to arrive from Algeria', trans. Prenowitz, *Stigmata: Escaping Texts* (London and New York: Routledge, 1998), 153–72.
Reveries of the Wild Woman: Primal Scenes, trans. Beverley Bie Brahic (Evanston: Northwestern University Press, 2000).
Portrait of Jacques Derrida as a Young Jewish Saint, trans. Beverly Bie Brahic (New York: Columbia University Press, 2003).
Selected Plays of Hélène Cixous, ed. Eric Prenowitz (London: Routledge, 2004).
'Enter the Theatre', *Selected Plays of Hélène Cixous*, ed. Eric Prenowitz (London: Routledge, 2004), 25–34.
The Perjured City, Or the Awakening of the Furies, trans. Bernadette Fort, in *Selected Plays of Hélène Cixous*, ed. Eric Prenowitz (London and New York: Routledge, 2004), 89–190.
Dream I Tell You, trans. Beverley Bie Brahic (Edinburgh: Edinburgh University Press, 2006).
The Day I Wasn't There, trans. Beverley Bie Brahic (Evanston: Northwestern University Press, 2006).
'This Stranjew Body', in *Questions for Jacques Derrida*, trans. Bettina Bergo and Michael B. Smith (New York: Fordham University Press, 2007), 52–77.

Insister of Jacques Derrida, trans. Peggy Kamuf (Edinburgh: Edinburgh University Press, 2007).

'Jacques Derrida as a Proteus Unbound', trans. Peggy Kamuf, *Critical Inquiry*, 33 (2007), 389–423.

'Tales of Sexual Difference', trans. Eric Prenowitz, *The Portable Cixous*, ed. Marta Segarra (New York: Columbia University Press, 2010), 48–60.

'A Kind of Magic', *Cixous, Derrida, Psychoanalysis*, ed. Mark Dawson, Mairéad Hanrahan and Eric Prenowitz, *Paragraph*, 36:2 (2013), 161–88.

Co-Authored Works

(with Catherine Clément) *The Newly Born Woman*, trans. Betsy Wing, intro. Sandra M. Gilbert (Minneapolis and London: University of Minnesota Press, 1986).

(with Mireille Calle-Gruber) *Rootprints: Memory and Life Writing*, trans. Eric Prenowitz (London and New York: Routledge, 1997).

(with Jacques Derrida) *Veils*, trans. Geoffrey Bennington (Stanford: Stanford University Press, 2001).

(with Frédéric-Yves Jeannet) *Encounters: Conversations on Life and Writing*, trans. Beverley Bie Brahic (Cambridge: Polity, 2013).

Interviews with Hélène Cixous

Makward, Christiane and Cixous, Hélène. 'Interview with Hélène Cixous', *SubStance*, 5:13 (1976), 19–37.

'Entretien avec Françoise van Rossum-Guyon', *Revue des Sciences humaines*, 44:169 (Octobre–Décembre 1977), 479–93.

Franke, Catherine and Chazal, Roger. 'Interview with Hélène Cixous', *Qui parle*, 3:1 (1989), 152–79.

O'Grady, Kathleen. 'Guardian of Language: An Interview with Hélène Cixous', *Women's education des femmes*, 12:4 (Winter 1996–7), 6–10.

Cixous, Hélène and Fort, Bernadette. 'Theater, History, Ethics: An Interview with Hélène Cixous on "The Perjured City, or the Awakening of the Furies"', *New Literary History*, 28:3 (Summer 1997), 425–56.

'Auteur au Théâtre du Soleil: Entretien avec Hélène Cixous', available online at http://www.theatre-du-soleil.fr/thsol/IMG/pdf/Auteur_au_Theatre_du_soleil. pdf.

'On Theatre: An Interview with Hélène Cixous', in *Selected Plays of Hélène Cixous*, ed. Eric Prenowitz (London: Routledge, 2004), 1–24.

Writing Not Yet Thought: Hélène Cixous with Adrian Heathfield (London: Performance Matters, 2011).

Other Works

Abbott, H. Porter. *The Cambridge Introduction to Narrative* (Cambridge: Cambridge University Press, 2002).

Abraham, Nicolas, and Torok, Maria. *L'Ecorce et le noyau* (Paris: Champs Flammarion, 1978).

Aristotle. *On the Art of Poetry* in *Aristotle, Horace, Longinus: Classical Literary Criticism*, trans. with intro. T. S. Dorsch (London and Harmondsworth: Penguin, 1965).

Artaud, Antonin. 'Ci-Gît', *Œuvres complètes*, tome 12 (Paris: Gallimard, 1974).

Augé, Marc. *Non-lieux: Introduction à une anthropologie de la surmodernité* (Paris: Seuil, 1992).

Barthes, Roland. *S/Z* (Paris: Éditions du Seuil, 1970).

Barthes, Roland. *S/Z*, trans. Richard Miller (New York: Hill & Wang, 1974).

Bellemin-Noël, Jean. *Psychanalyse et littérature* (Paris: PUF, coll. Que sais-je?, 1978).

Bennington, Geoffrey. 'Teleanalysis', in *Cixous, Derrida, Psychoanalysis*, ed. Mark Dawson, Mairéad Hanrahan and Eric Prenowitz, *Paragraph*, 36:2 (2013), 270–85.

Benveniste, Emile. 'De la subjectivité dans le langage', *Problèmes de linguistique générale I* (Paris: Gallimard (coll. Tel), 1966), 258–66.

Berger, Anne. 'Appels', in *L'événement comme écriture: Cixous et Derrida se lisant*, ed. Marta Segarra (Paris: Éditions Campagne Première, 2007), 85–107.

Berglund Hall, Elizabeth. 'Mundane Interruptions: The Insignificance of Hélène Cixous's *Le Jour où je n'étais pas là*', *Romanic Review*, 100:3 (May 2009), 329–44.

Binhammer, Katherine. 'Metaphor or Metonymy? The Question of Essentialism in Cixous', *Tessera*, 10 (1991), 65–79.

Bourcier, Marie-Hélène. *Sexpolitiques: queer zones 2* (Paris: La Fabrique, 2005).

Boyle, Claire. 'Writing Self-Estrangement: Possessive Knowledge and Loss in Cixous's Recent Autobiographical Work', *Dalhousie French Studies*, 68 (Fall 2004), 69–77.

Boyle, Claire. *Consuming Autobiographies: Reading and Writing the Self in Post-War France* (Oxford: Legenda, 2007).

Brooks, Peter. *Reading for the Plot: Design and Intention in Narrative* (Cambridge, MA: Harvard University Press, 1984).

Brooks, Peter. 'The Idea of a Psychoanalytic Literary Criticism', *Critical Inquiry*, 13:2 (1987), 334–48.

Calle-Gruber, Mireille (ed.). *Hélène Cixous: Croisées d'une œuvre, Actes du Colloque de Cerisy-la-Salle*, ed. Mireille Calle-Gruber (Paris: Galilée, 2000).

Calle-Gruber, Mireille. *Du café à l'éternité: Hélène Cixous à l'œuvre* (Paris: Galilée, 2002).

Carrera, Elena. 'Teresa of Avila and Hélène Cixous: Corps-à-corps with the Mother', *Journal of the Institute of Romance Studies*, 2 (1993), 409–28.

Conley, Verena Andermatt. *Hélène Cixous: Writing the Feminine* (Lincoln, NE and London: University of Nebraska Press, 1984).

Clément, Bruno. *L'Œuvre sans qualités. Rhétorique de Samuel Beckett* (Paris: Seuil, 1989).

Dawson, Mark, Hanrahan, Mairéad and Prenowitz, Eric (eds). *Cixous, Derrida, Psychoanalysis*, Special Number of *Paragraph*, 36:2 (2013).

Deleuze, Gilles and Guattari, Félix. *L'Anti-Œdipe* (Paris: Galilée, 1972).

Derrida, Jacques. *Glas* (Paris: Galilée, 1974).

Derrida, Jacques. *La Carte postale: de Socrate à Freud et au-delà* (Paris: Flammarion, 1980).
Derrida, Jacques. 'The Law of Genre', *Critical Inquiry*, 7:1 (Autumn 1980), 55–81.
Derrida, Jacques. 'La loi du genre', in *Parages* (Paris: Éditions Galilée, 1986), 249–87.
Derrida, Jacques. *The Post Card: From Socrates to Freud and Beyond*, trans. Alan Bass (Chicago: University of Chicago Press, 1987).
Derrida, Jacques. *Du droit à la philosophie* (Paris: Galilée, 1990).
Derrida, Jacques. 'Mochlos ou le conflit des facultés', *Du droit à la philosophie* (Paris: Galilée, 1990), 397–438.
Derrida, Jacques. 'Ponctuations: le temps de la thèse', in *Du droit à la philosophie* (Paris: Galilée, 1990), 439–59.
Derrida, Jacques. 'Les Pupilles de l'Université: Le principe de raison et l'idée de l'Université', in *Du droit à la philosophie* (Paris: Galilée, 1990), 461–98.
Derrida, Jacques. *Spectres de Marx: l'état de la dette, le travail du deuil et la nouvelle Internationale* (Paris: Galilée, 1993).
Derrida, Jacques. *Specters of Marx: The State of the Debt, the Work of Mourning and the New International*, trans. Peggy Kamuf, with intro. Bernd Magnus and Stephen Cullenberg (New York and London: Routledge, 1994).
Derrida, Jacques. 'Fourmis', in *Lectures de la Différence Sexuelle*, textes réunis et présentés par Mara Negrón (Paris: Éditions des femmes, 1994), 69–102.
Derrida, Jacques. *Mal d'Archive* (Paris: Galilée, 1995).
Derrida, Jacques. *De l'Hospitalité: Anne Dufourmantelle invite Jacques Derrida à répondre* (Paris: Calmann-Lévy, 1997).
Derrida, Jacques. *Archive Fever*, trans. Eric Prenowitz (Chicago: University of Chicago Press, 1998).
Derrida, Jacques. 'Un Ver à soie: Points de vue piqués sur l'autre voile', in Hélène Cixous and Jacques Derrida, *Voiles* (Paris: Galilée, 1998), 23–85.
Derrida, Jacques. *États d'âme de la psychanalyse* (Paris: Galilée, 2000).
Derrida, Jacques. 'H. C. pour la vie, c'est à dire . . .', *Hélène Cixous: Croisées d'une œuvre, Actes du Colloque de Cerisy-la-Salle*, ed. Mireille Calle-Gruber (Paris: Galilée, 2000), 13–140.
Derrida, Jacques. *Of Hospitality: Anne Dufourmantelle invites Jacques Derrida to respond*, trans. Rachel Bowlby (Stanford: Stanford University Press, 2000).
Derrida, Jacques. 'A Silkworm of One's Own', in Hélène Cixous and Jacques Derrida, *Veils*, trans. Geoffrey Bennington (Stanford: Stanford University Press, 2001), 17–92.
Derrida, Jacques. 'Psychoanalysis Searches the States of Its Soul', in *Without Alibi*, trans. Peggy Kamuf (Stanford: Stanford University Press, 2002), 238–80.
Derrida, Jacques. *Genèses, généalogies, genres et le génie: les secrets de l'archive* (Paris: Galilée, 2003).
Derrida, Jacques. *Geneses, Genealogies, Genres and Genius: The Secrets of the Archive*, trans. Beverley Bie Brahic (Edinburgh: Edinburgh University Press, 2003).
Derrida, Jacques. *Eyes of the University* (Stanford: Stanford University Press, 2004).
Derrida, Jacques. 'Punctuations: The Time of a Thesis', in *Eyes of the University: Right to Philosophy 2*, trans. Jan Plug and others (Stanford: Stanford University Press, 2004), 113–28.

Derrida, Jacques. 'Mochlos or the Conflict of the Faculties', in *Eyes of the University: Right to Philosophy* 2, trans. Jan Plug and others (Stanford: Stanford University Press, 2004), 83–112.

Derrida, Jacques. 'The Principle of Reason: The University in the Eyes of Its Pupils', *Eyes of the University* (Stanford: Stanford University Press, 2004), 129–55.

Derrida, Jacques. *H. C. for Life, That Is to Say . . .*, trans. with Additional Notes Laurent Milesi and Stefan Herbrechter (Stanford: Stanford University Press, 2006).

Dobson, Julia. *Hélène Cixous and the Theatre: The Scene of Writing* (Bern: Peter Lang, 2002).

Eagleton, Terry. *Sweet Violence: The Idea of the Tragic* (Oxford: Blackwell, 2003).

Felman, Shoshana. 'To Open the Question', *Literature and Psychoanalysis: The Question of Reading: Otherwise*, Special Issue, *Yale French Studies*, 55/56 (1977), 5–10.

Felman, Shoshana (ed.). *Literature and Psychoanalysis: The Question of Reading: Otherwise*, Special Issue, *Yale French Studies*, 55/56 (1977).

Felman, Shoshana. *Jacques Lacan and the Adventure of Insight: Psychoanalysis in Contemporary Culture* (Cambridge, MA and London: Harvard University Press, 1987).

Fisher, Claudine G. 'Cixous's Auto-Fictional Mother and Father', *Pacific Coast Philology*, 38 (2003), 60–76.

Forrester, John. 'Who Is in Analysis with Whom? Freud, Lacan, Derrida', *Economy and Society*, 13:2 (1984), 153–77.

Freeman, Barbara. '"Plus corps donc plus écriture": Hélène Cixous and the Mind-Body Problem', *Paragraph*, 11:1 (1988), 58–70.

Freud, Sigmund. *New Introductory Lectures on Psychoanalysis*, The Pelican Freud Library, Vol. 2 (Harmondsworth: Penguin, 1973).

Freud, Sigmund. *The Interpretation of Dreams*, The Pelican Freud Library, Vol. 4 (Harmondsworth: Penguin, 1975).

Freud, Sigmund. *Case Histories II*, The Pelican Freud Library, Vol. 9 (Harmondsworth: Penguin, 1979).

Freud, Sigmund. *The Complete Letters to Wilhelm Fliess (1887–1904)*, ed. Joseph M. Masson (Cambridge, MA: Belknap Press, 1985).

Genet, Jean. *Journal du voleur* (Paris: Gallimard, coll. Folio, 1949).

Genet, Jean. *Pompes funèbres* (Paris: Gallimard, collection 'Imaginaire', 1949).

Genet, Jean. *Miracle de la rose, Œuvres complètes* II (Paris: Gallimard, 1951).

Genet, Jean. *Œuvres complètes* IV (Paris: Gallimard, 1968).

Genet, Jean. 'What Remains of a Rembrandt Torn into Little Squares All the Same Size and Shot Down the Toilet', *Fragments of the Artwork*, trans. Charlotte Mandell (Stanford: Stanford University Press, 2003), 91–102.

Genette, Gérard. 'Frontières du récit', *Figures II* (Paris: Éditions du Seuil, 1969), 49–69.

Genette, Gérard. *Introduction à l'architexte* (Paris: Éditions du Seuil, 1979).

Genette, Gérard. 'Frontiers of narrative', *Figures of Literary Discourse*, trans. Alan Sheridan with intro. Marie-Rose Logan (New York: Columbia University Press, 1982).

Genette, Gérard. *Seuils* (Paris: Seuil, 1987).

Genette, Gérard. *Fiction et diction* (Paris: Éditions du Seuil, 1991).

Genette, Gérard. *The Architext: An Introduction*, trans. Jane E. Lewin with intro. Robert Scholes (Berkeley: University of California Press, 1992).

Genette, Gérard. *Fiction and Diction*, trans. Catherine Porter (Ithaca, NY and London: Cornell University Press, 1993).

Genette, Gérard. *Paratexts: Thresholds of Interpretation*, trans. Jane Lewin with foreword Richard Macksey (Cambridge: Cambridge University Press, 1997).

Goethe, Johann Wolfgang. *Faust 2*, ed. Helmut Kobligk (Frankfurt: M. Diesterweg, 1973).

Gombrich, E. H. 'Freud's Æsthetics', in *Literature and Psychoanalysis*, ed. Edith Kurzweil and William Phillips (New York: Columbia University Press, 1983), 132–45.

Gruber, Eberhard. 'Réécriture du tragique' in *Hélène Cixous: Croisées d'une œuvre, Actes du Colloque de Cerisy-la-Salle*, ed. Mireille Calle-Gruber (Paris: Galilée, 2000), 163–87.

Hamburger, Käte. *Logique des genres littéraires* (Paris: Éditions du Seuil, 1986).

Hanrahan, Mairéad. 'Hélène Cixous's Improper Name', *Romanic Review*, 90:4 (1999), 481–97.

Hanrahan, Mairéad. 'Genet and Cixous: The InterSext', *French Review*, 72:4 (March 1999), 719–29.

Hanrahan, Mairéad. 'Of Altobiography', *Paragraph*, 23:3 (2000), 282–95.

Hanrahan, Mairéad. 'Cixous's *Le Livre De Promethea*: A Diary in an Other Form', *French Studies*, 55:2 (2001), 195–206.

Hanrahan, Mairéad. '*Les Rêveries de la femme sauvage* ou le temps de l'hospitalité', *Expressions maghrébines*, 2:2 (2003), 55–69.

Hanrahan, Mairéad. 'The Place of the Mother: Hélène Cixous's *Osnabrück*', *Paragraph*, 27:1 (2004), 6–20.

Hanrahan, Mairéad. 'Where Thinking Is Not What We Think', *New Literary History*, 37:1 (2006), 179–95.

Hanrahan, Mairéad. 'Long Cuts', *parallax* 44, 13:3 (2007), 37–48.

Hippo, Saint Augustine of. *Confessions* (New York: Penguin Classics, 1961).

Jakobson, Roman. 'Modern Russian Poetry: Velimir Khlebnikov [Excerpts]', in *Major Soviet Writers: Essays in Criticism*, ed. Edward J. Brown (Oxford: Oxford University Press, 1973).

Jakobson, Roman. *Questions de poétique* (Paris: Éditions du Seuil, 1973).

Kamuf, Peggy. 'To Give Place: Semi-Approaches to Hélène Cixous', *Yale French Studies*, 87 (1995), 68–89.

Kamuf, Peggy. 'Outside in Analysis', *Mosaic*, 42:4 (December 2009), 19–34.

Kermode, Frank. *The Sense of an Ending: Studies in the Theory of Fiction* (Oxford: Oxford University Press, 1967).

Kierkegaard, Søren. *Fear and Trembling*, trans. Alastair Hannay (Harmondsworth: Penguin, 1985).

Kristeva, Julia. *Pouvoirs de l'horreur: Essai sur l'abjection* (Paris: Seuil, 1980).

Lacan, Jacques. *Écrits* (Paris: Éditions du Seuil, 1966).

Lacan, Jacques. 'L'Essence de la Tragédie: Un commentaire de l'*Antigone* de Sophocle', *Le Séminaire Livre VII: L'éthique de la psychanalyse* (Paris: Seuil, 1986), 283–332.

Lacan, Jacques. 'The Instance of the Letter in the Unconscious, or Reason since Freud', in *Ecrits: A Selection*, trans. Bruce Fink (New York: Norton, 2002), 138–68.

Laplanche, Jean and Pontalis, Jean-Bertrand. *Vocabulaire de la psychanalyse* (Paris: Presses Universitaires de France, 1967).

Laplanche, Jean and Pontalis, Jean-Bertrand. *The Language of Psychoanalysis* (London: Karnac, 1973).

Lie, Sissel and Ringrose, Priscilla. 'Personal and/or Universal? Hélène Cixous's Challenge to Generic Borders', *European Legacy*, 14:1 (2009), 53–64.

Lukacher, Ned. *Primal Scenes: Literature, Philosophy and Psychoanalysis* (New York: Cornell University Press, 1986).

Man, Paul de. 'Autobiography as Defacement', in *Modern Language Notes*, 94:5 (1979), 919–30.

Marder, Elissa. 'Birthmarks (Given Names)', *parallax* 44, 13:3 (2007), 49–61.

Michaud, Ginette. *Veilleuses: Autour de trois images de Jacques Derrida* (Québec: Éditions Nota bene, 2009).

Michaud, Ginette. *Battements du secret littéraire: Lire Jacques Derrida et Hélène Cixous 1* (Paris: Hermann, 2010).

Michaud, Ginette. '*Comme en rêve*': *Lire Jacques Derrida et Hélène Cixous 2* (Paris: Hermann, 2010).

Milesi, Laurent. 'Portraits of H. C. as J. D. and Back', *New Literary History*, 37:1 (2006), 65–84.

Moi, Toril. *Sexual/Textual Politics* (London: Routledge, 1988).

Montaigne, Michel de. *Œuvres complètes*, ed. Albert Thibaudet and Maurice Rat (Paris: Gallimard (Bibliothèque de la Pléiade), 1962).

Montaigne, Michel de. *The Complete Essays*, trans. and ed. with intro. and notes M. A. Screech (London: Penguin, 1993).

Motard-Noar, Martine. *Les Fictions d'Hélène Cixous: Une autre langue de femme* (Lexington: French Forum, 1991).

Nietzsche, Friedrich. *The Birth of Tragedy*, trans. Shaun Whiteside, ed. Michael Tanner (London: Penguin, 1993).

Nuttall, A. D. *Why Does Tragedy Give Pleasure?* (Oxford: Oxford University Press, 1996).

Picard, Anne-Marie. 'Writing Within the Secret Father', in *Hélène Cixous: Critical Impressions*, ed. Lee A. Jacobus and Regina Barreca (Amsterdam: OPA, 1999).

Poole, Adrian. *Tragedy: A Very Short Introduction* (Oxford: Oxford University Press, 2005).

Prenowitz, Eric. 'Make Believe: *Manhattan*'s *Folittérature*', *New Literary History*, 37 (2006), 147–67.

Rabaté, Jean-Michel. *Jacques Lacan: Psychoanalysis and the Subject of Literature* (Basingstoke: Palgrave, 2001).

Regard, Frédéric. 'AA!', *Le Rire et autres ironies* (Paris: Galilée, 2010), 9–22.

Rice, Alison. *Time Signatures: Contextualizing Contemporary Francophone Autobiographical Writing from the Maghreb* (Lanham, MD and Oxford: Lexington Books, 2006).

Ricœur, Paul. *Temps et récit 1* (Paris: Éditions du Seuil, 1983).

Ricœur, Paul. *Time and Narrative 1*, trans. Kathleen McLaughlin and David Pellauer (Chicago: University of Chicago Press, 1984).

Rosello, Mireille. *Postcolonial Hospitality: The Immigrant as Guest* (Stanford: Stanford University Press, 2001).

Rosello, Mireille. 'Frapper aux portes invisibles avec des mots-valises: la *malgériance* d'Hélène Cixous', in *Le Dire de l'hospitalité*, ed. Lise Gauvin, Pierre L'Hérault and Alain Montandon (Clermont-Ferrand: Presses Universitaires Blaise Pascal, 2004), 61–74.

Royle, Nicholas. *After Derrida* (Manchester and New York: Manchester University Press, 1995).

Running-Johnson, Cynthia. 'Genet's "Excessive Double": Reading *Les Bonnes* through Irigaray and Cixous', *French Review*, 63:6 (May 1990), 959–66.

Running-Johnson, Cynthia. 'The Medusa's Tale: Feminine Writing and "La Genet"', *Romanic Review*, 80:3 (1989), 483–95.

Rye, Gill. *Reading for Change: Interactions between Text and Identity in Contemporary French Women's Writing (Baroche, Cixous, Constant)* (Bern: Peter Lang, 2001).

Sartre, Jean-Paul. *Saint Genet: Comédien et martyr*, Vol. I of Jean Genet, *Œuvres complètes* (Paris: Gallimard, 1952).

Schipa, Mary E. 'Hélène Cixous: Sur la piste d'une autobiographie féminine', *Romance Review*, 5:1 (1995), 29–37.

Segarra, Marta (ed.). *L'événement comme écriture: Cixous et Derrida se lisant* (Paris: Éditions Campagne Première, 2007).

Segarra, Marta. 'Allégorie du voyage en Algérie', in *Rêver croire penser, Autour d'Hélène Cixous* (Paris: Hermann, 2010), 155–60.

Segarra, Marta and Clément, Bruno (eds). *Rêver croire penser. Autour d'Hélène Cixous* (Paris: Hermann, 2010).

Sellers, Susan. *Hélène Cixous: Authorship, Autobiography and Love* (Cambridge: Polity Press, 1996).

Shakespeare, William. *The Complete Works*, ed. Stanley Wells and Gary Taylor (Oxford: Clarendon Press, 1986).

Shiach, Morag. *Hélène Cixous: A Politics of Writing* (London: Routledge, 1991).

Steiner, George. *The Death of Tragedy* (Oxford: Oxford University Press, 1961).

Steiner, George. '"Tragedy", Reconsidered,' *New Literary History*, 35:1 (2004), 1–15.

Stevens, Christa. *L'Écriture solaire d'Hélène Cixous: Travail du texte et histoires du sujet dans* Portrait du soleil (Amsterdam: Rodopi (Faux Titre), 1999).

Still, Judith. *Derrida and Hospitality: Theory and Practice* (Edinburgh: Edinburgh University Press, 2010).

Syrotinski, Michael. *Deconstruction and the Postcolonial: At the Limits of Theory* (Liverpool: Liverpool University Press, 2007).

Szondi, Peter. *An Essay on the Tragic*, trans. Paul Fleming (Stanford: Stanford University Press, 2002).

Wallace, Jennifer. *The Cambridge Introduction to Tragedy* (Cambridge: Cambridge University Press, 2007).

Yee, Jennifer. 'The Colonial Outsider: "malgérie" in Hélène Cixous's *Les Rêveries de la femme sauvage*', *Tulsa Studies in Women's Literature*, 20:2 (2001), 189–200.

Zupančič, Alenka. 'Ethics and tragedy in Lacan', *The Cambridge Companion to Lacan*, ed. Jean-Michel Rabaté (Cambridge: Cambridge University Press, 2003), 173–90.

Index

À *la recherché du temps perdu*, 21
Abbott, H. Porter, 11, 18n
Abraham, Nicolas, and Torok,
    Maria, 29, 30, 53n
Æschylus, 136
Africa, 1, 26, 55n, 113
Akhmatova, Anna, 136
Aristotle, 4, 5, 6, 15n, 131, 142, 146,
    155n
Artaud, Antonin, 43, 55n
Augé, Marc, 27, 53n

Balzac, Honoré de, 20
Barthes, Roland, 10, 18n
Beckett, Samuel, 20
Bellemin-Noël, Jean, 52n
Benmussa, Simone, 16n
Bennington, Geoffrey, 56, 87n
Benveniste, Emile, 54n
Berger, Anne, 63, 89n, 90n
Berglund Hall, Elizabeth, 140, 155n,
    157
Bernhardt, Thomas, 160
Binhammer, Katherine, 121n
Bourcier, Marie-Hélène, 121n
Boyle, Claire, 157, 180n
Brooks, Peter, 10–11, 18n, 49, 52n,
    55n
brother, representation of, 25, 39, 45,
    55n, 169–75, 177

Calle-Gruber, Mireille, 15n, 17n, 57,
    147, 161, 181n; *see also* Hélène
    Cixous: writings: *Hélène Cixous,
    Photos de racines*
Carrera, Elena, 123n

Celan, Paul, 136, 181n
Chamisso, Adelbert von, 102
Chazal, Roger *see* Franke, Catherine
Cixous, Hélène
    and Algeria, 1, 15n, 16n, 31, 124,
        128, 129, 162–80, 183n
    archives, 21, 32, 40–1, 53n, 90n,
        91n, 92n, 99, 109–10, 113,
        116–18, 121n, 122n, 161
    and autobiography, 7–8, 17n
    dreams/dreaming, 20, 23, 51n,
        67–8, 69, 70, 72, 73, 74, 76,
        91n, 103, 106, 125n, 135, 145,
        147, 149, 164, 174
    and father, 1, 8, 15n, 23–4, 69, 84,
        127
    interviews, 14, 18n, 59, 124n, 129,
        153, 154n
    Jewishness, 1, 19, 55n, 124n,
        126n, 127, 163, 167, 169,
        171–2, 177
    and mother, 1, 69, 127, 161–2,
        163
    periodisation of work, 157–60
    practice of writing, 2–3, 7, 9,
        11–12, 20, 22, 24, 32, 39, 43,
        47, 51n, 57, 59, 65, 66, 71,
        83–7, 91n, 94, 96–7, 101, 104,
        109, 116, 127, 131–2, 147–50,
        161–2, 164, 176–7, 179–80,
        183n
    reception of, 2–3, 8, 61–3, 94–8,
        163, 182n
    and religion, 1, 113–14, 169,
        171–2, 176–7; *see also* Cixous:
        Jewishness

Cixous, Hélène *(continued)*
  signature, 95, 116–20
  the-book-she-does-not-write,
    160–2, 181n, 182n
  WRITINGS
  'A Kind of Magic', 19–21, 50, 51n,
    52, 55n, 90n; *Abstracts et brèves
    Chroniques du temps: I Chapitre
    Los*, 182n; *Anankè*, 51n;
    *Beethoven à jamais, ou
    l'existence de Dieu*, 180n;
    *Benjamin à Montaigne: Il ne faut
    pas le dire*, 181n; 'Ce corps
    étranjuif' ('This Stranjew Body'),
    88n; 'Ce qui a l'air de quoi', 88n;
    Ciguë: Vieille femmes en fleurs,
    182n; 'Contes de la différence
    sexuelle' ('Tales of Sexual
    Difference'), 9, 17n, 87n, 89n,
    90n; 'De la démoncratie en
    littérature ou Le Diable sans
    Confession', 88n, 91n; 'De la
    scène de l'Inconscient à la scène
    de l'Histoire', 24, 52n; *Dedans
    (Inside)*, 13, 23–50, 52n, 72, 127,
    129; *Déluge*, 13, 130–53, 154n,
    155n, 156n, 180n; 'En octobre
    1991…' ('In October 1991…'),
    136–7, 138, 161, 181n; 'Enter
    the Theatre', 13, 18n, 127, 136,
    137, 153n, 183n; *Entre l'écriture*,
    183n; *Entretien de la blessure:
    Sur Jean Genet*, 121n; *Et soudain
    des nuits d'éveil*, 128; *Ève
    s'évade*, 182n; 'Fichus et
    caleçons', 88n; *Hélène Cixous,
    Photos de racines (Rootprints:
    Memory and Life Writing)*, 7,
    16n, 87n, 88n, 147, 154n, 156n;
    Hyperrêve, 181n; *Insister: A
    Jacques Derrida (Insister of
    Jacques Derrida)*, 88n, 89n;
    'Jacques Derrida as a Proteus
    Unbound', 88n; *Jours de l'an
    (FirstDays of the Year)*, 156n,
    160–1, 181n; *La Fiancée juive: de
    la tentation*, 180n; *La Jeune née
    (The Newly Born Woman)*, 15n,
    60–1, 89n, 94–8, 120n; *L'Amour
    du loup et autres remords*, 6,
    66–7, 90n, 155n; *L'Ange au*

secret, 180n; *La Venue à
    l'écriture (Coming to Writing)*,
    11, 18n, 23; *La Ville parjure ou
    le réveil des Erinyes (The
    Perjured City, Or the
    Awakening of the Furies)*, 128,
    137, 153n; *Le Jour où je n'étais
    pas là (The Day I Wasn't There)*,
    159, 161, 181n; *Le Livre de
    Promethea*, 7, 16n; *Le Rire de la
    Méduse et autres ironies*, 6, 94–7,
    120n, 121n; 'Le Rire de la
    Méduse' ('The Laugh of the
    Medusa'), 94–8, 99, 104, 113,
    114–15, 120n, 121n; *Les
    Commencements*, 13, 65–87,
    90n, 91n, 92n, 93n, 96, 122n;
    *Les Rêveries de la femme
    sauvage: Scènes primitives
    (Reveries of the Wild Woman:
    Primal Scenes)*, 13, 124n, 157,
    163–80, 182n, 183n, 184n;
    'Lettre à Zohra Drif', 183n;
    *L'Exil de James Joyce ou l'art du
    remplacement (The Exile of
    James Joyce)*, 56, 87n; *L'Histoire
    (qu'on ne connaîtra jamais)*,
    155n; *L'Histoire terrible mais
    inachevée de Norodom Sihanouk,
    Roi du Cambodge (The Terrible
    But Unfinished Story of
    Norodom Sihanouk, King of
    Cambodia)*, 127, 128, 153n,
    154n; *L'Indiade ou l'Inde de
    leurs rêves et quelques écrits sur
    le théâtre*, 127, 128, 153n;
    Manhattan, 6; *Manne: aux
    Mandelstams aux Mandelas*, 11,
    159, 181n; *Messie*, 181n; 'My
    Algeriance, in other words: to
    depart not to arrive from
    Algeria', 15n, 32, 53n, 54n,
    126n, 162, 184n; *Neutre*, 51n,
    159, 162, 181n; *Or: Les letters
    de mon père*, 157, 180n;
    Osnabrück, 157, 163, 180n,
    181n; *Partie*, 51n; *Philippines*, 6;
    Portrait de Dora, 16n; *Portrait
    de Jacques Derrida en Jeune Saint
    Juif (Portrait Of Jacques Derrida
    as a Young Jewish Saint)*, 88n;

Portrait du soleil, 16n, 51n, 158, 159; *Prénom de Dieu*, 53n; 'Quelle heure est-il, ou La porte (celle qu'on ne passe pas)' ('What is it o'clock? or The door (we never enter)'), 87n, 136, 155n; *Rencontre terrestre* (*Encounters: Conversations on Life and Writing*), 11–12, 18n, 158–9, 160, 181n; *Rêve je te dis* (*Dream I tell you*), 20, 51n; *Revirements dans l'antarctique du cœur*, 182n; *Si près*, 161, 182n; *Souffles*, 7, 13, 98–120, 121n, 125n, 126n; *Tambours sur la digue*, 128, 129, 137, 153n; *Three Steps on the Ladder of Writing*, 17n, 23, 121n, 126n; *Tours promises*, 162, 181n, 182n; 'Une Virginité de mémoire', 182n; *Voiles* (*Veils*), 87n; *Writing Not Yet Thought*, 132, 154n

Clément, Bruno, 51n
Conley, Verena Andermatt, 2, 8, 15n, 57, 59–60, 88n, 89n, 126n

Dante, 160–1
Dawson, Mark *see* Cixous: writings: 'A Kind of Magic'
death, 8, 10–11, 23–4, 27–9, 30, 31, 33–4, 35, 38, 40–2, 45, 46, 48, 49, 56, 64, 75, 128, 130, 131, 136, 140, 141–4, 152, 155n, 160, 162, 176, 179, 181n
deconstruction, 8, 13, 57–9, 63, 65, 81, 85, 90n, 98, 163, 182n
Deleuze, Gilles and Guattari, Félix, 55n
Derrida, Jacques, 8, 12, 16n, 19, 23, 52n, 85
on hospitality, 166–7, 169, 177, 179, 182n, 183n, 184n
relations with Cixous, 59–60
works on Cixous, 9, 13, 17n, 56, 57, 61–5, 87n, 89n, 90n, 93n, 120n, 183n
WRITINGS
'Circonfession', 60; *De la Grammatologie*, 57; *De l'Hospitalité* (*Of Hospitality*), 166, 169, 179, 182n, 183n; *États*

d'âme de la psychanalyse ('Psychoanalysis Searches the States of Its Soul'), 90n; 'Fourmis', 106, 122n; *Genèses, généalogies, genres et le génie* (*Geneses, Genealogies, Genres and Genius*), 51n, 92n; *Glas*, 92n, 107–11, 122n, 123n, 125n; 'H. C. pour la vie, c'est à dire...' (*H. C. for Life, That Is to Say...*), 8–9, 13, 17n, 56, 57, 61–4, 87n, 89n, 90n, 93n, 120n, 183n; *La Carte postale: de Socrate à Freud et au-delà* (*The Post Card: From Socrates to Freud and Beyond*), 51n; 'La loi du genre' ('The Law of Genre'), 16n; 'Les Pupilles de l'Université: Le principe de raison et l'idée de l'Université' ('The Principle of Reason: The University in the Eyes of Its Pupils'), 59, 88n; *Mal d'Archive* (*Archive Fever*), 90n; 'Mochlos ou le conflit des facultés' ('Mochlos or the Conflict of the Faculties'), 58, 88n; 'Ponctuations: le temps de la thèse' ('Punctuations: The Time of a Thesis'), 58, 88n; *Spectres de Marx* (*Specters of Marx*), 53n; 'Un Ver à soie' ('A Silkworm of One's Own'), 87n
Dobson, Julia, 16n
Dostoevsky, 159
Drif, Zohra, 183n
Dufourmantelle, Anne *see* Derrida: writings: *De l'Hospitalité*
Duras, Marguerite, 61, 89n

Eagleton, Terry, 153n
Ecclesiastes, 33, 47

father, representation of, 25–31, 35–8, 41–2, 43–4, 45, 46, 48, 54n, 84, 122n, 168–9, 173
Felman, Shoshana, 22–3, 24, 52n, 65, 90n
fiction, 2–13, 16n, 17n, 20, 22–4, 32, 49–50, 53n, 65, 67, 82–5, 92n, 107, 128–30, 137, 154n, 157
Fisher, Claudine G., 17n

Fliess, Wilhelm, 14
Forrester, John, 52n
Fort, Bernadette, 128, 153n
Franke, Catherine and Chazal, Roger, 154n
Freeman, Barbara, 153n
Freud, Sigmund, 11, 14, 18n, 19–20, 23, 24, 40, 41, 43, 49, 50n, 51n, 52n, 53n, 73, 91n

Gandhi, Indira, 129
Genesis, 69, 70–1, 80, 91n
Genet, Jean, 98, 99, 101, 107–11, 113, 114, 115, 116, 118–19, 122n, 123n, 124n, 125n
Genette, Gérard, 3–6, 15n, 16n, 54n
genre, 3–9, 13, 16n, 17n, 61–2, 66, 81–2, 89n, 115, 127, 130–1, 147, 172, 176–7, 183n
Goethe, Johann Wolfgang, 101, 122n
Gombrich, E. H., 52n
Gruber, Eberhard, 154n
Guattari, Félix *see* Deleuze, Gilles

Hamburger, Käte, 15n
Hanrahan, Mairéad, 16n, 17n, 18n, 91n, 121n, 126n, 181n, 182n; *see also* Cixous: writings: 'A Kind of Magic'
Heathfield, Adrian, 132, 154n
Hegel, 92n, 125n
Hoft-March, Eilene, 157
hospitality, 166–9, 173, 176–80

irony, 6–7, 22, 94, 96

Jakobson, Roman, 4, 8, 15n
Jeannet, Frédéric-Yves, 11–12, 18n, 158–9, 160, 181n
Joyce, James, 107, 116, 124n

Kamuf, Peggy, 2–3, 15n, 52n, 57, 88n, 121n
Kermode, Frank, 10–11, 18n
Kierkegaard, Søren, 102–3, 122n
King Lear, 34, 54n, 55n
Kristeva, Julia, 67, 90n

Lacan, Jacques, 23, 24, 40, 41, 51n, 52n, 73, 75, 85, 91n, 93n, 155n, 173, 183n

language, 1, 3, 4, 8, 22, 24, 30, 31, 34, 38–45, 48, 55n, 60, 62, 65, 79, 89n, 90n, 95, 109, 117–18, 120, 126n, 177–80, 184n
Laplanche, Jean, and Pontalis, Jean-Bertrand, 29
Lie, Sissel, and Ringrose, Priscilla, 17n
Louis XV, 132
Lukacher, Ned, 181n

Makward, Christine, 124n
Man, Paul de, 7, 17n
Mandela, Nelson, 159
Mandelstam, Osip, 159
Marder, Elissa, 126n, 157, 161, 180n, 181n
metaphor, 2, 6–7, 8, 31, 35, 77, 98–9, 104, 109, 111, 113, 115–16, 120, 122n, 137, 143, 147, 172, 176–7, 183n
Michaud, Ginette, 17n, 51n, 57, 88n, 90n
Milesi, Laurent, 88n
Milton, 99, 104–5, 106
Mnouchkine, Ariane, 127
Moi, Toril, 2, 15n, 121n
Montaigne, Michel de, 36, 54n, 141
Moses, 14, 37, 54n
Motard-Noar, Martine, 17n, 54n
mother, representation of, 25, 35, 41, 45, 55n, 69, 70, 84, 92n, 98–109, 116, 118–20, 121n, 123n, 125n, 126n, 161–3, 167–8, 170, 171–3, 175, 177–8, 183n, 184n
mourning, 130, 132, 135, 145

narrative, 4, 5–6, 7, 9–12, 13, 20, 24, 25, 38–40, 43–4, 46–50, 77, 81, 129–30, 133, 137, 141, 144, 150, 152, 155n, 163, 164, 174–5, 180
Nibelungen, 141, 145, 155n
Nietzsche, Friedrich, 131, 152, 153, 154n
Nuttall, A. D., 153n

Œdipus, 105–6
O'Grady, Kathleen, 127, 129, 153n, 154n

Peñalver Vicea, Maribel, 157
Picard, Anne-Marie, 31, 53m, 55n
Plato, 5, 56
Pontalis, Jean-Bertrand *see* Laplanche, Jean
Poole, Adrian, 127, 130, 137, 138, 153n, 154n
postcolonial, 100, 113–15, 124n, 127, 163, 182n
Prenowitz, Eric, 91n, 129, 154n; *see also* Cixous: writings: 'A Kind of Magic' *and* 'Enter the Theatre'
proper name, 1, 2, 8, 37, 38, 62, 69, 82, 84, 86, 91n, 92n, 99, 101, 103, 105, 107–9, 114, 116–20, 121n, 125n, 126n, 132, 133–4, 135, 146, 147, 149, 154n, 156n, 157, 171, 181n
Proust, 37
psychoanalysis, 2, 8, 10, 13, 19–24, 29–30, 31, 38, 41–2, 49–50, 52n, 56, 73, 123n, 161

Rabaté, Jean-Michel, 52n, 155n
Racine, Jean, 179
Regard, Frédéric, 113, 124n
Rice, Alison, 126n
Ricœur, Paul, 10, 17n
Rilke, Rainer Maria, 99, 124n
Rimbaud, Arthur, 99, 105, 122n
Ringrose, Priscilla *see* Lie, Sissel
Rosello, Mireille, 182n, 183n
Rossum-Guyon, Françoise van, 14, 18n, 52n
Royle, Nicholas, 89n
Running-Johnson, Cynthia, 121n
Rye, Gill, 154n

St Augustine, 113, 124n
St Theresa of Avila, 99, 109–10, 123n
Samson, 101, 105, 111

Sartre, Jean-Paul, 107, 123n
Schipa, Mary E., 17n
Schumann, Robert, 102
Segarra, Marta, 51n, 57, 88n, 183n
Sellers, Susan, 17n, 31, 53n, 54n
Shakespeare, William, 20, 128–9, 131, 154n; *see also King Lear*
Shiach, Morag, 31, 53n, 55n, 57, 88n
Sophocles, 106
Sphinx, 40, 43, 45–6, 106
Steiner, George, 153n
Stendhal, 20, 159
Stevens, Christa, 51n, 57, 88n, 91n, 182n
Still, Judith, 88n, 182n, 183n
Suetonius, 179
Syrotinski, Michael, 182n
Szondi, Peter, 153n

theory, 2–3, 8, 12–13, 17n, 20, 21, 23, 41, 42, 54n, 57–61, 72–3, 75, 89n, 126n, 130, 182n, 183n
time, 10–11, 12, 13, 25, 26, 28, 31, 33–4, 42–3, 47, 49, 51n, 85, 86, 130–1, 139–45, 150–2, 156n, 157–66, 173–5, 180
Torok, Maria *see* Abraham, Nicholas
tragedy/the tragic, 13, 127–32, 135–42, 144, 145, 146, 150–3, 154n, 155n, 163, 179, 182n
trauma, 24, 25, 27, 29, 51n

Vinci, Leonardo da, 72
'vol'/'voler', 39, 40, 95–6, 107, 109, 111, 113–15, 120n, 124n, 125n

Wallace, Jennifer, 153n

Yee, Jennifer, 184n

Zupančič, Alenka, 155n